No Growth: Impacts on Metropolitan Areas

No Growth: Impacts on Metropolitan Areas

Edgar Rust

Lexington Books
D.C. Heath and Company
Lexington, Massachusetts
Toronto   London

Library of Congress Cataloging in Publication Data

Rust, Edgar.
    No growth: impacts on metropolitan areas.

    Bibliography: p. 223.
    Includes index.
    1. Cities and towns—Planning—United States. 2. Metropolitan
areas—United States. 3. Cities and towns—Growth. I. Title.
HT167.R87   309.2'62'0973   75-5193
ISBN 0-669-99705-6

Published simultaneously in Canada

Printed in the United States of America

International Standard Book Number: 0-669-99705-6

Library of Congress Catalog Card Number: 75-5193

Contents

List of Figures

List of Tables

xi

Preface

Metropolitan areas without population growth doubled in number with each decade from 1940 to 1970. Once limited to minor, out-of-the-way cities, episodes of population loss are now occurring in some of the largest metropolitan areas, including New York and Los Angeles. Most development and planning theory, however, is still based on assumptions of growth, not stability or decline. It is important, therefore, to learn what we can from the limited national experience with metropolitan non-growth in order to anticipate potential changes in newly declining areas, as well as to cope better with the problems associated with decline.

What happens to places that don't grow? Or does no growth even make any difference? If it does, to whom does it matter?

My first approach to these questions was to compare two handfuls of metropolitan areas, one rapidly growing and one non-growing in population (1960-1970) using summary data (Rust 1972). They were indeed different: the non-growing places proved to be exceedingly poor. Their people were also older, saved more money despite their smaller incomes, and were less frequently arrested. Their economies showed a tendency to become more specialized in slow-growth industrial sectors, and less specialized in services than their rapidly growing counterparts. There were many limitations to the study: it was small, superficial, and biased by regional differences between the growers and non-growers. I decided, therefore, to take on a larger, more structured study of the foregoing questions.

The next sample was a full set of all independent Standard Metropolitan Statistical Areas (SMSAs) which showed one percent or less population increase in any decade during the period 1940-1970. It was matched with another group of SMSAs having a similar distribution of locations (by Census division), population size, and industrial type. The other group was chosen for comparability rather than for large growth, and ended up somewhat slower-growing than average, yielding less spectacular but hopefully more valid contrasts. Statistical comparisons among these SMSAs confirmed the differences observed earlier and revealed some more subtle differences, seemingly related to the duration of no growth or the historical era in which they last grew.

Concurrently with the large sample studies, a subsample of ten non-growing SMSAs was selected representing a cross-section of types. I visited each in the field, toured it, and met with local officials and anyone else who seemed willing to discuss changes in the community during the no-growth period. (In St. Joseph, I met a man who had been a peanut vendor in one of the city's several burlesque houses until they were closed in 1929. He gave me a vivid description of a wide-open joy street, gesturing at its now empty buildings and vacant lots.) I investigated the catalogues, stacks, and clippings files of any public and university libraries in the area.

The field work led to a whole line of investigation that I had not anticipated. I began to see how early the die had been cast for many of these communities—not so much in the onset of decline for whatever reason, as in the character of growth which preceded it, which in turn was in large part a reflection of national forces operating at the time. I had discovered history.

After that, the study began to find its focus. The old question—does not growing make a difference—was answered strongly in the affirmative and a new set of more specific, historical and value-laden questions could be asked. The results follow.

Acknowledgments

The following persons made generous contributions of time and information to this study. Their kind assistance is gratefully acknowledged.

Jay D. Aldridge
J. Aronstein
LeRoy Bankston
Howard Bellinger
Susan Bernard
Austin Burke
Gordon Cameron
Fred Collins
Jack Daniels
James DeAngelis
William Deaton
Robert R. Drummond
Edgar Dunn
Albert Fishlow
John M. Hanley
Edward Heiselburg
Richard Hennessy
Don Hileman
Joseph Hinberger
Robert La Macchia
Milo Howard
Larry Long
Roy Lubove

Peter Marris
Mrs. Min Matheson
Art Maynard
Walt Newton
Evan Nolte
George F. Oliver II
Susan Peacock
Carl Pillion
Gabrielle Ramsauer
John Rousakis
Robert Savadge
Allen B. Schall
Roberta Seraf
Jim Sims
LeRoy Tillary
Ralph Tucker
Philip Tuhy
Bert Ward
Tom Warnagiris
Tony Warner
Reid Williamson
Leonard Ziolkowski

William Alonso first brought this subject to my attention and suggested so many ideas along the way that I have no way to separate his contribution from my own. Fred Collignon and Allan Pred gave valued advice and moral support. I am also indebted to Peter Morrison for his very complete and incisive critique, without which this version would be much less fully developed. Lois Kramer performed many of the computations, and Ann Reifman edited an earlier version of the manuscript.

Several valiant typists strained their eyesight and endurance for me beyond what anyone could reasonably ask. Norma Montgomery and Donald Abel, especially, have my admiration and gratitude. The Scientific Analysis Corporation of San Francisco helped me secure funding for the

This book is based upon research performed for the Behavioral Sciences Branch, Center for Population Research, National Institute for Child Health and Human Development, under Contract No. 1-HD-42806.

work and sheltered me from the harsh administrative realities of life for one short, happy year, thanks to the kindness and competence of Dorothy Miller, Setsu Gee, Bruce Jones, and their staff. The Center for Population Research gave us a contract under which much of the research was done, and even better, gave us Wendy Baldwin to monitor it in a graceful and totally supportive manner.

**Part I
Observations**

The first twelve chapters of this book describe what it is like for a metropolitan area not to grow. Three complementary perspectives are employed: first a statistical snapshot of the current incidence and distribution of the "no-growth" condition among the metropolitan areas of the United States, then a historical overview of the large national forces influencing local growth and decline, and finally, a series of case studies of selected no-growth areas which were investigated by a combination of field observation, interviews, readings and data analysis.

1

The Stable and Declining Metropolitan Areas of the United States of America

A great deal is known about what goes on in rapidly growing American metropolitan areas. Stability and decline have had less attention. The intent of this study is to explore the limited experience with no growth which exists in metropolitan areas of the United States, to learn how well or badly they have coped with it and what lessons there may be in that experience.

The growth of a metropolitan area has many possible measures. Its land area, labor force, employment, income, production, property value, daytime population and number of households all are reasonable indexes of size. Capital investment, housing starts, and migration rates highlight the process by which growth occurs. But resident population change is the most convenient growth index. It is available over long periods of time, has nearly the same meaning in any period, and can be related by simple, predictable ratios to many other aspects of the community.

The particular cases selected for this study are Standard Metropolitan Statistical Areas (SMSAs), as defined by the Bureau of the Budget as of April 1970. Specifically, they are the thirty SMSAs outside the New York Consolidated Area which had less than 1 percent population increase in one or more decades since 1940 (table 1-1). They contain 7 1/2 million people in 1970, and about 5 percent of the United States metropolitan population.

The sample does not fully coincide with everybody's notion of "no growth." Because births exceeded deaths in all SMSAs, this sampling criterion defines a study universe which is limited to cases of substantial outmigration. It excludes a large number of slowly growing SMSAs with declining central city populations (like Boston and San Francisco), and others often regarded as "declining areas" because of falling employment, dismal living conditions, and strong outmigration (like Lowell, Mass.), which nevertheless have shown nominal population increase. It does not represent the whole "no growth" condition. There are also SMSAs in the sample whose citizens will vigorously deny the "no growth" label despite the census figures. They will point to rising indicators of size such as building permits, utility connections, or bank deposits, but overlook other sectors of their communities which are shrinking more rapidly: the company town built outside city limits for a failing or rapidly automating factory, the military bases with clusters of private services, the generations of unusually large graduating high school classes for whom there are no job vacancies in the area. They are right that their world is expanding, but they

5

Figure 1-1. Non-Growing SMSAs in the Study

Table 1-1
Non-Growth Areas in the Study*

SMSAs		Decades of 1% or Less Population growth	
	1940s	1950s	1960s
1. Abilene			x
2. Altoona	x		x
3. Amarillo			x
4. Brownsville-Harlingen-San Benito			x
5. Charleston, W. Va.			x
6. Duluth-Superior	x		x
7. Fall River		x	
8. Fort Smith	x	x	
9. Gadsden			x˙
10. Huntington-Ashland			x
11. Johnstown	x	x	x
12. Lake Charles			x
13. McAllen-Pharr-Edinburg			x
14. Midland			x
15. Montgomery			x
16. New Bedford		x	
17. Odessa			x
18. Pittsburgh			x
19. Pueblo			x
20. St. Joseph		x	x
21. Savannah			x
22. Scranton	x	x	x
23. Sioux City	x		x
24. Steubenville-Weirton			x
25. Terre Haute	x	x	
26. Texarkana		x	
27. Waco			x
28. Wheeling	x	x	x
29. Wichita Falls			x
30. Wilkes-Barre-Hazleton	x	x	x

*Included are all independent SMSAs which had 1% or less population increase between successive decennial censuses 1940-70, using constant 1970 area boundaries. Excluded is Jersey City, SMSA, which lost population in the 1960s but as a part of the New York Consolidated Area cannot be considered independently.

are trapped, perhaps arbitrarily in the same statistical aggregate with others whose world is not.

Historically very low, the incidence of metropolitan non-growth is increasing. Within the set of SMSAs defined by 1970 boundaries, twenty-six SMSAs had less than 1 percent population growth in the 1960s, up from ten in the '50s and five in the '40s. In the period 1970-72, twenty-seven SMSAs failed to grow.

The incidence of metropolitan non-growth in those three decades was greatest among small cities, and smallest in the West. Pittsburgh (with 2.2

million people) was the only one of the 84 independent SMSAs over 350,000 population to decline in any of those decades, but 29 of the 159 areas under 350,000 population did so. No metropolitan area west of the Rockies lost population between decennial censuses since 1940, but ten of the 18 SMSAs in Appalachia did so, as did eleven of the 37 SMSAs in the West South Central Division (table 1-2).

The present decade shows very different trends, however. Twenty-seven SMSAs lost population between 1970 and 1972, including eight over a million population and three on the West Coast (table 1-3).

A historical perspective reveals close economic similarities among the non-growing areas (see Chapter 2). All areas on which historical data were found are former boom towns. The older ones boomed on coal, iron, railroads, cotton or beef, the younger ones on petroleum, defense or aerospace. Most were dominated by a single industry in their growth phase, and many by a single firm. To be sure, not all former boom towns with these industries have declined. The ones which did so typically had three interrelated disadvantages: they were competitively weak within those industries, they were absentee controlled, and they were highly specialized. They failed for these or other reasons to develop new growth sectors in other industries during the boom period and had to diversify later in a far weaker bargaining position.

The non-growing metropolitan areas of the United States are far from being a homogeneous class. They reflect the social, economic, and historical diversity of the nation, and belong as much to their regions and industrial sectors as to the class of non-growing SMSAs. While much of the study will concentrate on their similarities or their unique case histories, a few broad classifications are useful in describing the sample, particularly their geographic locations, historical origins, and growth paths.

The major geographic distinction to be made is between North and South. Southern cities in the sample, like Southern cities generally, tend to have both lower incomes per capita and a more polarized income distribution than Northern cities of similar size, with a considerably larger part of their population below poverty level. They tend to have smaller and more recently developed manufacturing sectors than their Northern counterparts, but proportionally larger trade and service sectors. Few of them have had as long periods of no growth as those in the North. They have nearly average proportions of black and Chicano populations for their regions. Black, Chicano, and Puerto Rican populations are strikingly absent from non-growing SMSAs of the North, as the latter have generally been bypassed in the recent northward migration of those groups.

Overlapping the North-South distinction are several other geographic regions whose cities share a common character. The Appalachian no-growth cities are largely products of coal, the railroad-building era of the

Table 1-2
Distributions of Non-Growth Areas by Location, Size and Type, 1940s, 1950s, and 1960s Combined

Geographic Divisions*	Non-Growth	U.S. Total	Number of Non-Growth Areas As % of U.S. Total
New England	2	26	8
Middle Atlantic	5	25	20
South Atlantic	3	37	8
East No. Central	3	48	6
West No. Central	3	20	15
East So. Central	2	13	15
West So. Central	11	37	30
Mountain	1	17	7
Pacific	—	22	—
*1950 Population**			
Less than 100,000	9	73	12
100,000 - 149,999	8	47	17
150,000 - 349,999	11	67	16
350,000 - 999,999	1	40	3
1,000,000 - 2,499,999	1	10	10
2,500,000 or more	—	5	—
*1960 Population**			
Less than 100,000	5	36	14
100,000 - 149,999	10	48	21
150,000 - 349,999	14	86	16
350,000 - 999,999	—	48	—
1,000,000 - 2,499,999	1	17	6
2,500,000 or more	—	7	—
*Industrial Type, 1960***			
Nodal	4	52	8
Manufacturing	9	97	9
Government	2	27	7
Mixed	15	53	28
Other	—	13	—

*1970 Census of Population
**Stanback and Knight (1970)

late nineteenth century, and the early growth of the steel industry. They include the biggest non-growing SMSAs. Cramped in narrow valleys, they have some of the dirtiest air and water in the country, and the most ravaged landscape. Smaller groupings include the midwestern river cities like Terre Haute, Sioux City, and St. Joseph, with histories of trading, meat packing, and the gradual eclipse by places with better rail connections, and the oil,

Table 1-3
Distributions of Non-Growth Areas by Location and Size, 1960s and 1970-73

	SMSAs Not Growing* By Person		SMSAs, U.S. Total
	1960-70	1970-73	
Geographic Division			
New England	0	2	26
Middle Atlantic	5	5	25
South Atlantic	4	6	37
East North Central	1	7	48
West North Central	3	2	20
East South Central	2	0	13
West South Central	9	5	37
Mountain	1	0	17
Pacific	0	3	22
1970 Population			
Less Than 100,000	5	2	26
100,000 - 149,999	9	5	42
150,000 - 349,999	10	8	91
350,000 - 999,999	0	7	51
1,000,000 - 2,499,999	1	5	25
2,500,000 or more	0	3	8

*1960-70: Less than 1.0% increase
 1970-73: Less than 0.1% increase

gas, military or farming centers in Louisiana and Texas which were still booming as recently as the 1950s and the early 1960s.

The non-growing SMSAs (like the most rapidly growing ones) tended in the past three decades to be out on the fringes of larger urban concentrations. The northern Appalachian cities—Wheeling, Pittsburgh, and Charleston, in the upper Ohio River System, as well as Altoona, Johnstown, Wilkes-Barre, and Scranton in the highlands—lie in a sort of backyard between chains of industrial cities that extend between Buffalo and Chicago and between Boston and Washington. Gadsden, Montgomery, and Savannah ring Atlanta at a radius of 150 and 200 miles and the declining Texas cities ring Dallas-Fort Worth at about the same distance.

Why Are So Many Metropolitan Areas Not Growing?

The incidence of population stability or decline among the 242 areas classed as SMSAs within the continental United States as of the 1970 Census roughly doubled from the 1940s to the 1950s and again from the 1950s to the 1960s. The reasons for the change are not simple demographics. Rates of natural increase actually increased in most of the period. Gross internal migration rates changed little. Migration from non-metropolitan areas and abroad declined and was a small but significant factor in the change. Evidently what changed most was the *directionality* of migration which resulted in greater variance of SMSA net migration rates even though overall mobility stayed about the same. Several historical trends seem to contribute to this change.

The non-growing metropolitan areas typically had possessed a temporary advantage over alternative locations in some earlier era which permitted them to grow to a larger population size than they can presently support. In a sense, their root problem is a history of excessive growth relative to their long-term prospects. The first American "boomtowns" were trading centers for farms, forests, and fisheries. Some enjoyed gateway locations at breakpoints in the westward settlement of the interior, a drastic but sometimes self-extinguishing advantage as the process on which they fed gradually transformed their locations from central to peripheral with respect to the new markets, transportation networks, and production centers. Between 1840 and 1890, the coastal cities, then Pittsburgh and Wheeling, Terre Haute and finally St. Joseph, Fort Smith, and Sioux City had their eras as jumping-off points.

The next generation of major urban growth centers were industrial cities. Local economic boosting is still largely based on the perception of that era that manufacturing is the surest source of wealth and growth. Some trading centers like Pittsburgh made the transition to manufacturing in time but many did not. The inefficient technology and the large component of heavy industrial goods in the national product of the early industrial period, 1880-1920, required huge raw material inputs and particularly favored · locations near coal or iron ore deposits, whereas more recently the value of raw materials inputs has steadily dwindled as a proportion of national product.

In the period since 1920, the composition of national demands has shifted further from agricultural and material resource commodities and heavy industrial products to durable consumer goods and to services. Industrial cities with a weak service sector and a small local consumption market often found themselves unable to attract or generate firms and institutions supportive of stable growth. During the same period the absorption of large parts of the economy into major corporations increased the mobility of capital, entrepreneurship, and innovations under the control of administrative headquarters. These headquarters became increasingly clustered in a few major metropolitan areas, eroding the ties of investors, managers, and professionals to their home areas.

Whereas most of the no-growth before 1970 occurred in a time of rising fertility, there has since been a sharp reduction. What are likely to be the effects of reduced national fertility upon the distribution of metropolitan population growth rates, and on the incidence of non-growth and related problems?

Local SMSA rates of natural increase do tend to move up and down parallel to national rates, but also to be influenced by prior net migration (Alonso 1973, p. 10). Other things being equal, the number or size of non-growing SMSAs should increase as birthrates decline. If age-specific fertility were to decline equally in all places, the areas showing the greatest effect on their total growth rates would be those with the largest proportions of young adults in their ages of highest fertility. These are precisely the areas which have had the most rapid recent net inmigration. Those with older populations would be less affected and those whose young adult population has been depleted by decades of outmigration and low fertility, the least of all.

Fertility changes will have a significant short-run effect upon mobility, however. If young families tend to be smaller, the typical migrant family head will take fewer children with him and have a correspondingly smaller effect upon the populations at the origin and destination of his or her move. (Young children are the most mobile age class after young adults, as Chapter 13 shows.) The migration system may begin to "cool off" reducing net migration primarily in areas having a strong imbalance of flows in or out. This effect would be upward on the growth rates of areas with strong net outmigration—the newly stable or declining areas, but not those which have grown little for decades—and downward on the growth rates of the fastest growing areas.

About 1985, the small age cohorts born since the early 1970s would begin to enter their period of highest and most economically motivated mobility. At this point total mobility might be further depressed for a long period. What migration occurred, furthermore, would contain a higher proportion of returns to home towns, retirement, and other non-economically motivated moves which characterize much migration of older people (Lansing and Mueller 1967) so that migration would become substantially less effective in redistributing population toward areas of economic growth than it is now. This effect would tend to accentuate labor shortage conditions in boom areas and labor surplus conditions in non-growth areas, and to accentuate the divergence of incomes per capita.

In sum, the main effects of reduced national fertility upon the distribution of metropolitan growth rates, non-growth and related problems are likely to be:

1. a downward tendency for most SMSA population growth rates, with a greater reduction in the very large rates and little impact upon the growth of areas that have been nearly stable or declining for long periods.

2. a smaller demographic multiplier of labor migration and a depressing effect upon overall mobility.

3. beginning about 1985, a reduced capacity of spontaneous labor migration to compensate for unequal growth of labor demand: this may be the beginning of a period in which a large proportion of the labor force is immobile.

Although a greater number of areas (or a few larger ones) may become susceptible to population stability or decline, the initial problems of non-growth would be somewhat softened in the short run by the reduced demographic multipliers of labor movements. If steps are not taken to moderate growth differences or to expedite and rationalize migration within the next decade, however, the problems of chronic labor surplus we now associate exclusively with long depressed areas may begin to spread into many more places.

Why Are Non-Growing Metropolitan Populations so Poor?

Non-growing metropolitan populations relative to growing ones are poor and getting poorer. The fact is beyond question (table 1-4). Less clear is the function of non-growth itself in the predicament of these people. Are the non-growing places merely not growing because they are poor, or are they also to some extent poor because they are not growing? The difference has profound ethical and policy implications.

It is well established that local economic conditions influence migration

Table 1-4
Income and Income Growth in Growing and Non-Growing SMSAs of the Study Sample*

	Decades of Less than 1% Population Increase Prior to 1970		
	0	*1 or 2*	*4 or 5***
1969 per capita income, $	2,934 (348)	2,630 (480)	2,680 (130)
Growth of per capita income 1959-69, %	72 (10)	62 (9)	68 (9)

*The sample include sixty SMSAs of which thirty had at least one decade of less than 1% population growth since 1940.

**No areas in the sample had three decades.

Note: Figures are class means with standard deviations in parentheses.

14

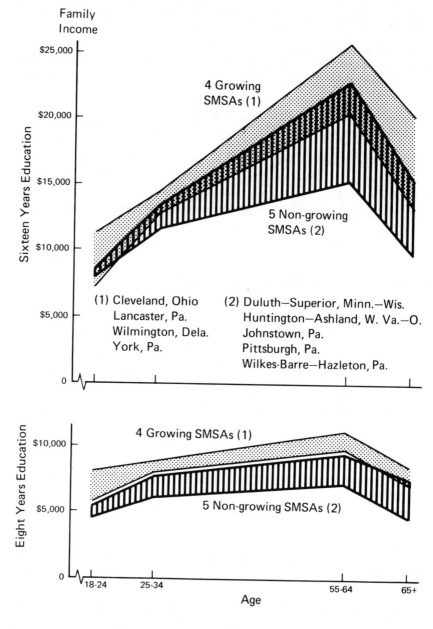

Source: 1970 Census of Population Vol. PC-1 Table 202

Figure 1-2. 1969 Family Income Range by Age and Education of Head, Selected Areas

patterns of people and firms. Poor local areas tend to be less attractive to migrants than rich ones. On the other hand, they are more attractive to some expanding industries, particularly those seeking workers with low wage demands. This far, the traditional economic view is confirmed. If these were the only relations between population and income, then metropolitan non-growth might be no problem: it would merely reflect a healthy redistribution of population and sources of wealth, contributing to an equalization of incomes, and to a more efficient performance of the national economy. There are two difficulties with this view, however: selective migration and institutional changes.

All people and firms are not affected the same way. Instead, younger, richer, and upwardly mobile persons tend to cluster together with the better-paying jobs in the growing areas, leaving poorer people as a non-mobile residue together with the more intermittent or lower-paying jobs in the stable or declining areas (Blau and Duncan 1967, pp. 255-266). The resulting differentiation of people and jobs according to levels and trends of income results in lower income per capita in non-growing places (table 1-4). However, income per capita can be a misleading statistic when it is applied to a changing group of people. The effect of selective migration on observed income per capita could mask strong gains in individual welfare. Loss of population could, for example, help both the outmigrants, to the extent that they move to areas of greater labor demand, and those who remain and face less competition for their jobs.

If, on the other hand, non-growth itself and the accumulation of the less mobile people into non-growing areas foster institutional differences which depress the levels of real income the people there are able to achieve, then non-growth contributes at least to an unjust distribution between migrants and non-migrants, and quite possibly to an overall loss for society. It is this possibility that would justify calling metropolitan non-growth a problem in itself and not merely the reflection or locus of other problems. Empirically, such differences seem to exist. For example, based on a comparison of the five non-growing SMSAs in the sample for which data are available in sufficient detail, with four growing SMSAs of similar size and location, persons of any given age and education levels earn less in non-growing areas than in growing ones (figure 1-2). Further confirmation of this view will be found in the case studies.

2 The Historical Context

Most non-growing metropolitan areas fit a common historical pattern. The shifting spatial distribution, product composition and organization of the national economy have set the stage for the cessation of growth in those metropolitan areas which enjoyed disproportionately greater advantages in one era than in the next.

Internal transportation improvements, cheap land under the Homestead Acts, new agricultural technology, and the rise of protectionist foreign trade policies combined to insure that large parts of the vast national growth of the mid-nineteenth century would occur in the interior of the United States. The older port cities, especially those lacking inland trade routes beyond the Appalachian ridges, were vulnerable to decline if their immediate hinterlands became less productive. At each stage of the frontier's advance, temporary gateway locations along its length would boom until the frontier moved on. About 1890, the frontier disappeared. By 1920, the rail transportation network was filled in and essentially completed. Industrial locations which were once unique mineral sources lost their special advantages when more flexible metallurgy, more efficient energy conversion and cheaper transportation evolved.

As the composition of the national product shifted from agriculture and natural resource commodities (which had been largely for export), to an increasingly prosperous and diverse domestic consumption market, the key sources of U.S. urban growth changed. Before 1860, the most rapidly growing cities generally specialized in commerce; from 1860 to 1910 the most rapidly growing areas specialized in manufacturing; and since World War I, the quickly growing cities specialized increasingly in services (Pred 1966). The eras and probable sources of growth of several areas under study are summarized in table 2-1.

Like those areas still growing, many presently non-growing metropolitan areas were built on a rapidly growing industry of the time (commerce, mining or manufacturing); unlike the growing ones, the non-growing areas failed to develop the significant specialties of subsequent eras until decline was well established. By this point, relative wage levels had dropped; serious unemployment existed; and substantial outmigration of higher-skilled young people had occurred. When and if nationally growing industries eventually moved into these cities, the existence of a low-skilled, relatively captive (i.e., immobile) labor force and a business community desperate for any trade whatever attracted firms most in need of cheap

Table 2-1
Main Growth Sources and Their Eras of Expansion in Selected* Non-Growing SMSAs

	Trade and Transportation	Cotton and Textiles	Food and Food Processing	Coal or Iron Mining	Iron and Steel Manufacturing	Other Manufacturing	Oil and Gas	Military Installations	Periods of Population Stability or Decline
Amarillo	1887-		1887-1920				1920-1950	1950-1968	1968-1970
Altoona	1880-1920								1930-1970
Brownsville-Harlingen-San Benito			1920s 1940s						1960s
Charleston, W. Va.	1860-			1860-1920				?-1960	1960s
Duluth-Superior				1880-1910					1920-1970
Fall River		1870-1900							1910-1940 1960s
Fort Smith	1820s 1880s						1900-1910	1941-1946	1920s, 1946-1960
Johnstown				1860-1920	1870-1920				1920-1970
Lake Charles							1900-1910, 1940-1960		1910-1920 1960-1970
Midland							1950-1960		1910-1920 1960-1970

Montgomery		1850-1900						1950-1963	1910-1920, 1963-1970
New Bedford	1820-1840	1860-1910							1840s, 1920-1940, 1960s
Odessa							1900-1910, 1940-1960		1900-1910, 1960s
Pittsburgh	1810-1860			1860-1920	1860-1920				1960s
Pueblo					1880-1920				1960s
St. Joseph	1859-1895		1880-1900						1900-1920, 1930-1970
Savannah	1840-1860	1734-1820				1921-1950		1940-1962	1962-1972
Scranton				1840-1900					1930-1970
Sioux City			1870-1890						1890s, 1930-1950, 1960s
Terre Haute	1820-1924		1880-1923	1900-1923	1860-1880				1923-1960
Wheeling	1812-1880				1860-1920				1930-1970
Wichita Falls		1880-1920						1940-1960	1930s, 1960s
Wilkes-Barre-Hazelton				1840-1920					1930-1970

*Omitted are the following areas for which historical sources of growth were not identified in the general studies on which this chapter is based: Abilene, Huntington-Ashland, Steubenville-Weirton, McAllen-Pharr-Edinburg, Texarkana, and Waco.

labor, financial aid and political concessions, and least in need of forward or backward linkages with local firms, or of a local consumption market. Some few firms in this condition were "infant" industries, with the potential to have substantial positive impact on the community, but the great majority were likely to perpetuate or worsen the distressed conditions which drew them there, and would lead eventually to the city's further decline.

Organizational factors were as important as geographic and structural factors in affecting the development of the non-growing areas. The parallel rise of large corporations and the federal government in the twentieth century nurtured the stability of favored administrative centers and greatly increased the mobility of certain resources (including money, entrepreneurship, technology, and a small technical-managerial elite), enabling massive fluctuations of local economic growth with the opening and closing of branch plants and military installations and the letting of government contracts.

The interweaving of access, national demand, and institutional changes in the development of recently non-growing metropolitan areas is sketched below. The narrative is separated into three overlapping eras: the period of westward settlement and agricultural expansion of roughly 1830 to 1890, the period in which domestic heavy industry was developed and the frontier closed, 1860-1930, and the period since 1920 in which consumer products and services increasingly dominated national demand, white-collar occupations moved from a minority to a majority of the labor force and very large urban areas captured the greatest increases of population and material welfare.

**Westward Settlement, Growth of Agriculture and the
Pre-industrial Trading Cities: 1830-1890**

The regions of most rapid economic growth shifted progressively from the East Coast to the Great Lakes, the interior plains and the Far West just behind the frontier of settlement. They moved, not as a smooth flow, but in a series of jumps which abruptly shifted locational advantages among series of "gateway" cities. Agriculture made tremendous advances in volume, income, and productivity in the newly opened lands. During the period 1840-1860, per capita income in the West South Central region (now the nation's second lowest) was above the U.S. average (North 1966).

The extension of rail access permitted development of lands devoted to corn and hogs beyond the Ohio from the 1830s, wheat across the Great Plains in the '40s to 1919, cotton from Georgia in 1815 to eastern Texas by 1860, and range cattle west of the advancing frontier. Due to the flexible routing of rail lines in these relatively flat lands, the early river ports lost much of their former advantage. For example, Indianapolis, now the largest land-locked American city, could eclipse Terre Haute, a nearby river city (McCarty 1971). The same flexibility of routing created large rewards for successful promotion of a particular route by property owners in the towns it would serve. The resulting competition, vividly described by Glaab and Brown (1967) was one of the early beginnings of the persistent tradition of civic boosterism which grew up with the newer Midwestern towns and later spread back to the major cities.

The older Southern farm lands east of the Appalachian chain were in many cases unable to compete, because their small fields and lack of capital inhibited mechanization. These regions entered into a long decline which has left many of them depressed today. The ratio of foreign trade to GNP fell from 15-30 percent in the colonial period and remained below 7 percent for every decade from 1830 to the present except for the 1914-1918 war, with further declines since World War II (Davis et al. 1972, pp. 554-555), further reducing the relative importance of Eastern locations. Thus, although most of the South suffered from the successive waves of over-planting of cotton in reaction to the boll weevil infestation after 1905, the central and eastern growers, trading through cities like Montgomery and Savannah, were the hardest hit.

Only a few of the recently non-growing metropolitan areas achieved their maturity as pre-industrial commercial centers: Savannah and New Bedford on the Atlantic, and St. Joseph and Sioux City on the upper Missouri. (Others, like Pittsburgh, New Bedford, and Terre Haute, were founded as trading cities but grew to their present size and character by successfully industrializing as their agricultural trade declined.) They grew up when tariffs were low, and a great proportion of U.S. production was sold abroad. In addition to foreign trade, a large part of domestic commerce was also carried by water; consequently the domestic market was concentrated near the larger cities of the Eastern Seaboard. At that time, overland transportation was slow and expensive so that closely spaced shipping ports were required. All the presently declining areas with commercial origins could be described as former shipping ports, which first fell to minor positions as the interior transportation network evolved and then were hit by a decline in the specialized products they handled.

Sioux City and St. Joseph were bypassed by the East-West trunk railways, and later by the East-West Interstate Highway routes. Savannah and New Bedford, although they had early rail access, were remote from the interior markets, had poor, sparsely populated service areas, and had limited highway access westward. Savannah specialized in Georgia cotton and naval stores, both of which were severely depressed in the early years of this century. New Bedford's whaling industry was eclipsed by petroleum, although the area was successfully industrialized in textiles. The decline of the four cities' commercial sectors was due to a combination of slow growth in the industries they served (agriculture, forestry, and fisheries), a competitive loss within those industries to neighboring centers, and a failure to develop new industrial sectors of their own until decline had firmly set in. Rapid industrialization and better inland transportation attracted the trade of parts of their former hinterlands to other areas. At this point wage levels were low, unemployment was high, and local property interests were desperate for outside investment. As a result, the industrialization which did take place—primarily in food processing, paper, textiles or apparel—was encouraged to use labor at low productivity and to contribute little to the public environment. Fallows (1970) documents one such case in the exploitation of Savannah's labor force, waterways, and tax base by Union Camp Paper Co.

The opening and settlement of the interior created a succession of "gateway" locations, often at natural barriers although sometimes simply where funds ran out temporarily in the westward extension of a particular route. "Gateway" locations were particularly vulnerable to overgrowth and decline because the same process of interior development on which they fed in their heyday often transformed their locations to peripheral ones. Wheeling occupied this position as the terminus of the Cumberland Road from 1820 to 1830 and as the supply point for its push westward to Illinois in the 1830s; Terre Haute was also a temporary terminus until the road crossed the Wabash in 1840 (Shepherd 1957). Other former "gateway" cities are found at the heads of navigation of many rivers flowing out of the Appalachian chain (Pittsburgh; Charleston, West Virginia; Montgomery, Alabama), and on the Missouri at the heads of the Pony Express route (St. Joseph) and the Long Trail (Ft. Smith, Arkansas) (Shepherd 1957).

Urbanization and Growth of Capital-Products Industries: 1860-1930

Either nationwide decline or massive relocation (i.e., localized decline) occurred in all the major growth industries of the early industrial period of 1840-1890; cotton textiles, coal, railroads, iron and steel, food processing. The largest group of recently non-growing metropolitan areas grew up on one or more of these industries. (Terre Haute had, by unique misfortune, almost all of them in its heyday, plus a brewing and distilling industry which ended with Prohibition.)

The earliest major American manufacturing industry was the production of cotton textiles, which reached a very substantial scale by the time of the Civil War. The growth of the cotton industry was enhanced in the 1870s by the Civil War innovation of ready-to-wear clothing. The industry was dependent in these years upon limited local supplies of mechanical energy, mainly water power, and so it tended to support the development of numerous small mill towns rather than a few major cities (Vance 1955).

Food processing, another early industry, was again largely decentralized in its early phase because of the large costs of transportation, the perishability of most raw produce, and the lack of significant technological economies of scale, and so was generally not a source of major urban growth. (A possible exception would be the large concentration of grain storage and milling at Buffalo, although general commerce, steel, and machinery also figured in that city's early growth.)

Anthracite coal mining created the first American "boom towns" in the modern sense. Although anthracite did not overtake charcoal for iron smelting (its main early market) until about 1854, its potential was recognized much earlier and wild land rushes in the 1830s preceded the extension of rail access into the Northeast Pennsylvania fields which became the Wilkes-Barre-Hazleton-Scranton metropolitan areas (Glaab 1963, pp. 194-195). As the only anthracite source in the continent accessible to industrial and household markets at the time, the area grew to support over half a million persons among dozens of small to medium-sized company towns. Some coal-burning industries were attracted to the area but the main source of income was mining itself during the growth period.

Anthracite was gradually replaced by coke, a bituminous coal product, for iron smelting by around 1870. Although other uses of anthracite as a domestic and industrial fuel continued to expand for a few decades, the boom phase of growth was over.

Bituminous coal was a more widespread resource, but highly variable in quality. In many areas it was exploited only for local consumption except in times of peak national demand. Where it was cheap enough and accessible to other resources like suitable sand, clay or metal ores, it supported the growth of glass, tile or smelting industries, such as at Terre Haute and at Charleston, West Virginia. Only a few deposits, notably those of western Pennsylvania and southeastern Colorado, proved to make coke of suitable composition for the somewhat inflexible Bessemer process which was used in early large-scale steel-making.

Steel was the first American industry in which potential scale economies coincided for a while with geographically concentrated resources to produce major urban growth based only on a single industry. The thermal efficiency of steel-making increased both with the size of the individual batch (less surface from which to lose heat) and with the integration of metallurgical and forming processes to avoid reheating. Labor and inventory costs also declined with scale. In the period 1870-1914, this potential was exploited with the development of increasingly large integrated steel smelting and rolling mills, and explosive urban growth in the cities of the coal or ore-bearing regions such as Pittsburgh, Youngstown, Wheeling, Johnstown, Duluth, Pueblo, Birmingham, and others.

In the early years of the industry the major market was rails, a simple uniform product. As more diversified products were demanded in later years, the advantages of immense scale declined. Ownership of the industry became concentrated in a few owners, most notably Pittsburgh interests, including Andrew Carnegie and later the U.S. Steel Corporation, who could control the pricing so as to extend the competitive life of the old installations until their "Pittsburgh Plus" basing point policy (all steel was priced as if shipped from Pittsburgh) was struck down in 1924.

Limited liability incorporation laws were adopted in most industrial states in the same period, making possible the financing and organization of very large-scale industrial firms. Protectionist trade policies designed to foster the growing manufacturing industries prompted foreign retaliations which mainly affected agricultural exports, accelerating both the shift from farm to city and the decline of the older agricultural regions.

The emergence of large multi-plant corporations represented not only a concentration of economic power and a restructuring of employment relations, but a tremendous increase in the mobility of capital. Reinforcing this trend was the growth of the stock markets from the 1890s. Private and institutional savings could flow more readily into the industrial structure, and could easily pass from cities and states of slow growth and capital surplus to others where a higher return was offered. This increase was not matched by a corresponding increase in labor mobility and tended to leave the slow-growing areas, paradoxically, with persistent labor surpluses and capital shortages.

Unlike the major Northern trading cities with their substantial industrial sectors, there was little industrial growth to offset the decline of commerce for the Southern trading centers which began to decline in the late nineteenth century. Their early rail lines and railroad yards, mills and foundries had been systematically destroyed during the Civil War. Southern credit and currency were worthless and most local investors found better returns in agriculture than in industry in spite of rising foreign tariffs (Bolino 1961). The beginnings of Southern industrialization—the blast furnaces at Birmingham about 1872 and cotton textile mills in the Coastal Plains about 1880—were quickly followed by the first Northern industrial investment in the South, other than in railroads; Carnegie and others moved in 1885 to control the emerging iron and steel industries (Schlesinger 1933).

Savannah's cotton and naval stores trade, controlled largely from New York, had been declining for several decades before the city began to industrialize. The concessions given by the city to Union/Camp Paper Company (Fallows 1970) show how Savannah's impoverished condition contributed to the marginal type of firms the city attracted as well as the exploitive behavior of these firms toward the city, its resources, and its physical environment (see chapter 9).

Metropolitan Concentration and the Growth of Consumer Goods and Service Industries: 1920-1974

The technology of manufacturing and the development of transportation and public utilities evolved jointly in a way which shifted the balance of industrial location forces from a strong raw material orientation in the late nineteenth century to a strong market orientation by the mid-twentieth century. Raw materials had composed a decreasing proportion of total costs in most industries due to a greater use of semi-finished manufactured inputs and services, an increasing proportion of complex products with high value in relation to their mass, and more efficient use of energy and materials. Energy cost differentials fell by orders of magnitude with the development of electrical transmission and pipelines. At the same time, marketing and distribution costs took on increasing importance with the rise of personal incomes, product differentiation, mass merchandising, and advertising, and since World War I, the innovations of market research and consumer financing.

Thus, some cities which grew up in the early industrial period by capitalizing on local raw material or energy supplies faced a waning of these advantages, especially if their locations were remote from the emerging clusters of major metropolitan areas in the Northeast, the Great Lakes and California. Relatively isolated cities like Duluth-Superior, Johnstown, and Pueblo, which grew up on mining combined with steel and related industries, not only lost large parts of their mining employment with automation and the depletion of the better mineral deposits, but were unable to sustain growth in their mineral-using industries, such as metallurgy, metal fabrication, and machinery. Food processing similarly declined in cities like Terre Haute, Montgomery, St. Joseph, and Sioux City.

With the growth of large corporations and labor organizations in certain industries came the evolution of internal labor markets, "providing relative job security, fringe benefits and seniority ladders at the expense of restricted entry and a growing duality between labor conditions in industries characterized by open and closed markets" (Doeringer and Piore 1970). Social legislation as it evolved in the twentieth century tended to reinforce the resulting disparities between industries, regions, and social classes with exemptions for industries such as agriculture and mining in which the required wage levels, employment practices, and working conditions were not commonly met, and with the dependence upon local initiative and financing of most social services, increasing the gap between rich and poor cities. In addition, the federal budget rose as a distributor of capital infrastructure, notably highways, military activities, and social services.

Construction of the American system of the interconnected railways as it exists today was essentially complete by the end of World War I. It had been a vast capital investment which permanently transformed the geography of agriculture and temporarily supported vast growth and geographic concentration of the steel industry in the Pittsburgh-Cleveland region, as well as the growth of temporary rail operations centers such as those of Altoona and Terre Haute. Since 1920 more capital investment went annually into public roads, exclusive of vehicles and the fuel and maintenance industries, than into the entire railroad system (Davis et al. 1972, pp. 534-535).

The resulting diffusion of personal accessibility had and still has countless ramifications. In the family-farm districts of the Midwest and South, the truck and tractor contributed to the technological obsolescence of the hired hand and the creation of a persistent labor surplus which accumulated in local cities and towns.

The spatial reorganization of food processing and distribution by grocery chains increased disparities between rich and poor places. The creation of virtually total interurban vehicular access on paved roads by the 1930s has helped larger urban areas far more than the smaller and more remote ones, by opening the latter to competition from outside, encouraging the outmigration of capital and entrepreneurship to the prosperous metropolitan areas without exposing the relatively immobile remaining labor forces to commensurate income opportunities.[a]

Labor migration not only lagged behind the movement of income sources into the biggest cities, but in bad times has actually tended to go the other way. There was a substantial slowing of big-city growth in the Great Depression as discouraged workers moved back to their home areas. Population trends in the current recession are similar. Even though jobs are even more scarce in the rural and small town areas to which the people return, there is still a human, if not economic, rationale in the pattern: if one has to be poor, one might as well be poor among family and old friends.

Boom industries of the period included automobiles, aircraft, appliances, chemicals, defense, electronics, government, paper, and petroleum. Many of those were involved in non-growing areas prior to their fall, but stagnated or moved on. Many like petroleum production were

---

[a] This "backwash effect" remarked by Hirschman (1965) is simply the back side of the cycle of cumulative advantage predicted by the Janelle model of spatial reorganization. See Pred (1974a), p. 56.

labor-intensive only in the development stage, stimulating rapid population increases but not providing commensurate permanent employment in places like Midland, Odessa, and Lake Charles. Paper for packaging and consumer durables provided longer periods of growth, but in places like Savannah it was growth punctuated by severe layoffs because of the disproportionate response of these industries to the business cycle, and especially of the more remote, absentee-owned plants within the industry.

Dramatic impacts of shifts in federal spending with military exigency and congressional seniority were seen in the spurts and falls of growth in Fort Smith in the 1940s, in Amarillo, Montgomery, Wichita Falls, Savannah, and other air base locations in the 1950s and 1960s, and the more recent impacts of military, space program, and SST procurement cutbacks upon Seattle-Tacoma, Los Angeles, Wichita, and the Cape Kennedy vicinity.

Another important trend of the mid-century period was the temporary reversal of the long-term decline of birth rates that accompanied the process of urbanization and industrialization since the mid-nineteenth century and reached very low levels in the depression of the '30s. An exceptionally large generation born from the latter 1940s through the early 1960s resulted in positive population growth even in areas with little employment growth and low incomes. Growing up in prosperous years this generation was better educated than any before. As it began to reach its most mobile years of age in the 1960s and attempted to enter the labor force, the areas lacking attractive job opportunities abruptly began to lose population as large fractions of their young generations moved away in search of fortunes commensurate with their educations. The number of non-growing metropolitan areas (as defined in Chapter 1) increased from nine in the 1940s to eleven in the '50s and twenty-five in the '60s. Fertility rates have declined, however, since the late 1960s, and the reverse sequence of effects can be anticipated. Local crude birthrates will probably tend to converge, because young populations will be more affected by the change, and local population changes will be more strongly affected by net migration than natural increase for a while. When the relatively small recent cohorts begin to enter their job-seeking years, total mobility probably will fall slightly, reducing again the rate at which local populations can adjust to economic changes.

3 Change Without Growth: Ten Cases

Ten non-growth SMSAs were visited for several days each by the author between November 1973 and July 1974. They were Pueblo, Amarillo, Fort Smith, Montgomery, Savannah, Wilkes-Barre, Scranton, Pittsburgh, Terre Haute, and St. Joseph. Most of the major regional groupings, industrial types, size classes, and historical situations found among non-growing SMSAs are represented within this group.

Each report presents a short history of the area's growth and decline, identifying where possible the major sources of change and describing the general character of the community. Demographic and economic changes in recent decades are then examined more closely, with particular emphasis on the period 1960-1970.

The purpose of the case studies is to explore the dynamics of changing community size and its human impacts in the chronological development of the ten areas. The treatment of areas is not uniform: rather, promising sources of insight are pursued opportunistically wherever they are found.

For the reader interested in comparative analysis, Chapter 14 will treat the full sample and a comparison group in a more structured way. In this chapter, however, the overriding objective is to get a sense of the human and historical experience of population stability or decline.

A number of themes will reappear with variations in the cases: the succession of boom to bust, and in a larger perspective the succession of one boom and bust cycle to another; the demographic "momentum" of rapid growth and the lag of population growth in adjusting to the loss of its underlying economic sources; the subtle and sometimes overt institutional deterrents against economic transformation of these places toward a more stable livelihood; the cumulative vulnerability of the areas' people and natural environments to destructive exploitation. The picture is bleak when one concentrates on such areas: the disequilibrating, divergent influences seem to dominate local levels of well being. Is the world of traditional economics, which constantly seeks an equilibrium, not applicable here? Its implications run seriously counter to present public policy and would seem to justify much more active government involvement in area growth management and stabilization.

The periods 1940-1970 and 1960-1970 were examined in somewhat more detail in the case studies because all the areas experienced decline in this

29

period, and because special data were available for these periods. It may be helpful to preview some of the methods and major conclusions of the analyses performed.

Detailed employment breakdowns by industry, employment shift analyses, and components of population change were assembled for the SMSAs by decades beginning in 1940. In addition, for the decade of the 1960s, population age profiles were made from Census data, and analyses of employment, mean wages, and wage changes by migration status and industry were derived from the Social Security Continuous Work History Sample.

The components of population change for the ten areas are summarized in table 3-1: natural increase, which is the excess of births over deaths, and net migration, which is the excess of inmigration over outmigration. Their sum is population growth. All figures are expressed as a percentage of the area's total population at the beginning of the decade. Net migration shows a larger range within the group, but natural increase varies surprisingly much, from 1.3 percent for St. Joseph in the 1960s to 28 percent for Amarillo in the 1950s. There is a discernible rise in natural increase rates in the 1950s and fall afterwards, consistent with national trends. There also appears to be a tendency for natural increase rates to fall following periods of strong net outmigration. There are strong regional and historical differences, the oldest and longest-declining areas having the lowest natural increase rates.

Shift-share analyses of employment changes in the last three decades were obtained from the Bureau of Economic Analysis for seven of the case study areas[a] through the generosity of Edgar Dunn of Resources for the Future, Inc. These analyses use the Esteban-Marquillas method, which differs from the conventional method of shift-share analysis (cf. Isard 1960; Perloff et al. 1960) in that it decomposes the "shift" or "competitive" component of growth into two components, one of which is independent of the local industry mix, in order to express better the "contribution to growth due to the special dynamism of the sector in that region compared with the average growth that such a sector has at the national level" (Esteban-Marquillas 1972, p. 250).

Table 3-2 summarizes the results of the analysis. It gives the components of total employment change, but not of individual sectors. Each number is expressed in units of workers. The first five columns, the starting population, and the four "effects," add up to the sixth, the total employment at the end of the decade. The total "effects" may be interpreted as follows:

Size Effect (Col. 2): U.S. Normal Distribution × U.S. Normal Rates.

[a] The BEA analyses grouped some SMSAs together, so that Wilkes-Barre and Scranton are combined in this analysis and Pueblo and St. Joseph data could not be obtained separately from nearby growing SMSAs.

Table 3-1
Components of Population Change for Case Study Areas, by Decade, 1940-1970

		Initial Population	Population Growth Rate (%)	Natural Increase Rate (%)	Net Migration Rate (%)
Amarillo	1940-50	61,430	41.9	21.8	20.1
	1950-60	87,140	71.6	28.0	43.6
	1960-70	149,493	−3.4	16.1	−19.5
	1970	144,396			
Fort Smith	1940-50	155,733	−9.0	12.8	−21.8
	1950-60	141,978	−4.8	16.0	−20.8
	1960-70	135,110	18.7	11.4	7.3
	1970	160,421			
Montgomery	1940-50	148,966	14.5	12.5	2.0
	1950-60	170,614	17.1	18.8	−1.7
	1960-70	199,734	0.8	11.9	−11.1
	1970	201,325			
Pittsburgh	1940-50	2,084,376	6.4	10.6	−0.2
	1950-60	2,213,236	8.7	12.0	6.8
	1960-70	2,405,435	−0.2	−4.7	−7.0
	1970	2.401,245			
Pueblo	1940-50	68,870	31.0	13.6	17.4
	1950-60	90,188	31.6	23.5	8.1
	1960-70	118,707	−0.4	8.1	−12.3
	1970	118,238			
St. Joseph	1940-50	94,067	2.9	1.3	1.6
	1950-60	96,826	−6.5	7.5	−14.0
	1960-70	90,581	−4.1	5.2	−9.2
	1970	86,915			
Savannah	1940-50	117,970	28.4	16.0	12.4
	1950-60	151,481	24.3	22.5	1.8
	1960-70	188,299	−0.3	13.0	−13.3
	1970	187,767			
Scranton	1940-50	301,423	−14.6	4.5	−19.1
	1950-60	257,396	−8.9	6.3	−15.6
	1960-70	234,531	−0.2	1.6	−1.8
	1970	234,107			
Terre Haute	1940-50	173,875	−0.8	7.1	−7.9
	1950-60	172,468	−0.2	6.8	−6.6
	1960-70	172,069	1.8	3.8	−2.1
	1970				
Wilkes-Barre	1940-50	441,518	−11.2	6.4	−17.6
	1950-60	392,241	−11.6	6.0	−17.6
	1960-70	346,972	−1.4	2.1	−3.5
	1970				

Sources: Population from U.S. Censuses of 1940 and 1970, calculated from county data; Components of change, 1960-70, from 1970 Census Report PHC(2)-2; Components of change, 1950-60 and net migration rates, 1940-50, from Current Population Reports P-23 #7; Natural Increase Rates 1940-50 calculated by residual method.

Table 3-2
Summary of Shift-Share Analysis: Effects on Total Employment

		Employment at Start Period	Size Effect: US Normal Distrib. × US Rates	Ind. Mix: Differential Distribution × US Rates	Allocation: Differential Distribution × Diff. Rates	Competitive: US Distribution × Diff. Rates	Employment at End of Period
Amarillo	1940-50	23,406	6,242	1,490	-3,361	9,158	36,938
	1950-60	36,938	5,716	827	-150,101	170,406	63,789
	1960-70	63,789	12,432	784	-48,508	31,680	60,177
Fort Smith	1940-50	38,147	10,172	-4,403	-7,007	6,179	42,981
	1950-60	42,981	6,668	-4,109	-7,082	2,682	41,110
	1960-70	41,110	8,040	-1,403	-10,519	18,692	55,866
Montgomery	1940-50	53,156	14,176	-1,914	-6,363	7,137	66,188
	1950-60	66,188	10,249	52	-17,703	15,179	73,965
	1960-70	73,965	14,413	-2,472	-6,942	-2,151	76,817
Pittsburgh	1940-50	862,355	229,939	44,702	-277,262	170,997	1,030,731
	1950-60	1,030,731	159,569	37,467	-48,857	-140,573	1,038,337
	1960-70	1,038,337	202,360	16,184	-40,893	-123,916	1,092,075
Savannah	1940-50	42,692	11,384	2,502	-7,041	7,742	57,284
	1950-60	57,284	8,866	2,952	-3,610	2,645	68,140
	1960-70	68,140	13,281	-1,314	-6,679	-1,183	72,244
Terre Haute	1940-50	47,698	12,715	-561	-6,626	8,820	62,047
	1950-60	62,047	9,607	-1,978	-14,122	4,352	59,905
	1960-70	59,905	11,675	-942	-4,248	13	66,400
Scranton-Wilkes-Barre-Hazleton	1940-50	201,116	53,626	-7,900	-26,617	11,188	231,410
	1950-60	231,410	35,823	-14,930	-43,775	-2,630	205,896
	1960-70	205,896	40,128	1,316	-5,601	-12,508	229,233

Source: Bureau of Economic Analysis, U.S. Department of Commerce.

The growth which would have occurred if the region grew at the same rate as the nation.

Industry Mix Effect (Col. 3): Differential Distribution × U.S. Normal Rates. The additional growth which would have occurred if each *sector* grew at its national rate.

Allocation Effect (Col. 4): Differential Distribution × Differential Rates. The growth in addition to the size and mix effects which would have occurred due to higher-than-normal growth rates in larger-than-normal industries. When negative, it reflects a failure to specialize in industries which grew at higher rates in the area than the nation, or a specialization in industries which grew at abnormally low rates. The Industry mix and Allocation effects may be added to reflect the total contribution of the area's specialization to its growth.

Competitive Effect (Col. 5): U.S. Normal Distribution × Differential Rates. The additional growth which would have occurred if each industry were the same proportion of total employment as in the nation. It indicates how well industry does in the area generally, reflecting "the special dynamism" of the region, if any. As discussed below, this and the preceding term are very sensitive to growth in sectors which are very small at the beginning of the period.

The new "competitive effect" and "allocation effect" terms provide a refinement on previous shift-share formats, but must be interpreted with caution. The concept of growth by multiplication which underlies them is not always appropriate. It assumes that there will be a causal relation of existing activities in a place and sector with future additions to that sector. It disregards the open character of the regional economy and the resulting ease with which new additions can be made from the outside, independently of what is already there. Thus, the "competitive effect" term reflects fairly plausibly the relative weakness of Pittsburgh in the steel industry, but gives a meaningless number, four times the area's total employment, to describe the competitive component of the rise of military employment in Amarillo in the 1950s. The term expresses the differential growth which would have occurred in this sector due to the differential growth rates if the sector had started the decade at a size proportional to its place in the national economy. A sector which was new to a region, then, shows very large actual and differential growth rates since its initial value was near zero, and a colossal "competitive effect" term when applied to the much larger theoretical U.S. normal value. By the same token, the "allocation effect" becomes a very large negative number for a newly developing sector in a region. This behavior does not invalidate the concepts, but calls for a knowledge of the communities when making comparisons.

Calculations of each term were obtained for thirty-one employment sectors for the periods 1940-1950, 1950-1960, and 1960-1970, in the SMSAs of Amarillo, Fort Smith, Montgomery, Pittsburgh, Savannah, Terre Haute, and Scranton-Wilkes-Barre-Hazleton. The resulting analysis is suggestive of fairly consistent processes of structural change which may be associated with metropolitan non-growth.

The allocation effect was strongly negative in every area for every period, regardless of whether the area was growing or declining at the time. This expresses a strong and consistent tendency of those communities toward faster than normal growth in the deficient sectors and slower than normal growth in the excessive ones, relative to the national structure. The effect illustrates a convergence mechanism, but not necessarily a stabilizing one unless the response of sectoral growth rates to an abnormal distribution is appropriate in timing, size, and duration. Large negative allocation effects suggest the possibility of a deviation-amplifying (boom and bust) mode of development, in which new sectors are pioneered, overdeveloped, and abandoned in an ongoing cycle.

The industry mix effects showed a negative or declining value in most cases. The failing industry mix reflected a general failure to keep up with national trends in the growth of trade and service industries and a tendency to attract slow-growing manufacturing sectors.

The competitive effect was negative in some episodes of employment stability or decline, positive in others. However, the sum of the competitive and allocation effects, equivalent to the traditional version of the competitive effect, is negative in all periods of decline observed. In effect, these non-growing areas are losing out both because their economic base is specialized in nationally slow-growing industries, and because they are competitively weak even in these industries.

Population age profiles for the case study areas showed curiously high shoulders, pinched waists, and bulging hips. In less anthropomorphic terms, the non-growing areas had large proportions of older people with relative deficits of young people in certain age groups. In recently declining areas the deficits tended to be limited to the age groups 0-5 and 20-25 years. In areas which had declined for some time the deficient age cohorts spread upward to include, in the extreme cases of Wilkes-Barre and Scranton, large parts of the working age span, but usually retained a characteristic projecting "shelf" just below age twenty. Comparisons of age profiles for 1960 and 1970 revealed strong age stratification of net migration, with most of the net movement in ages 0-5 and 15-30.

Analyses of migration industry and wage histories the Social Security Work History Sample revealed some surprising patterns in the ways people adapt to local economic changes. The least expected was the relatively small role of migration compared with flows in and out of the covered work force in accommodating job growth and decline in the case study areas, even in areas of moderate ''official'' unemployment. Wage gains of outmi-grants tended to exceed those of non-migrants, although non-migrants who changed industries during periods of local expansion tended to do well. The trade and service sectors sometimes appeared to be serving as reservoirs for underemployed workers, absorbing people from other industries in bad times and emitting them in good times. New entries to the work force tended to go disproportionately into the trade sector at very low wage levels.

These empirical themes will appear with variations throughout the following case studies. Generalizing from them is tempting, but will be reserved until Part II, after a hopefully better-rounded view has been presented of the human circumstances in which they occur.

4

Case Study: Amarillo SMSA, Texas

Figure 4-1 shows that a large part of the Amarillo SMSA is very recently developed. Steady growth from 1887 to 1950 was overshadowed by a massive population increase from 1950 to 1968 due to the establishment and growth of an air force base in the area. Net migration alone added 44 percent to the population in the decade of the 1950s and natural increase added another 28 percent. Equally striking is the precipitous fall of the area's relative income per capita, beginning in the boom phase and continuing more gradually after it passed. The air base was closed in 1968, approx-

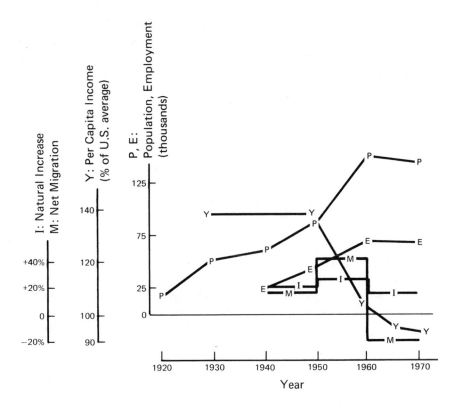

Figure 4-1. Composite of Trends: Amarillo SMSA

imately 10,000 families quickly left the area, and by 1970 the area's population was almost back down to the 1920-1950 trend line.

General Character

Civilian Amarillo is a pleasant, well-to-do prairie city, as its high pre-boom income suggests. It has several growing industries to supplement its agriculture-oriented trade and service base. As table 4-1 shows, its population is better educated than average for the division and holds a greater proportion of white-collar jobs. Incomes are more equally distributed than usual. Homeownership is high. Although the Census was taken in the midst of severe outmigration (note the high vacancy rates), unemployment and poverty rates were low and home values normal for the division.

A strikingly persistent characteristic of the Amarillo community has been its speed and aggressiveness in adopting new industries and converting old ones or abandoning them before they become obsolete. In the three decades for which shift-share data are available, it consistently shows very large positive competitive effects and negative allocation effects, reflecting the area's tendency to grow rapidly from a small base in new fast-growing sectors (table 3-2). Much the same pattern would characterize the area's earlier growth as well.

Amarillo has always been a cattle town. It used to receive steers, now calves. Its feedlot industry, founded in 1960, exists symbiotically with feed grain production on newly irrigated prairie within the county and with fertilizer production using natural gas. Water scarcity may threaten the beef industry's growth in a decade or two if importation schemes fail, but there is apparently still some capacity for expansion. The Amarillo area gas fields fire a smelter and supply a plant which makes most of the country's helium (Hammond 1971; Archambeau 1970). The city's trade and service region extends well beyond its immediate vicinity. The small rural towns of the area are dying out, and their trade seems to be going mostly to the row of shopping centers on the city's southwest frontier. Amarillo's steadily growing service sector includes West Texas State University, with 7,000 students in the south part of the SMSA, a handsome community college in the central area, and a technical college on part of the former air base. Wholesale distribution is also growing, with a large Levi Strauss distribution center now the area's largest private employer.

Chronological Development to 1940

Amarillo was founded as a cattle trading center at the intersection of the

Table 4-1

Selected 1970 Population and Housing Characteristics: Amarillo, Texas, SMSA

	SMSA	W.S. Central Division	243 SMSAs
Black	4.7%	4.3%	12.0%
Under 5 years	8.6%	8.2%	8.5%
65+ years	8.0%	11.8%	9.3%
Median years of education[1]	12.3	11.5	12.2
Unemployment	3.4%	4.2%	4.3%
White collar[2]	53.4%	47.0%	52.4%
Crafts and Foremen[2]	14.4%	14.3%	13.6%
Laborers and other	32.2%	38.7%	34.0%
Family incomes $15,000+	15.9%	16.8%	24.5%
Family incomes below low income	9.2%	10.1%	8.5%
Housing owner-occupied	68.1%	65.3%	59.5%
Median house value[3]	$12,304	$12,385	$19,027
Median gross rent	$86	$88	$117
Homeowner vacancy rate	5.2%	1.8%	1.1%
Rental vacancy rate	14.7%	10.7%	6.0%

Source: *County and City Data Book*, U.S. Bureau of the Census, 1972.

Notes:

1. Persons 25 years and over
2. Percentage of employed civilian labor force
3. Single family owner-occupied

Santa Fe Railroad with Fort Worth and Denver in 1887. It gradually diversified and grew as a minor but wealthy center of trade and finance (table 4-2). Natural gas discoveries in 1918, together with good rail access, induced the Guggenheims to establish a zinc smelter here about 1920, in the same period that they abandoned their coal-fired smelters in Pueblo. Local gas deposits were found to contain a large part of the world's stored helium, and the U.S. Bureau of Mines opened its Amarillo Helium Plant in 1929 to extract and store the gas. The area grew from 20,000 to 53,000 population in the '20s, but added only 8,000 people—less than the probable natural increase—in the '30s.

Census industrial data for 1940 (table 4-3) show the Amarillo area was still strongly specialized in trade, transportation, finance, and services, which accounted for 69 percent of the total employment. Thirty years later, at over twice the size, these sectors would still contain 69 percent of the area's total employment. Some radical changes were to be involved, however, in staying much the same: the conversion from rail to truck and air transportation, the suburbanization of much of the trade and service activity, the rationalization of the beef industry to feedlots and grain production, the rise and fall of a huge military base.

Table 4-2

Historical Population and Employment, Amarillo SMSA (Potter & Randall Counties, Texas)

Year	Population	% Change of Population	Employment	% Change of Employment	% of Employment Female
1880	31	—			
1890	1,036	—			
1900	2,783	168.6			
1910	15,736	465.4			
1920	20,385	29.5			
1930	53,150	160.6	18,228	—	21.8
1940	61,430	15.6	23,406	28.4	26.7
1950	87,140	41.9	36,895	57.6	29.2
1960	149,493	71.6	53,909	46.1	33.6
1970	144,396	−3.4	82,553	53.1	39.4
1973	150,400	1.0			

Sources:

Population: 1880-1920: 1920 *Census of Population*, Vol. 1, Table 49; 1930-1940: 1940 *Census of Population*, Vol. 1; 1950-1970: 1970 *Census of Population*, State reports; 1973: *Current Population Reports*, Ser. P25, No. 537.

Employment: 1930, 1940, 1950, 1960, and 1970 *Censuses of Population*.

Note: Employment is for ages 10+ in 1930, for ages 14+ 1940 to 1970.

Development in the 1940s and 1950s

The wartime and early postwar years saw steady expansion in the transportation, trade, and service sectors, but more rapid growth in construction and manufacturing, particularly smelting, machinery, and petroleum (natural gas) refining (table 4-3). In transportation, motor freight was the main source of growth and began to catch up with rail employment. Population within the present SMSA boundaries grew by 42 percent in the 1940s and relative income remained high.

Amarillo's 72 percent expansion from 1950 to 1960 in both population and employment provides the only recent example of extreme growth in the case studies. Acceleration of growth was due to the construction of the Amarillo Air Force Base, although there was also continued strong growth of manufacturing with great expansion of the area's beef processing industry and of fabricated metals and ordinance manufacture. West Texas State University's growth as well as air base demands were probably factors in the near-doubling of professional service employment in the 1950s. The other established trade, service, and transportation sectors expanded less rapidly, declining temporarily in their share of total employment. The air base and its associated services brought much lower-income people than the previous population, indicated by a 38-point drop in the area's relative income per capita from 1949 to 1965.

Development in the 1960s

The phasing out of the Amarillo Air Force Base was announced in 1964, but its personnel actually increased until 1967. It was finally closed in 1968, resulting in the departure of about 10,000 families. Meanwhile, the area was renewing itself in many ways, and preparing to make the most of the base closing. Some economic changes are not visible in the aggregate data of table 4-3, like the transformation of the beef industry from grazing to feedlots, which occurred in this period. Others are visible but misleadingly classified. The establishment of a Levi Strauss Co. national distribution center, by 1974 the area's largest employer, is registered under "apparel manufacturing." The area's traditional sectors—transportation, trade, and services—continued their steady growth and transformation, regaining their dominant position in the area's profile by 1970. Air replaced surface transportation as a source of growth in this decade. Trade and service development, which had previously been drawn along the "strip" leading to the air base, moved strongly toward the more attractive residential areas of the northwest suburbs.

When the base was finally closed, the city acquired most of the property, building a grandiose air terminal (giving Amarillo "the most airport terminal space per capita of any city in the world," *Airline Management,* August 1971), and leasing the hangars and shops as an "industrial park." The first major tenant was Bell Helicopters, which in 1969 moved in to repair helicopters damaged in Vietnam; its employment peaked at 1,700 in 1970, and was back down to 300 in 1972.

The impact of these losses also appears to have been geographically more localized than the large numbers would suggest. The air base was located outside of the city beyond the stockyards. The directly linked commercial and service activities grew up along the connecting highways—bars, pawnshops, motels—and apparently drew little trade from other parts of the city. Many were still empty in 1973, but the strip seemed to be slowly recovering with growth in the adjacent industrial district.

It is also noticeable that in the period of adjustment, 1968-1972, the local economy was able to shed over 10,000 jobs without a substantial rise in unemployment (table 4-4). Even given rapid growth in other sectors, explanations are needed for the community's seemingly painless adaptation.

Table 4-3
Employment by Selected Industrial Sectors, 1940-1970 Amarillo SMSA

	1940	1950	1960	1970
TOTAL EMPLOYMENT (FULL AND PART TIME)	23,406	36,938	63,789	60,177
AGRICULTURE,FORESTRY,FISHERIES AND OTHER	1,313	1,713	1,569	1,649
AGRICULTURE	1,305	1,710	1,560	1,649
FORESTRY,FISHERIES AND OTHER	8	3	9	
MINING	382	282	869	770
CONTRACT CONSTRUCTION	1,463	3,817	5,086	4,154
MANUFACTURING	2,389	3,687	6,180	6,642
FOOD AND KINDRED PRODUCTS	634	754	1,526	943
TEXTILE MILL PRODUCTS	2	8	7	27
APPAREL AND OTHER FABRICATED TEXTILE PRODUCTS	21	19	32	988
PRINTING,PUBLISHING AND ALLIED INDUSTRIES	300	629	770	1,018
CHEMICALS AND ALLIED PRODUCTS	127	242	403	310
LUMBER AND FURNITURE	106	181	399	368
MACHINERY	155	453	497	480
MACHINERY EXCEPT ELECTRICAL	--	402	401	387
ELECTRICAL MACHINERY	--	51	96	93
TRANSPORTATION EQUIPMENT	31	90	115	322
MOTOR VEHICLES AND MOTOR VEHICLES EQUIPMENT	28	72	36	48
TRANSPORTATION EXCLUDING MOTOR VEHICLES	3	18	79	274
OTHER MANUFACTURING	1,013	1,311	2,431	2,186
PAPER AND ALLIED PRODUCTS	--	13	20	23
PETROLEUM REFINING AND RELATED PRODUCTS	--	303	494	287
PRIMARY METALS INDUSTRIES	--	614	469	478
FABRICATED METALS + ORDNANCE		136	1,006	804
MISCELLANEOUS MANUFACTURING		245	442	594
TRANSPORTATION,COMM.,+PUB. UTILITIES	2,675	5,332	6,064	6,791
TRANSPORTATION	2,111	3,613	3,864	4,493
RAILROAD TRANSPORTATION	1,402	2,041	1,873	1,613
MOTOR FREIGHT TRANSPORTATION AND WAREHOUSING	436	882	1,388	1,429
OTHER TRANSPORTATION SERVICES	273	690	603	1,451
COMMUNICATIONS	289	795	867	974
ELECTRIC,GAS,AND SANITARY SERVICES	275	924	1,333	1,324

WHOLESALE AND RETAIL TRADE	6,894	11,105	14,138	16,098
WHOLESALE TRADE	1,602	2,993	3,541	4,381
RETAIL TRADE	5,292	8,112	10,597	11,717
EATING AND DRINKING PLACES	1,000	1,559	2,018	2,343
FOOD + DAIRY STORES	875	1,155	1,322	1,390
OTHER RETAIL TRADE	3,417	5,398	7,257	7,984
FINANCE,INSURANCE AND REAL ESTATE	1,090	1,538	2,623	3,401
SERVICES	6,133	8,274	13,524	17,549
BUSINESS SERVICES	4,157	4,783	6,774	6,901
LODGING PLACES AND PERSONAL SERVICES	1,848	2,142	2,785	2,807
BUSINESS AND REPAIR SERVICES	679	1,140	1,783	2,265
AMUSEMENTS AND REC. SERVICES	285	289	388	597
PRIVATE HOUSEHOLDS	1,345	1,212	1,818	1,232
PROFESSIONAL SERVICES	1,976	3,491	6,750	10,648
TOTAL GOVERNMENT	1,067	1,190	13,736	3,123
CIVILIAN GOVERNMENT	1,067	1,147	3,565	2,951
FEDERAL MILITARY	--	43	10,171	172

Source: Regional Economics Information System, Bureau of Economic Analysis, From Census Data.

Table 4-4
Civilian Employment and Unemployment Estimates, 1960-1972: Amarillo SMSA

	Annual Average			
	1960	*1967*	*1970*	*1972*
Civilian Labor Force	53,360	63,880	64,995	69,455
Employment	52,260	62,380	62,595	61,930
Unemployment	1,100	1,300	1,400	2,525
% Unemployed	3.9	2.3	3.7	3.9

Source: Texas Employment Commission.

To what extent can it be attributed to the high mobility of the recently arrived part of the population and the fact that most military personnel and some civilian employees were transferred elsewhere by the government, to the availability of jobs in other sectors, or to a lucky slackening in labor supply? Apparently, each of these factors had some importance.

The superimposed population age profiles for 1960 and 1970 (figure 4-2) show that the major population losses were in the cohorts aged under 15 and 25-40 in 1970. Surprisingly, there is only a small deficit in the cohort aged 20-25 in 1970, which would normally be expected to have been the most mobile one at the time of the cutbacks. The apparent reason is that the same cohort was already relatively small in size in 1960 (age 10-15) compared with the cohorts above and below it. Supply pressure from new entrants to the labor force could therefore have been falling off in the late '60s compared with the early part of the decade.

The Social Security Continuous Work History Sample provides a partial view of the interactions between demographic and economic change during the period (tables 4-5 and 4-6). It omits military and railroad workers, important sectors in Amarillo, and uses too small a sample (1 percent) to permit fine subdivisions of the data, but still permits some conclusions about the broad directions of change. Its perspective is that of the individual worker's experience over two successive five-year periods.

Overall wage movements for SSI covered workers according to their migration and work status are summarized in table 4-5. It confirms the point made earlier that inmigrants of the 1960-65 period earned about average mean wages at the beginning of the period but gained by only 12.5 percent. The greatest wage gains in the growth phase were made by experienced workers who changed jobs between industries, but in the declining half of the decade that group's gains were exceeded by those who left the area.

The industry breakdown, table 4-6, shows a rough correspondence with the aggregate trends described above: strong growth 1960-1965, slowing

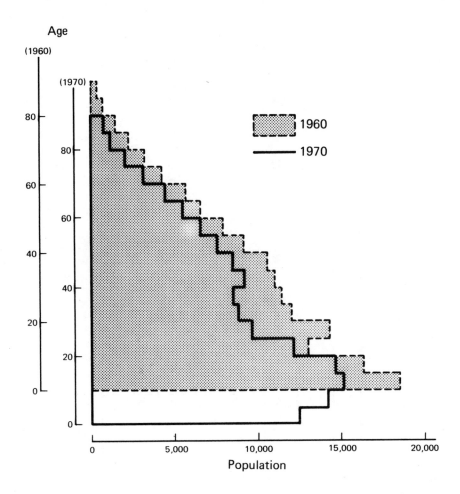

Figure 4-2. Population Age Profiles, 1960 and 1970 Amarillo, Tex. SMSA

1965-1970, with losses in trade and construction but with continued expansion in manufacturing and "government and other," which includes services. The analysis of migration and employment status may be grouped into three "components of change": net migration, changes of employment from one industry to another, and net entries to the covered work force, subtracting out retirements, draftees, etc.

In both halves of the decade the largest single component of change was "entered covered work force." The flood of new workers was not influenced by falling demand either in number or distribution: it went disproportionately into trade, even when that sector was contracting. Exits from the

Table 4-5
Migration Summary, All Industries, Amarillo SMSA (Based on Social Security Continuous Work History Sample (1%) First Quarter of 1960-65-70)

	THOUSANDS OF WORKERS	% OF TOTAL	1960-1965		
			1960 MEAN WAGES	1965 MEAN WAGES	% CHANGE MEAN WAGES
INITIAL COVERED WORK FORCE	38.7	100.0	3,721		
INMIGRANTS	11.5	29.7	3,892	4,377	12.5
OUTMIGRANTS	8.8	22.7	4,348	5,753	32.3
NET MIGRATION	2.7	7.0			
NONMIGRANTS:					
SAME INDUSTRY	12.4	32.0	4,453	5,507	23.7
DIFFERENT INDUSTRY	4.2	10.9	3,174	4,567	43.9
NET MILITARY AND OTHERS	.6	1.6			
ENTERED COVERED WORK FORCE	14.6	37.7		2,318	
LEFT COVERED WORK FORCE	12.9		2,834		
FINAL COVERED WORK FORCE	43.7	112.9		4,042	

1965-1970

	THOUSANDS OF WORKERS	% OF TOTAL	1965 MEAN WAGES	1970 MEAN WAGES	% CHANGE MEAN WAGES
INITIAL COVERED WORK FORCE	43.7	100.0	4,042		
INMIGRANTS	8.4	19.2	4,264	6,201	45.4
OUTMIGRANTS	13.3	30.4	4,162	7,319	75.9
NET MIGRATION	-4.9	-11.2			
NONMIGRANTS:					
SAME INDUSTRY	13.2	30.2	5,043	6,993	38.7
DIFFERENT INDUSTRY	4.8	11.0	3,069	4,730	54.1
NET MILITARY AND OTHERS	-.4	-.9			
ENTERED COVERED WORK FORCE	19.2	43.9		3,319	
LEFT COVERED WORK FORCE	11.0		3,139		
FINAL COVERED WORK FORCE	46.6	106.6		5,087	

Source: Regional Analysis Information System, Bureau of Economic Analysis.

Table 4-6
Migration Summary by Industry, Amarillo, Texas SMSA: (Based on Social Security Continuous Work History Sample (1 Percent), First Quarter of 1960-65-70) (in thousands of workers)

	Construction	Manufacturing	TPU	Trade	F.I.R.E.	Government and Other	All Industries
Initial covered work force 1960	3.4	4.4	4.9	13.1	2.8	9.5	38.7
1960-65:							
Immigrants	1.9	1.1	1.0	4.2	*	2.7	11.5
Outmigrants	.8	*	2.3	3.1	.7	1.5	8.8
Net migration	1.1	.8	-1.3	1.1	-.3	1.2	2.7
Non-migrants:							
Same industry	1.2	2.6	.9	3.3	.8	3.6	12.4
Left this industry	*	*	*	1.9	*	1.0	
Entered this industry	.6	1.3	*	1.1	*	.6	4.2*
Net transients	.6	1.3		-.8		-.4	
Net military and others	*	*	-.1	.1	*	.5	.6
Entered covered work force	1.2	1.8	.5	5.4	.9	4.8	14.6
Left covered work force	1.0	1.1	1.3	4.6	1.0	3.4	12.9
Net entries less exits	.2	.7	-.7	.7	-.1	.9	1.1

Final covered work force 1965	4.9	6.8	2.8	14.3	2.4	12.2	43.7
1965-70:							
Inmigrants	.8	1.4	1.8	1.6	.7	1.7	8.4
Outmigrants	2.0	2.1	.8	4.6	1.0	2.7	13.3
Net migration	-1.2	-.7	1.0	-3.0	-.3	-1.0	-4.9
Non-migrants:							
Same industry	1.1	3.4	.6	3.0	*	4.5	13.2
Left this industry	*	.8	*	2.3	*	1.1	
Entered this industry	*	1.1	*	1.0	.6	1.0	4.8**
Net transients		.3		-1.3	.6	-.1	
Net military and others	-.1	.3	-.5	-.1	.1	-.1	-.4
Entered covered work force	1.7	2.6	.6	7.1	.7	5.8	19.2
Left covered work force	1.3	.5	.8	4.0	.9	3.5	11.0
Net entries less exits	.5	1.8	.3	3.1	-.3	2.4	7.8
Final covered workforce 1970	4.0	8.8	3.3	13.0	2.5	13.3	46.6

*Statistically Insignificant
**Changed Industries.

covered work force—retirements, military draft, layoffs, etc.—were also a large component. Exits were stable or declined in every sector but construction, where new entries increased as well.

The aggregate work force adjustments, however, were accomplished mainly by migration. Inmigration fell and outmigration increased in the years of decline. Net migration within each industry tended to parallel the total for all industries rather than the growth or decline of the particular industry. New entries actually increased in the second half of the decade.

Structural adjustments were accomplished differently according to the industry, new entries dominating the rapid gainers like manufacturing, government, and other, but outward net migration dominating the major downward adjustments of construction and trade in the second half-decade. Net transfers between industries were a relatively small part of the structural adjustment process, but tended to flow from trade, government, and other, which had the highest gross entry rates by far, into manufacturing, where average earnings were much higher but where apparently some work experience was required.

In sum, the relatively successful accommodation of the Amarillo area to a severe job and population loss in the late 1960s may be credited to a happy combination of institutional, demographic, and economic circumstances. Many of the workers affected were transferred directly to non-local jobs, and their families relocated at government expense. Others not receiving this help nevertheless showed a high rate of spontaneous mobility. The number of young people reaching working age in the community slacked at the right time to relieve one source of supply pressure. And armed in advance with information that permitted investments in businesses and property linked with the air base to be amortized over a few years, the aggressively innovative local economy went right on spawning new sources of growth.

5

Case Study: Fort Smith SMSA, Arkansas-Oklahoma

The recent growth of the Fort Smith SMSA departs from a twenty-year trend of decline. In a fifty-year perspective, however, it does little to change the picture of long-term stagnation in figure 5-1. The urban parts of the area were largely developed just before the First World War, and total population fluctuated around 140,000 to 150,000 ever since. Income per capita rose from 52 percent of the U.S. average in 1929 to 73 percent in 1960, but its rank position among SMSAs in income per capita remained near bottom. Natural increase rates have been low for a southern SMSA, and net migration rates were strongly negative until the 1960s. While the Amarillo case study illustrated a mode of decline that was apparently not very harmful, Fort Smith seems to present the other side of the coin, a case of growth which seems to have done little good.

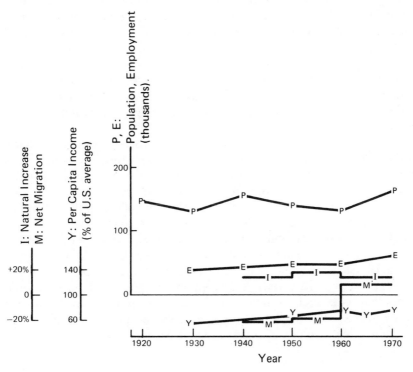

Figure 5-1. Composite of Trends: Fort Smith SMSA

General Description

The Fort Smith metropolitan area, like that of many cities on state or county borders, is somewhat exaggerated by the SMSA boundaries, which by convention follow county lines. The resulting statistical aggregate of four counties in two states includes a number of depressed and isolated small towns (2,500 persons or less) and rural areas, as well as the few true suburbs. The SMSA is, thus, over twice as populous as the Fort Smith urbanized area, but is even poorer and slower growing.

The central Fort Smith business area, a few blocks along Garrison Street before it crosses the Arkansas River, is a sad row of decrepit late nineteenth century commercial buildings. The former shopping street backs onto small run-down houses on one side, cavernous factories and warehouses on the others.

Driving out toward the edges of the city and adjacent Van Buren, one encounters occasional well-maintained neighborhoods and a very prosperous park-like district, but the dominant impression is of pervasive decay. There are unexplained gaps, probably over-optimistic subdivisions of the '20s. On the perimeter of the more or less continuous part of the city are a few small factories and shopping centers of recent vintage. The remainder of the area is largely farmland and second growth forest, with occasional small towns, typically containing a food processing plant, an equipment store, a school, and a gas station. Compounding long-term decline of urban employment, the rural portions of the SMSA have the added problem of seasonal unemployment. Alma, Arkansas, for instance, twelve miles west of Fort Smith, exists for a single large pickling plant which operates summers only.

The area's present character is a curious blend of western and southern. Its black population is only 4 percent and falling. Historically its trade was with the West, but it sided with the Confederacy and suffered under Reconstruction. It is in a right-to-work state. Its recent growth in low-wage, non-union manufacturing jobs is reminiscent of the textile mill towns of the Coastal Plains and the sewing shops of Appalachia.

Its 1970 population and housing profile (table 5-1) shows a poor and aging community. The area's 1970 population, like that of the West South Central Division as a whole, had a greater proportion of old people than the average of metropolitan areas. An exceptional proportion of the labor force is unskilled. One family's income in five is below poverty level and very few are over $15,000. Clearly more than a decade's growth was needed to overcome a half century of stagnation and decline.

Table 5-1

Selected Population and Housing Characteristics Fort Smith SMSA 1970

	SMSA	West South Central Division	243 SMSAs
Black %	4.2	4.3	12.0
Under 5 years %	8.4	8.2	8.5
65 years and over %	12.3	11.8	9.3
Median years of education[1]	10.8	11.5	12.2
Unemployed %	4.8	4.2	4.3
White collar[2] %	39.6	47.0	52.4
Crafts and Foremen[2] %	14.9	14.3	13.6
Laborers and other %	45.5	38.7	34.0
Family incomes over $15,000 %	7.3	16.8	24.5
Family incomes below low income	19.8	10.1	8.5
Housing owner occupied %	70.1	65.3	59.5
Median house value[3]	$9,416	$12,385	$19,027
Median gross rent	$ 69	$ 88	$ 117
Home owner vacancy rate %	1.8	1.8	1.1
Rental vacancy rate %	8.7	10.7	6.0

Source: *County and City Data Book*, U.S. Bureau of the Census, 1972

Notes:

1. Persons 25 years and over

2. Percentage of employed civilian labor force

3. Single family owner-occupied

Chronological Development to 1940

Conventional local histories emphasize Fort Smith's long period as riverport gateway to the Western Frontier from 1817 to the 1880s, dispensing gear to the forty-niners, justice and whiskey to the Indian territories. For all that, it was only a small town of 3,000 in 1880, struggling belatedly to secure a westward rail connection which might allow it to survive despite the declining river traffic (Patton 1967; Butler 1972). The Arkansas portion of the area was largely farmland by then, and had a population of 29,200 (table 5-2). The connections were made and a modest boom followed; Fort Smith remained a minor, if exceptionally rowdy city.

The present city was essentially built in one mad scramble in the years around 1910 to exploit the Massard Prairie natural gas field. Gas was found there in 1901 and distributed in the city in 1905. One hundred and twenty-

Table 5-2

Historical Population and Employment, Fort Smith SMSA (Crawford & Sebastian Counties, Arkansas; LeFlore & Sequoyah Counties, Oklahoma)

Year	Population	% Change in Population	Employment	% Change in Employment
1860*	14,158	—		
1870*	16,811	18.7		
1880*	28,975	72.3		
1890*	47,140	62.7		
1900*	58,205	23.5		
1910*	76,220	31.0		
1910**	130,352	—		
1920**	152,039	16.6		
1930**	139,376	−8.3	35,237	—
1940**	155,733	11.7	38,147	8.3
1950**	141,978	−9.0	42,981	12.7
1960**	135,110	−4.8	41,110	−4.4
1970**	160,421	18.7	55,866	35.9
1973**	170,000	3.7		

Sources:

Population: 1880-1920: 1920 *Census of Population*, Vol 1, Table 49; 1930-1940: 1940 *Census of Population*, Vol. 1; 1950-1970: 1970 *Census of Population*, State reports; 1973: *Current Population Reports*, Ser. P25, No. 537.

Employment: 1930, 1940, 1950, 1960, and 1970 *Census of Population*.

*Arkansas counties only.
**Present total SMSA.

six wells had been drilled in the field by 1911, the city's population was near 30,000, and local industries included "steel and iron works, smelters, glass works, brick works, cotton oil plants, furniture factories, and the largest sorghum mill in the world," with such amenities as opera, an amusement park, and legalized prostitution (Butler 1972). By 1920 the present SMSA contained 152,000 people, only 8,000 less than in 1970. The energy-based industries declined in the 1920s and 1930s, although the last big smelter was not torn down until 1966.

During the next forty years of decline, there were two complete transformations of the gradually degenerating energy-based economy, first to a military economic base and then to manufacturing.

Development in the 1940s and 1950s

Camp Chaffee Army Base was built in 1941 and soon contained over 30,000 persons. It served as an armored division training camp and a mustering-out point. It became the main industry of the area. Closed in 1946, it reopened for the periods 1948-1950, 1950-1956, 1956-1959, and 1961-1965, and is now only a reserve camp. During this period agricultural employment declined and the area became increasingly specialized in military and military-linked trade and service activities (table 5-3). Virtually the only large employers to survive from the early period were two large makers of wood furniture (Fort Smith Clipping File, Fort Smith Public Library). By the late 1950s the area was in severe economic distress.

Development in the 1960s

Industrial promotion was seriously undertaken in 1957. It was given a boost by Act 9 of the Arkansas legislature in 1960, enabling municipal revenue bond financing of both plant construction and equipment, which Fort Smith and nearby Van Buren used heavily to develop industrial sites and bring in manufacturing and food processing plants.

The massive Arkansas River Waterway Project opening navigation past Fort Smith to Tulsa apparently had little to do with the growth in the 1960s; there are still no important waterfront facilities in the area. The typical new jobs are in food, appliance, and furniture manufacturing, relatively low-wage sectors.

The 18 percent population gain in the 1960s reflected a period of superficially successful industrial promotion, but the area's falling income rank (from 222nd to 228th out of 243 SMSAs) reflected more poignantly the very low wages the jobs brought. Twenty percent of Fort Smith's families still had incomes below poverty level in 1970, and only 7 percent earned $15,000 or more. Unemployment rates improved moderately in the decade (table 5-4).

Fort Smith's age profile (figure 5-2) changed strikingly little in shape between 1960 and 1970, considering the substantial increase of total population. Inmigrants tended to be substantially older than outmigrants and probably included a large proportion of returning former residents. There was a net gain in population only for the cohorts aged 30-55 and under 20 in 1970 (the spaces marked "G" in figure 5-2). The age profile, therefore, remained high-shouldered with the characteristic projecting shelf just below the normal age of entering the labor market which is typical of labor surplus areas.

The Social Security Continuous Work History Sample shows a small net outmigration of workers for both halves of the 1960s (tables 5-5 and 5-6). Very large numbers of people entered the covered work force—more than the area's total employment at the start of the decade—and relatively few left it. The mean wage levels of new entrants were low, particularly in the second half of the decade.

Table 5-3
Employment of Selected Industrial Sectors, 1940-1970, Fort Smith SMSA

	1940	1950	1960	1970
TOTAL EMPLOYMENT (FULL AND PART TIME)	38,153	43,094	41,261	56,069
AGRICULTURE, FORESTRY, FISHERIES AND OTHER	13,119	9,198	2,975	2,019
AGRICULTURE	13,089	9,150	2,852	1,938
FORESTRY, FISHERIES AND OTHER	30	48	123	81
MINING	973	1,272	611	723
CONTRACT CONSTRUCTION	1,358	2,829	2,853	4,562
MANUFACTURING	6,090	7,668	10,080	16,548
FOOD AND KINDRED PRODUCTS	1,291	1,708	1,820	2,404
TEXTILE MILL PRODUCTS	8	35	12	47
APPAREL AND OTHER FABRICATED TEXTILE PRODUCTS	174	192	300	360
PRINTING, PUBLISHING AND ALLIED INDUSTRIES	366	525	655	789
CHEMICALS AND ALLIED PRODUCTS	185	181	95	147
LUMBER AND FURNITURE	2,678	2,646	3,511	4,389
MACHINERY	45	122	760	3,944
MACHINERY EXCEPT ELECTRICAL	—	106	146	629
ELECTRICAL MACHINERY	—	16	614	3,315
TRANSPORTATION EQUIPMENT	29	73	116	383
MOTOR VEHICLES AND MOTOR VEHICLES EQUIPMENT	21	35	19	169
TRANSPORTATION EXCLUDING MOTOR VEHICLES	8	38	47	214
OTHER MANUFACTURING	1,314	2,186	2,811	4,085
PAPER AND ALLIED PRODUCTS	—	341	954	1,058
PETROLEUM REFINING AND RELATED PRODUCTS	—	53	72	29
PRIMARY METALS INDUSTRIES	—	280	70	89

FABRICATED METALS + ORDNANCE	—	332	369	904
MISCELLANEOUS MANUFACTURING	—	1,180	1,346	2,005
TRANSPORTATION, COMM., + PUB. UTILITIES	2,366	3,396	3,025	3,414
TRANSPORTATION	1,804	2,363	1,949	2,030
RAILROAD TRANSPORTATION	1,146	1,386	746	556
MOTOR FREIGHT TRANSPORTATION AND WAREHOUSING	489	550	708	1,067
OTHER TRANSPORTATION SERVICES	169	427	495	407
COMMUNICATIONS	208	461•	452	593
ELECTRIC, GAS, AND SANITARY SERVICES	354	572	624	791
WHOLESALE AND RETAIL TRADE	6,280	9,126	9,715	11,930
WHOLESALE TRADE	-1,125	1,914	1,844	2,442
RETAIL TRADE	5,155	7,212	7,871	9,488
EATING AND DRINKING PLACES	715	1,250	1,296	1,843
FOOD + DAIRY STORES	1,228	1,462	1,206	1,605
OTHER RETAIL TRADE	3,212	4,500	5,371	6,040
FINANCE, INSURANCE AND REAL ESTATE	607	887	1,249	1,844
SERVICES	6,492	7,258	8,940	12,840
BUSINESS SERVICES	3,883	3,995	4,371	4,342
LODGING PLACES AND PERSONAL SERVICES	1,179	1,449	1,336	1,592
BUSINESS AND REPAIR SERVICES	672	971	1,176	1,493
AMUSEMENTS AND REC SERVICES	223	314	230	307
PRIVATE HOUSEHOLDS	1,809	1,261	1,629	950
PROFESSIONAL SERVICES	2,609	3,263	4,569	8,498
TOTAL GOVERNMENT		1,460	1,813	2,189
CIVILIAN GOVERNMENT	908	1,346	1,658	1,986
FEDERAL MILITARY	—	114	155	203

Source: Regional Economics Information System, Bureau of Economic Analysis, from Census Data.

Table 5-4
Selected Annual Average Unemployment Rates, Fort Smith SMSA

1963	1966	1969	1971	1973
7.0	6.1	4.3	5.8	4.6

Source: Arkansas Department of Employment Security

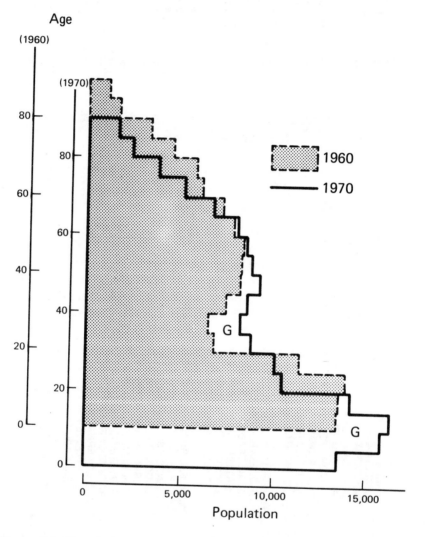

Figure 5-2. Population Age Profiles, 1960 and 1970 Fort Smith, Ark. SMSA

Employment growth in the first half decade was mainly in the trade and government sectors (the latter includes services). The major increases of manufacturing employment occurred in the second half of the decade, accompanied by a slowing of growth in trade and government and other. All three sectors showed strong excesses of entries over exits, but trade and government and other had net outmigration, and in the second half-decade also had net losses of employees to other sectors, mainly manufacturing. The transportation, communication, and public utilities sector, which paid by far the highest wages, declined sharply, but made a partial recovery.

In conclusion, it appears that the Fort Smith area's heavy investment in growth inducements from 1958 on succeeded, by the late 1960s, in stimulating a spurt of employment growth. The new jobs, mostly in manufacturing, were taken largely by new entrants to the covered work force who would otherwise very likely have left the area. Whether they were better off not leaving must be seriously questioned: clearly, for example, outmigrants leaving the area ended up making more money. As new entrants to the work force they were at the bottom of their pay scales, which together with the relatively lower wage levels in the industries that grew helps explain the failure of income per capita to rise significantly. A harder question will be whether the area can provide this new generation of workers with advancement opportunities in the years to come: in other words, whether the bulk expansion of the 1960s can be transformed into qualitative improvements of life opportunities.

Table 5-5

Migration Summary, All Industries, Fort Smith SMSA (Based on Social Security Continuous Work History Sample (1%) First Quarter of 1960-65-70)

	THOUSANDS OF WORKERS	% OF TOTAL	1960-1965		
			1960 MEAN WAGES	1965 MEAN WAGES	% CHANGE MEAN WAGES
INITIAL COVERED WORK FORCE	30.4	100.0	2,933		
INMIGRANTS	4.6	15.1	3,166	4,055	28.1
OUTMIGRANTS	5.0	16.4	2,499	3,998	60.0
NET MIGRATION	-.4	-1.3			
NONMIGRANTS:					
SAME INDUSTRY	13.9	45.7	3,754	4,996	33.1
DIFFERENT INDUSTRY	2.7	8.9	2,285	3,659	60.1
NET MILITARY AND OTHERS	.4	1.3			
ENTERED COVERED WORK FORCE	15.4	50.7		2,360	
LEFT COVERED WORK FORCE	8.4		2,127		
FINAL COVERED WORK FORCE	37.4	123.0		3,650	

1965-1970

	THOUSANDS OF WORKERS	% OF TOTAL	1965 MEAN WAGES	1970 MEAN WAGES	% CHANGE MEAN WAGES
INITIAL COVERED WORK FORCE	37.4	100.0	3,650		
INMIGRANTS	6.7	17.9	3,845	5,162	34.3
OUTMIGRANTS	7.1	19.0	4,082	6,690	63.9
NET MIGRATION	-.4	-1.1			
NONMIGRANTS:					
SAME INDUSTRY	16.9	45.2	3,902	5,808	48.8
DIFFERENT INDUSTRY	3.8	10.2	3,190	5,644	76.9
NET MILITARY AND OTHERS	.8	2.1			
ENTERED COVERED WORK FORCE	18.7	50.0			
LEFT COVERED WORK FORCE	9.3		3,091	2,838	
FINAL COVERED WORK FORCE	47.2	126.2		4,484	

Source: Regional Analysis Information System, Bureau of Economic Analysis.

Table 5-6
Migration Summary by Industry, Fort Smith SMSA (Based on Social Security Continuous Work History Sample (1%) First Quarter of 1960-65-70)

THOUSANDS OF WORKERS

GOVERNMENT AND OTHER, INCLUDING UNCLASSIFIED

FINANCE, INSURANCE AND REAL ESTATE

WHOLESALE AND RETAIL TRADE

TRANSPORTATION, COMMUNICATION AND PUBLIC UTILITIES

MANUFACTURING

CONTRACT CONSTRUCTION

MINING

AGRICULTURE, FORESTRY AND FISHERIES

	5.5	.6	7.5	2.6	12.0	1.4	.5	*
INITIAL COVERED WORK FORCE, 1960	5.5	.6	7.5	2.6	12.0	1.4	.5	*
1960-1965								
IMMIGRANTS	.8	*	.7	.5	1.6	.7	*	.
OUTMIGRANTS	.9	*	1.5	.6	1.1	.7	*	*
NET MIGRATION	-.1	.1	-.8	-.1	.5	.0	.	-.1
NONMIGRANTS:								
SAME INDUSTRY	2.9	*	3.1	1.3	6.1	*	.	*
LEFT THIS INDUSTRY	*	.	.8	*	1.5	*	.	.
ENTERED THIS INDUSTRY	1.0	.	.8	.	.5	*	*	.1
NET MILITARY AND OTHERS	.1	*	.1	*	.0	.1	.	.9
ENTERED COVERED WORK FORCE		4.9	.5	4.1	*	4.6	*	*
LEFT COVERED WORK FORCE	1.5	*	1.9	.6	3.1	.5	.5	
FINAL COVERED WORK FORCE, 1965	9.7	1.0	9.0	2.2	13.0	2.0	*	*
1965-1970								
INMIGRANTS	1.1	.	.9	.7	3.4	*	*	*
OUTMIGRANTS	1.7	*	1.6	.6	2.1	.7	*	*
NET MIGRATION	-.6	-.3	-.7	.1	1.3	-.3	.	.1
NONMIGRANTS:								
SAME INDUSTRY	4.3	*	3.8	1.0	7.1	*	*	.
LEFT THIS INDUSTRY	.7	*	1.2	*	1.0	*	*	*
ENTERED THIS INDUSTRY	.6	*	.6	.5	1.4	*	.1	.
NET MILITARY AND OTHERS	.1	*	.0	*	.5	.1	.	*
ENTERED COVERED WORK FORCE	5.1	.7	4.9	*	6.7	.7	*	*
LEFT COVERED WORK FORCE	3.0	*	2.2	.5	2.7	.8	.	.
FINAL COVERED WORK FORCE, 1970	11.2	1.3	10.4	2.5	19.2	1.9	*	*

Source: Regional Analysis Information System, Bureau of Economic Analysis.
*Statistically insignificant

6

Case Study: Montgomery SMSA, Alabama

The Montgomery area experienced two decades of non-growth in this century. It declined slightly in the decade 1910-1920 (not shown in figure 6-1), grew slowly for forty years and then stopped near 200,000 in the 1960s (figure 6-1). Slow growth resumed in the early 1970s. Its income per capita was consistently low. Population growth since 1940 was due largely to high rates of natural increase, as net migration moved from a weak positive rate to one that is strongly negative, and employment growth showed no upturn.

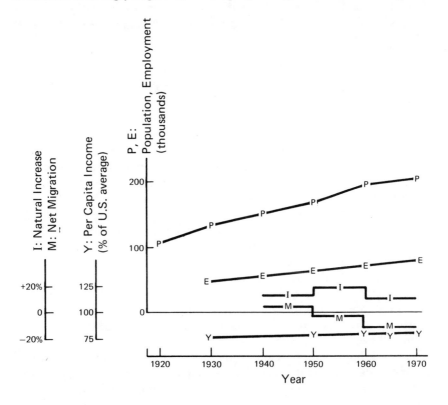

Figure 6-1. Composite of Trends, Montgomery SMSA

General Description

The Montgomery area has four major parts, and four corresponding cultures. There are two distinct rural parts, Appalachian and Black Belt. The northern rural part is Appalachian in character with marginal farmland, much of it returning to pine forest, with hills and lakes, summer resort areas, and a few small textile mill towns. The southern rural part is black soil farm land, once the best cotton-growing land in the South but now producing corn, peanuts, and other crops (as well as cotton) from the more productive bottom lands. These are occupied by large, prosperous, highly mechanized farms, white-owned and -run. The poorer land is in small holdings or tenant farms, occupied largely by blacks. The farm areas, rich and poor, have been slowly depopulating for most of this century.

There are also two distinct urban parts, depressive-central and manic-suburban. Central Montgomery includes the tombstone-white Alabama State Capitol buildings and a surrounding area of former merchants' houses, a commercial district dominated by grandiose, 1890s-style warehouses and offices, a small industrial area, and a ring of progressively smaller housing.

A ring-road surrounds the city, connecting Maxwell Air Force Base, the Air War College, and the former Gunter Air Force Base with a nearly continuous eruption of shopping centers—the newer ones air-conditioned—and condominium or apartment complexes. Hospitals, hotels, and office buildings are all found on the ring-road as well. Proprietors and customers are virtually all white. The area's developers, wooing a transient military market, could not have more firmly repudiated, symbolically and economically, the older more troubled Montgomery.

A population and housing profile of the area based on the 1970 Census (table 6-1) distinguishes the area from most of the other case studies. It has relatively more black people, but their numbers are declining. It has more young and fewer old people, reflecting both military and rural components of the population. Its large number of white-collar workers are associated mainly with state and local government. It has less homeownership than is typical for other non-growing areas or for the East South Central Division because of a very low rate for black families, who also have high rates of crowding and very low median income. In only five SMSAs do black families have lower median incomes.

The low homeowner vacancy rates, contrasted with the very high rental vacancy rate, reflects the fact that the major groups to leave in the 1960s were blacks and military personnel, which are both predominantly non-homeowner groups.

Very high rates of female employment have prevailed since the earliest Census employment data for the area (table 6-2), in part because of the large

Table 6-1

Selected Population and Housing Characteristics, Montgomery SMSA, 1970

	Montgomery SMSA	East South Central Division	243 SMSAs
Black %	34.9	20.0	12.0
Under 5 years %	8.9	8.6	8.5
65 years and over %	9.1	9.9	9.3
Median years of education[1]	12.1	10.5	12.2
Unemployed %	3.8	4.6	4.3
White collar[2] %	50.7	40.5	52.4
Crafts and Foremen[2] %	12.4	14.5	13.6
Operatives, laborers and other %	36.9	45.0	34.0
Family incomes over $15,000 %	15.1	10.9	24.5
Family incomes below low income[3] %	19.3	21.0	8.5
Housing owner occupied %	61.5	66.7	59.5
Median house value[4]	$16,395	12,534	19,027
Median gross rent	$74	76	117
Home owner vacancy rate %	1.9	1.3	1.1
Rental vacancy rate %	12.0	8.3	6.0

Montgomery SMSA by Race

	Black	White & Other
Population change, 1960-70	−6.1%	+4.9%
Median family income	4010	9854
Housing units owner-occupied	41.0%	70.3%
Housing units with 1.01 or more persons/rm.	27.1%	4.2%
Housing units with no automobile available	48.3%	8.4%

Source: *County and City Data Book*, U.S. Bureau of the Census, 1972.

1. Persons 25 years and over.
2. Percentage of employed civilian labor force.
3. As defined by 1970 Population Census Based on Family Size
4. Single family owner-occupied.

number of black women employed as domestics and as farm laborers. In 1930, for example, 41.3 percent of blacks employed were women, a very high proportion even by contemporary norms. Further increases in recent decades have reflected growth in government, textiles and apparel employment, and continued large numbers of domestic service workers.

Chronological Development to 1940

In the early nineteenth century, a series of southern inland cities were

Table 6-2
Employment by Sex, 1930-1970, Montgomery, Alabama SMSA

	1930	1940	1950	1960	1970
Employment	47,343	53,156	62,659	67,516	73,253
Male	29,115	36,425	40,041	40,615	42,494
Female	18,228	16,731	22,618	26,901	30,759
% Female	38.5	31.5	36.5	39.8	42.0
(U.S. % Female)	(22.1)	(24.7)	(28.0)	(32.8)	(37.7)

Source: *Census of Population*, 1930, 1940, 1950, 1960, 1970.

Note: 1930 data are for ages 10 and older.
　　　1940-70 data are for ages 14 and older.

developed as shipping points at the heads of navigation of the major rivers flowing out of the Appalachian Mountains (Vance and Demerath 1954, p. 10). Accommodating only shoal-draft river boats, they served to extend inland the agricultural hinterlands of the major port cities of the Atlantic and Gulf Coasts, but in most cases they did not begin to erode the coastal cities' trade and financial dominance for half a century. The restoration of the southern railway systems in the 1870s, and their interconnection in the 1880s along the piedmont rather than the coast, gave these cities a new lease on life and in some respects inverted the whole geography of the region (Vance and Demerath 1954, p. 40). The region's greatest markets were by then in the northern cities of the United States, not Europe. With rail access, the inland capitals, which had always been closer to the richest land, now became the more favored spots for shipping and trade as well. If it had not been for the decline of the area's cotton industry soon after, the growth of the Piedmont cities might have been truly spectacular. Atlanta was the strongest of them—after the cotton crash it was unchallenged—and might have captured the bulk of Piedmont trade anyway. As it was, the Piedmont cities all saw some very prosperous years around the turn of the century. This transformation involved two of the case study areas. Montgomery, at the head of the Alabama River above Mobile, briefly surpassed its coastal counterpart, but being totally dependent on one product was harder hit by the decline of cotton after around 1900 and failed to keep pace thereafter. Savannah, a coastal city, was reduced to the status of a subregional center by the growth of Atlanta 300 miles inland.

　　Montgomery lies on the Alabama River below the confluence of the Coosa and the Tallapoosa. There was steamboat traffic down the Alabama to the gulf at Mobile from 1821 (with regular service until 1910) and sometimes up the Coosa to Wetumpka; flatboats could be poled down the Coosa from Rome, Georgia. Nevertheless, Montgomery was for its first

Table 6-3

Historical Population and Employment, Montgomery SMSA (Montgomery & Elmore Counties, Alabama)

Data	Population	% Change in Population	Employment	% Change in Employment
1870	58,151	—		
1880	69,858	20.1		
1890	77,904	11.5		
1900	98,146	26.0		
1910	110,423	12.5		
1920	108,938	−1.3		
1930	132,951	22.0	47,343	—
1940	148,966	12.0	53,156	12.3
1950	170,614	14.5	62,659	17.9
1960	199,734	17.1	67,516	7.8
1970	201,325	0.8	73,253	8.5
1973	240,600	3.4		

Sources:

Population: 1870-1920: 1920 *Census of Population*, Vol. 1, Table 49; 1930-1940: 1940 *Census of Population*; 1950-1970: 1970 *Census of Population*, State reports; 1973: *Current Population Reports*, Ser. P25, No. 537.

Employment: 1930, 1940, 1950, 1960 and 1970 *Census of Population*

twenty years just another of the 200 or so steamboat landings along the river system (*The Rivers of Alabama,* pp. 80-152).

Montgomery became significant among the Piedmont cities only after 1840 (Vance and Demerath 1954). It was incorporated in 1837, grew rapidly as a market town, and was selected as the state capital in 1846. A yellow fever epidemic reduced the population for the decade of the 1850s. The Civil War, while catastrophic to the South's economy generally, saw some growth of the area—it was for a while the capital of the Confederacy—and in 1870 Montgomery County "was considered the one (remaining) agricultural county in the State" (*Montgomery Guide*), with a population of 58,000 (table 6-3).

The great boom of Black Belt cotton production occurred in the 1880s and 1890s. The latter part of the boom coincided with the interconnection of five rail lines with the national system at Montgomery, and the creation of what are now the major urban and rural features of the area.

The boom years at the end of the century must have been extraordinary. The "nation's first electric street railway" (one of several) was built. In 1900 Montgomery claimed "the second highest white male literacy rate in the nation" (Gay 1957, p. 20)—a claim notable for its exclusions: the area's population was nearly 70 percent black at the time. The immense Commercial Street warehouses and office buildings, bombastic in style, and the large, handsomely finished railroad station, were completed. Several industries were established, of which only furniture manufacturing remains significant. The Wright Brothers were brought in to set up an airport and flying school in 1911. Cotton farming had already reached its peak in 1900, however, and was soon afterwards decimated by pests, soil depletion, and overplanting. Today the warehouses stand empty; the station is padlocked.

The area was apparently carried on by entrepreneurial and demographic momentum for a decade's growth after the decline of cotton set in, but there was little to sustain it. The area declined slightly in total population from 1910 to 1920. The brunt of the downturn was borne by black people. Black population declined by 8,000, from 70 percent to 60 percent of the total, while white population increased by 5,700. As the rural population of surrounding central Alabama slowly declined in succeeding years, Montgomery's population became swollen with an impoverished, semirural labor surplus, a condition that was to persist half a century.

In the 1920s a cotton yarn mill was established in Montgomery by the West Boylston Manufacturing Co. to take advantage of the labor surplus, and became for a while the area's largest employer (*Montgomery Guide,* p. 13). Industrial growth slowed in the 1930s, but Montgomery extended its trade and service area as the smaller towns of central Alabama declined, and state government grew as it took on more public works and service functions.

Racial separation was also reinforced in this era. In 1937, the city's principal newspaper began to publish a separate edition for black readers, a practice that was continued into the 1960s.

Development in the 1940s and 1950s

In 1940 nearly one-fourth of the area's employment was still in agriculture. About half was in transportation, utilities, finance, trade and services, and one-tenth in government (table 6-4).

According to the shift-share analysis, the only sectors significantly above national proportions were agriculture, government, and private household services.

The most important economic changes of these two decades were the growth of state, local, and military government employment, and the precipitous decline of agriculture. By 1960, agriculture employed only 5 percent, but government nearly one-fifth. Transportation, utilities, finance, trade and services increased their share of the growing total employment from 48 percent to 55 percent, but remained below national average proportions.

The city was aggressive in securing new and expanded federal installations during and after World War II. It leased the site of Gunter Air Base and the Air University to the government. Maxwell Air Base grew. A large V.A. hospital was established after the war, located like the others on the perimeter of the city.

The Civil Rights Movement caused exceptional bitterness in Montgomery, possibly because it was so unexpected to the complacent white bureaucratic class that dominated state and local government, finance, and the press. They must have been shocked and hurt to be displayed to a national audience as the oppressors in the Montgomery Bus Boycott, the bombing of Dr. King's house in 1956, and the March to Selma in 1957. W. T. Gay's curious blank-verse book, *Montgomery, Alabama: A City in Crisis* (1957), evokes some of their feelings, in fascinating contrast with Dr. King's book, *Stride Towards Freedom: The Montgomery Story*. The white response, however, was ultimately negative and self-destructive. The public parks and recreation facilities of the central city, rather than be integrated, were closed, fenced, and padlocked until 1967. On the insistence of local advertisers, the newspaper was turned over to a conservative editor after the Selma march: local news was to be played down, controversy ignored. White Montgomery headed precipitously for the outer neighborhoods.

Development in the 1960s

The same major trends continued into the early 1960s at a slowing pace: the decline of agricultural employment, the growth of the military, the explosion of white suburbs, and erosion of the urban core. According to the 1 percent Social Security Work History sample, total trade employment declined somewhat. Then Gunter AFB was phased out and both Maxwell AFB and the Air University stopped growing. Military employment fell by about 3,000 over the decade, but probably by considerably more from 1965 to 1970. The relative magnitude of the military cutbacks was not so severe as in the Amarillo and Fort Smith cases, however.

There was slow growth in most other sectors, except for a substantial increase in professional services. (This increase, due in part to the expansion of Auburn University in the late 1960s, still left the professional services sector underrepresented relative to national proportions.)

While major government employers were cutting back there was some expansion in machinery, textiles and apparel manufacturing, and a moderate growth in state government, trade and services.

Like Amarillo, Montgomery used the site of the closed air base (which it still owned) for an industrial park, and with the help of an EDA grant, attracted a number of small branch plants to it. Much of the recent indus-

Table 6-4
Employment by Selected Industrial Sectors, 1940-1970, Montgomery SMSA

	1940	1950	1960	1970
TOTAL EMPLOYMENT (FULL AND PART TIME)	53,156	66,188	73,965	76,817
AGRICULTURE,FORESTRY,FISHERIES AND OTHER	12,918	8,136	4,094	1,874
AGRICULTURE	12,890	8,086	4,040	1,825
FORESTRY,FISHERIES AND OTHER	28	50	54	49
MINING	143	150	77	166
CONTRACT CONSTRUCTION	2,314	4,751	4,912	5,432
MANUFACTURING	6,624	8,479	9,711	9,873
FOOD AND KINDRED PRODUCTS	1,100	1,473	2,359	1,641
TEXTILE MILL PRODUCTS	2,316	2,334	1,770	1,869
APPAREL AND OTHER FABRICATED TEXTILE PRODUCTS	207	337	220	611
PRINTING,PUBLISHING AND ALLIED INDUSTRIES	432	606	958	965
CHEMICALS AND ALLIED PRODUCTS	699	601	535	266
LUMBER AND FURNITURE	1,289	2,030	1,418	1,441
MACHINERY	107	171	672	842
MACHINERY EXCEPT ELECTRICAL	--	150	457	747
ELECTRICAL MACHINERY	--	21	215	95
TRANSPORTATION EQUIPMENT	86	76	257	353
MOTOR VEHICLES AND MOTOR VEHICLES EQUIPMENT	82	72	191	248
TRANSPORTATION EXCLUDING MOTOR VEHICLES	4	4	66	105
OTHER MANUFACTURING	388	851	1,522	1,885
PAPER AND ALLIED PRODUCTS	--	42	61	212
PETROLEUM REFINING AND RELATED PRODUCTS	--	24	60	38
PRIMARY METALS INDUSTRIES	--	73	91	82
FABRICATED METALS + ORDNANCE	--	10P	294	358
MISCELLANEOUS MANUFACTURING		604	1,016	1,195
TRANSPORTATION,COMM.,PUB. UTILITIES	3,354	4,645	4,203	4,946
TRANSPORTATION	2,392	3,315	2,538	2,639
RAILROAD TRANSPORTATION	1,652	2,061	1,269	861
MOTOR FREIGHT TRANSPORTATION AND WAREHOUSING	372	494	632	1,011
OTHER TRANSPORTATION SERVICES	368	760	637	767
COMMUNICATIONS	465	589	863	1,099
ELECTRIC,GAS,AND SANITARY SERVICES	497	741	802	1,208

WHOLESALE AND RETAIL TRADE	7,700	12,046	13,705	15,986
WHOLESALE TRADE	1,318	2,376	2,595	3,958
RETAIL TRADE	6,382	9,670	11,110	12,028
EATING AND DRINKING PLACES	996	1,795	1,772	1,887
FOOD + DAIRY STORES	1,416	1,874	1,773	1,993
OTHER RETAIL TRADE	3,970	6,001	7,565	8,148
FINANCE INSURANCE AND REAL ESTATE	1,236	2,161	3,047	3,945
SERVICES	13,457	16,774	20,116	22,342
BUSINESS SERVICES	10,599	11,087	11,832	9,080
LODGING PLACES AND PERSONAL SERVICES	2,131	2,676	2,895	2,555
BUSINESS AND REPAIR SERVICES	670	1,255	1,428	1,880
AMUSEMENTS AND REC. SERVICES	286	410	450	442
PRIVATE HOUSEHOLDS	7,512	6,746	7,059	4,203
PROFESSIONAL SERVICES	2,858	5,687	8,284	13,262
TOTAL GOVERNMENT	5,410	9,046	14,100	12,253
CIVILIAN GOVERNMENT	3,514	5,484	7,547	8,689
FEDERAL MILITARY	1,896	3,562	4,553	3,564

Source: Regional Economics Information System, Bureau of Economic Analysis, from Census Data.

Table 6-5
Selected Annual Average Unemployment Rates, Montgomery SMSA

1960	1966	1972
4.8	3.1	3.0

Source: Alabama Department of Industrial Relations

trial growth has gone into the smaller towns and villages of the SMSA where cheap labor is more readily available and managers can live conveniently in the Montgomery suburbs.

The development of a physically separate white suburban Montgomery described early in this chapter was accomplished largely in the years since 1960. Other dramatic physical improvements have been made in the same period: the construction of a series of locks and dams along the Alabama River, interstate highway connections, industrial parks, urban renewal, and reconstruction of historic houses in the Capitol area. Social and economic change have not accompanied these improvements, however. A sampling of firms newly located in the area reads much as it would have twenty years ago: sewing shops, small assembly plants, food processing. The press remains bland but conservative, labor essentially unorganized, community organizations complacent. By standing still, Montgomery lags ever farther behind.

Labor force participation rose in the Montgomery area much as in the rest of the nation during the 1960s, the largest factor being an increase in the proportion of working women. The 4 percent employment gain was therefore associated with only 0.8 percent population increase. Unemployment rates remained moderate (table 6-5) and many employers complained of labor shortage, suggesting that non-economic pressures might be retarding inmigration to or hastening outmigration from the area. The very poor job and housing prospects for blacks, the low pay scales in Alabama civilian government employment, and the bad press received nationally in the prior decade are plausible contributing factors.

The population loss of the decade was more black than white, more male than female. Montgomery's age profiles (fig. 6-2) show the greatest loss of population in the cohort aged 20 to 24 in 1970. Of the population aged 20 to 24, 47.9 percent migrated away from the SMSA between 1965 and 1970 (1970 *Census of Population,* Vol. PC(2)-2E). There is evidence of considerable net outmigration up to age 50. A falling fertility rate combined with the net outmigration of young parents with their offspring explains the small cohorts under ten years in 1970.

Valid data from the Social Security Continuous Work History Sample (tables 6-6, 6-7) exist only for the first half-decade, due to a classification

Table 6-6
Migration Summary, All Industries, Montgomery SMSA (Based on Social Security Continuous Work History Sample (1%)
First Quarter of 1960-65)

	THOUSANDS OF WORKERS	% OF TOTAL	1960-1965		
			1960 MEAN WAGES	1965 MEAN WAGES	% CHANGE MEAN WAGES
INITIAL COVERED WORK FORCE	58.5	100.0	3,134		
INMIGRANTS	11.6	19.8	3,441	4,416	28.3
OUTMIGRANTS	12.0	20.5	3,524	5,380	52.7
NET MIGRATION	-.4	-.7			
NONMIGRANTS:					
SAME INDUSTRY	26.8	45.8	3,554	4,667	31.3
DIFFERENT INDUSTRY	3.6	6.2	2,232	3,244	45.3
NET MILITARY AND OTHERS	1.0	1.7			
ENTERED COVERED WORK FORCE	21.2	36.2		2,203	
LEFT COVERED WORK FORCE	15.7		2,333		
FINAL COVERED WORK FORCE	64.6	110.4		3,708	

Source: Regional Analysis Information System, Bureau of Economic Analysis.

Table 6-7
Migration Summary by Industry, Montgomery SMSA (Based on Social Security Continuous Work History Sample (1%) First Quarter of 1960-65-70)

THOUSANDS OF WORKERS

GOVERNMENT AND OTHER, INCLUDING UNCLASSIFIED

FINANCE, INSURANCE AND REAL ESTATE

WHOLESALE AND RETAIL TRADE

TRANSPORTATION, COMMUNICATION AND PUBLIC UTILITIES

MANUFACTURING

CONTRACT CONSTRUCTION

MINING

AGRICULTURE, FORESTRY AND FISHERIES

1960-1965

INITIAL COVERED WORK FORCE, 1960	.7	*	4.3	9.1	2.7	14.9	4.0	22.8
INMIGRANTS	*	.	2.2	1.9	.5	3.0	.6	3.3
OUTMIGRANTS	*	*	1.4	2.7	*	3.8	1.1	2.3
NET MIGRATION	-.2	.	.8	-.8	.1	-.8	-.5	1.0
NONMIGRANTS:								
SAME INDUSTRY	.	*	1.5	4.7	1.2	4.6	1.4	13.4
LEFT THIS INDUSTRY	.	.	*	.5	*	1.8	*	*
ENTERED THIS INDUSTRY	.	*	*	*	*	*	*	1.8
NET MILITARY AND OTHERS	.1	.	.1	.1	*	.0	.2	.5
ENTERED COVERED WORK FORCE	*	.	2.6	2.6	.6	6.2	.6	8.3
LEFT COVERED WORK FORCE	*	*	1.2	1.1	.7	4.4	1.2	6.7
FINAL COVERED WORK FORCE, 1965	.5	*	6.7	9.8	2.6	14.5	3.2	27.3

Source: Regional Analysis Information System, Bureau of Economic Analysis

*Statistically Insignificant

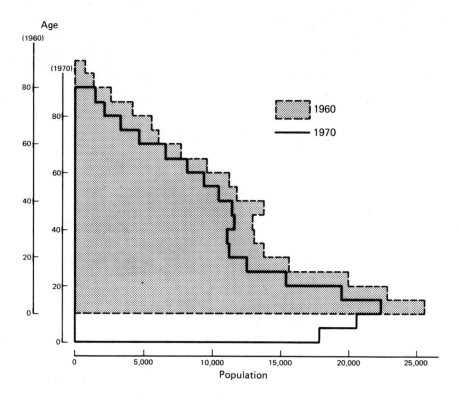

Figure 6-2. Population Age Profiles, 1960 and 1970 Montgomery, Ala. SMSA

error in the original tables. They confirm the expected trends of net outmigration and slow growth or decline in most sectors except construction, government, and services. The excess of entries over exits was the major factor in growth of the work force, but had little effect on industry mix. Interindustry transfers and difference in net migration contributed about equally to the differing growth rates between industries. The higher-wage sectors, manufacturing and finance-insurance-real estate, offered few entry opportunities and declined in relative importance. Outmigrants' wages were nearly the best off to begin with, and they made the greatest wage gains.

7

Case Study: Pittsburgh SMSA, Pennsylvania

Figure 7-1 shows that Pittsburgh is another SMSA whose population and employment have been growing slowly for a long time. It is distinguished, however, by its large size, with over two million people, and high income per capita when decline first set in in the 1930s. The steep decline of the area's relative income per capita symbolizes both the passage of steel from the center of American industry, and Pittsburgh from the center of American steel.

General Description

The Pittsburgh SMSA is primarily a group of small to medium sized steel

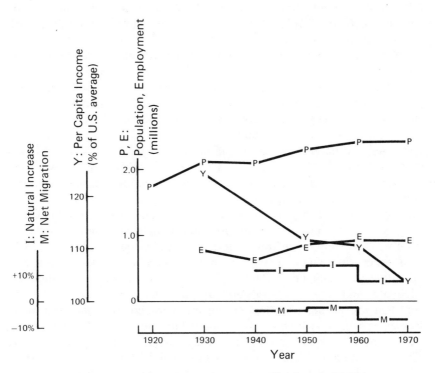

Figure 7-1. Composite of Trends, Pittsburgh SMSA

and coal mining cities, many of them in severe economic distress. Less than one-fourth of the region's 2.4 million population is in the central city, which has been declining steeply for several decades.

The digest of population and housing data (table 7-1) shows it has fewer black people, fewer high incomes, fewer white-collar workers and more homeownership than is common, but otherwise is very close to the Division and 243 SMSA averages. An SMSA this large, however, would ordinarily have more blacks, high incomes, and white-collar workers, and less home-ownership than average. In other words, the SMSA as a whole differs from the average, not in being more like a metropolis of two million people, but in being more like a small industrial city. The incidence of poverty incomes was similar to that of the smaller declining cities of the state at 7.2 percent. The number of larger incomes, 16.8 percent of families over $15,000, was greater than in other declining areas but exceptionally low for a major metropolitan area: Cleveland, for example, had 27.1 percent.

Historical Background

Pittsburgh is an outstanding example of the "gateway" phenomenon dis-cussed in Chapter 2. It lies at the eastern-most head of deep-draft naviga-tion of the Ohio River system, and was therefore an important shipping point from the earliest years of Ohio Valley settlement. It was not among the thirty most populous cities in 1810, but ranked twenty-third in 1820, seventeenth in 1830, and thirteenth in 1850. After 1850 its position slipped as river traffic gave way to rail, but railroads with their enormous iron and steel demands were later to give Pittsburgh a second chance.

Trading, particularly in manufactured goods (which, unlike farm pro-duce, were sufficiently valuable and durable to justify the overland ship-ment from New York, Baltimore or Philadelphia rather than the river route via New Orleans) increased. Pittsburgh developed a light manufacturing industry quite early in the nineteenth century, presumably capitalizing on the impatience of farmers waiting for overland shipments from the Coast. As was common in most cities at this time, small local foundries made iron from whatever grades of raw materials could be found in the immediate area. Steel was refined in small quantities and metal-working was a craft operation. As it happened, Pittsburgh area ores were quite poor, limestone adequate, and coal was very good. In particular, the Connellsville area coal had the proper chemical composition for coking coal used in the Bessemer process, which was the principal technology used in the massive expansion and centralization of the American steel industry in the 1890s. This was a point in history at which a large advantage would go to those who expanded first and fastest, because of the economies of scale inherent

Table 7-1
Selected Population and Housing Characteristics Pittsburgh, Pennsylvania SMSA 1970

	SMSA	Middle Atlantic Division	243 SMSAs
Black %	7.1	10.6	12.0
Under 5 years %	7.4	8.1	8.5
Sixty-five years and over	10.7	10.6	9.3
Median years of education[1]	12.1	12.1	12.2
Unemployed %	4.3	3.9	4.3
White collar[2] %	49.1	51.6	52.4
Crafts and foremen[2] %	15.5	13.3	13.6
Operatives, laborers and other %	35.4	35.1	34.0
Family incomes over $15,000 %	18.8	24.5	24.5
Family incomes below low income %	7.2	7.9	8.5
Housing owner occupied %	67.7	56.6	59.5
Median house value[3]	$15,416	$19,037	$19,027
Median gross rent	$ 96	$ 112	$ 117
Home owner vacancy rate %	.8	.8	1.1
Rental vacancy rate %	5.9	3.5	6.0

Source: *County and City Data Book*, U.S. Bureau of the Census, 1972

Notes:

1. Persons 25 years and over.

2. Percentage of employed civilian labor force.

3. Single family owner-occupied.

in the new technology. Economical large-scale steel-making was feasible at several other points in the country lacking the coking coal but having superior ore supplies. The technology was European and had first been adapted to American ores, not in Pittsburgh, but in Eastern Pennsylvania. Nevertheless, the critical combination of resources, technology, and entrepreneurial talent were ultimately assembled in the Pittsburgh area steel firms.

One factor which may have tipped the balance may have been access to the interior markets via the Ohio River system. According to the *Economic Study of the Pittsburgh Region* (Hoover et al. 1960), its steel companies were in the best possible location to control the vast interior market during the late nineteenth century when steel track was replacing iron in the continental railway systems, and the Midwestern industrial centers were being built.

Pittsburgh and the surrounding region were built up to an extraordinary size and degree of specialization in order to exploit its transitory advantages in the steel industry. Population nearly tripled from 1880 to 1910 (table 7-2). The city's steel mills manufactured the means of their own

Table 7-2

Historical Population and Employment, Pittsburgh SMSA (Allegheny, Beaver, Washington and Westmoreland Counties, Pennsylvania)

Year	Population	% Change in Population	Employment	% Change in Employment	% of Total Employment Female
1850	261,644				
1860	308,512	17.9			
1870	405,554	31.4			
1880	528,928	30.4			
1890	786,010	48.6			
1900	1,083,846	37.9			
1910	1,471,800	35.8			
1920	1,759,989	19.6			
1930	2,023,269	15.0	757,382	—	19.5
1940	2,082,556	2.9	662,384	−12.5	22.2
1950	2,213,236	6.3	808,811	22.1	24.7
1960	2,405,435	8.7	832,138	2.9	28.8
1970	2,401,362	−0.2	877,806	5.4	33.9
1973	2,366,800	−1.4			

Sources:

Population: 1870-1920: 1920 *Census of Population*; 1930-1940: 1940 *Census of Population*; 1950-1970: 1970 *Census of Populatio,*; 1973: *Current Population Reports*, See P. 25 No. 537.

Employment: 1930, 1940, 1950, 1960 and 1970 *Censuses of Population*

obsolescence, just as the outfitters, traders, and land speculators did a half-century earlier. The new manufacturing centers and the rail network gradually eroded the realm in which they could be the unique suppliers. The Pittsburgh steel industry has expanded slightly during the past sixty years only by upgrading the capacity of existing plants, while new growth in the industry nationally has located mainly in growing metropolitan centers. Steel production since the early twentieth century has no longer been dependent upon the formerly indispensible Connellsville coking coal except for specialized metallurgical processes, while scrap supplies and concentrated local markets have become increasingly important locational factors.

Another factor in the extraordinary localization of the industry and the growth of Pittsburgh into a nearly one-industry city around the turn of the century may have been the organization of U.S. Steel Corporation in the 1890s as a vertically integrated producer, headquartered in Pittsburgh. Its powerful political and financial influence over transportation rates, prices of intermediate goods, wages, and capital markets inhibited for a while both non-Pittsburgh steel-making and the making of anything but steel or heavy steel-using products in Pittsburgh.

The historical oddity, however, is not that Pittsburgh's leading industry stopped growing so fast, but that other sectors failed to grow in its place. It was the only SMSA of anywhere near its size, except Boston, not to grow faster than the national rate for most of this century. Its trade and service sectors have grown but remain unusually small for an SMSA of its size (partly a reflection of the small size of the central city), and much of its employment growth has still been in heavy industry, particularly within existing local firms. Despite having gained several new corporate headquarters through vigorous promotion in the past decade, the number of jobs controlled by Pittsburgh-based firms has declined. It was the only SMSA over one million population which did not gain from 1960 to 1970 in total jobs controlled by major corporations headquartered there, as reported in *Fortune* magazine's "500 Industrial Corporations" (Allan Pred, Unpublished Data, 1973). Conditions which characterized the region in the period and contributed to the failure of new activities to grow in Pittsburgh included the following:

1. Insularity: the gradually contracting geographic realm within which the city's firms and institutions were exchanging goods or information;
2. The lack of desirable building sites: the topography of the region is very rough, and the river frontage, valley bottoms and even some of the steepest slopes were occupied within several miles of the city center, while access to outlying land was limited by topography to a few routes which were poorly developed;
3. The extreme discomfort and ugliness caused by industrial air pollution, greatly reduced since 1950;
4. The area's reputation, whether or not warranted, for an expensive, highly organized, and disputatious labor force;
5. The concentration of economic power in a few aging and non-diversified organizations, particularly the Mellon metallurgical interests;
6. The highly integrated style of heavy manufacturing as developed in the huge Pittsburgh plants, which bought few goods or services from local organizations outside the parent firm, and stimulated little technological or intellectual development.

Three additional points made by the historian Roy Lubove (1969) are:

7. The shortage and decrepit condition of housing and the difficulty of financing it. This is consistent with the low vacancy rates, in spite of slow growth and low costs (table 7-1);
8. Inadequate medical and educational services contrasting with generously endowed school and hospital buildings;
9. Ingrained resistance to the use of public powers in dealing with social problems, an ethic of volunteerism.

The Pittsburgh SMSA grew more slowly than most after 1920, losing employment sharply in the 1930s. Pittsburgh's SMSA was still a relatively wealthy area in 1929, ranking thirty-fifth with 125 percent of the U.S. income per capita. It declined to sixty-ninth rank and 103 percent by 1969, making it the poorest SMSA over 1.2 million population.

Development in the 1940s and 1950s

Total employment in the Pittsburgh SMSA recovered during the 1940s to slightly more than its 1930 level, as shown in figure 7-1.

The shift-share analysis shows the area to be highly specialized in two industries, steel and machinery, which are growing nationally at a moderate rate, but are not sharing locally in that growth. Despite a half century's erosion, the area remains extremely specialized in those sectors, and deficient in most other manufacturing sectors, as well as in government and services.

The area continued to become more specialized in plants and industries which were passing toward the end of their life cycles, with little progress toward diversification. There was to be no significant growth of total employment for the next two decades. Changes in the industry distribution were also small, but relative to national trends, this lack of structural change had the effect of further increasing the relative degree of specialization. As in the Great Depression, the area responded to the recessions of the 1950s and 1960s with sharply fluctuating unemployment rates (table 7-3).

The so-called "Pittsburgh Renaissance" of 1946 to the mid-sixties was an impressive but essentially cosmetic approach to Pittsburgh's problems, dealing forcefully with the few aspects which were physical, tractable, and promising of substantial gain to owners of downtown real estate. The "Renaissance" included smoke control, the clearance and redevelopment of the Gateway Center (without federal assistance), a civic auditorium with a retracting roof (never open), new in-city expressway links, and a number of large urban renewal clearance projects. It did not include any significant lower-income housing or social service components in this period, although a major effort to back middle-income housing was made in the 1960s. The immediate stimulus of the "Renaissance" was the threat of large corporations to move their headquarters to other cities. This was finally enough to galvanize the Mellon family, which had very large interests in Pittsburgh business and real estate as well as several major corporations, into cooperative civic action. The break with their past tradition of strictly private charity was made possible by a temporary, limited-purpose alliance between Mellon-controlled interests, organized by Richard King

Table 7-3
Selected Annual Average Unemployment Rates, Pittsburgh SMSA

1951	1954	1957	1962	1969	1971
3.5	8.6	5.3	9.4	2.5	5.3

Source: Pennsylvania Bureau of Employment Security.

Mellon in 1943 as the Allegheny Conference for Community Development (ACCD), with the Democratic, labor-oriented city political apparatus headed by Mayor David Lawrence, and by a considerable influx from other cities of high level executives and professionals on both sides (Lubove 1969; Clipping files, Carnegie Library).

During the 1950s, total employment grew little in the SMSA (table 7-2) despite the "Renaissance." The resulting outmigration (fig. 7-1) was masked by a relatively high birthrate.

ACCD has continued to act as a seedbed for new public/private community programs such as the Regional Industrial Development Corporation, which builds industrial parks, and Penn's Southwest Association, which promotes these parks. More recently ACCD's announced emphasis has shifted toward health services, education, and minority enterprise (*Post-Gazette,* October 13, 1971).

Development Since 1960

The decade of the 1960s brought little basic change to the Pittsburgh SMSA, despite some drastic changes in appearance due to urban renewal, and highway and suburban construction. Total population and employment were virtually constant. The mix of industries, while showing some growth in government trade and services, lagged further behind national trends in those sectors (table 7-4). There was substantial suburban population growth in some sectors of Pittsburgh's outskirts, but this was balanced by population losses in the central city (by 13 percent) and in many of the smaller industrial or mining cities included within the SMSA, like McKeesport, which lost 16 percent of its 1960 population.

The Continuous Work History Sample (tables 7-5 and 7-6) shows no growth in the covered work force in the period 1960-1965, but moderate growth from 1965 to 1970. The major component of the change was an increase in net entries to the covered work force, with only a slight rise in net migration. Structural changes were in the expected directions with a moderate gain in government and service balanced by decline in manufacturing and mining. Wages and wage gains of migrants exceeded those of

Table 7-4
Employment by Selected Industrial Sectors, 1940-1970, Pittsburgh SMSA

	1940	1950	1960	1970
TOTAL EMPLOYMENT (FULL AND PART TIME)	862,355	1,030,731	1,038,337	1,092,075
AGRICULTURE,FORESTRY,FISHERIES AND OTHER				
AGRICULTURE	27,715	22,858	13,927	10,004
FORESTRY,FISHERIES AND OTHER	27,636	22,682	13,802	9,908
MINING	79	176	125	96
CONTRACT CONSTRUCTION	79,529	64,829	23,798	19,229
MANUFACTURING	35,117	53,528	53,763	55,882
FOOD AND KINDRED PRODUCTS	311,321	382,324	393,595	351,672
TEXTILE MILL PRODUCTS	19,580	22,529	27,176	16,827
APPAREL AND OTHER FABRICATED TEXTILE PRODUCTS	1,616	1,958	631	725
PRINTING,PUBLISHING AND ALLIED INDUSTRIES	3,286	5,775	7,349	9,764
CHEMICALS AND ALLIED PRODUCTS	8,712	11,230	15,287	15,774
LUMBER AND FURNITURE	4,607	8,210	11,174	11,109
MACHINERY	5,558	4,409	4,509	4,478
MACHINERY EXCEPT ELECTRICAL	30,313	46,792	56,614	58,473
ELECTRICAL MACHINERY		14,966	18,443	28,344
TRANSPORTATION EQUIPMENT		31,826	38,171	30,129
MOTOR VEHICLES AND MOTOR VEHICLES EQUIPMENT	4,338	8,531	10,487	10,519
TRANSPORTATION EXCLUDING MOTOR VEHICLES	1,151	2,530	3,581	2,428
OTHER MANUFACTURING	3,187	6,001	6,906	8,091
PAPER AND ALLIED PRODUCTS	233,311	272,890	260,368	224,003
PETROLEUM REFINING AND RELATED PRODUCTS		4,080	4,674	5,619
PRIMARY METALS INDUSTRIES		6,608	2,096	3,335
FABRICATED METALS + ORDNANCE		192,959	182,016	144,582
MISCELLANEOUS MANUFACTURING		25,949	34,569	33,723
TRANSPORTATION,COMM.,+PUB. UTILITIES	67,557	43,294	37,013	36,744
TRANSPORTATION	46,185	94,034	81,359	77,357
RAILROAD TRANSPORTATION	30,075	64,249	50,630	46,649
MOTOR FREIGHT TRANSPORTATION AND WAREHOUSING	8,893	39,929	26,693	16,676
OTHER TRANSPORTATION SERVICES	7,217	11,818	14,247	17,174
COMMUNICATIONS	7,037	12,502	9,690	12,799
ELECTRIC,GAS,AND SANITARY SERVICES	14,335	12,625	12,601	13,583
		17,160	18,128	17,125

WHOLESALE AND RETAIL TRADE	143,806	189,798	192,370	218,306
WHOLESALE TRADE	18,616	31,028	33,593	40,201
RETAIL TRADE	125,190	158,770	158,777	178,105
EATING AND DRINKING PLACES	19,401	27,260	27,815	34,302
FOOD + DAIRY STORES	33,869	37,419	31,133	33,393
OTHER, RETAIL TRADE	71,920	94,091	99,829	110,410
FINANCE,INSURANCE AND REAL ESTATE	24,995	30,698	38,837	45,674
SERVICES	147,602	159,569	201,984	269,427
BUSINESS SERVICES	83,264	77,031	79,368	79,539
LODGING PLACES AND PERSONAL SERVICES	26,317	28,264	28,028	27,035
BUSINESS AND REPAIR SERVICES	14,253	20,535	23,023	32,720
AMUSEMENTS AND REC. SERVICES	6,751	8,755	9,358	8,526
PRIVATE HOUSEHOLDS	35,943	19,477	18,959	11,258
PROFESSIONAL SERVICES	64,338	82,538	122,616	189,888
TOTAL GOVERNMENT	24,713	33,093	38,704	44,524
CIVILIAN GOVERNMENT	24,676	31,531	36,747	42,269
FEDERAL MILITARY	37	1,562	1,957	2,255

Source: Regional Economics Information System, Bureau of Economic Analysis, from Census Data.

Table 7-5
Migration Summary, All Industries, Pittsburgh SMSA (Based on Social Security Continuous Work History Sample (1%) First Quarter of 1960-65-70)

	THOUSANDS OF WORKERS	% OF TOTAL	1960-1965		
			1960 MEAN WAGES	1965 MEAN WAGES	% CHANGE MEAN WAGES
INITIAL COVERED WORK FORCE	747.1	100.0	4,860		
INMIGRANTS	73.6	9.9	6,102	7,662	25.6
OUTMIGRANTS	80.6	10.8	4,998	6,592	31.9
NET MIGRATION	−7.0	−.9			
NONMIGRANTS:					
SAME INDUSTRY	410.4	54.9	5,503	6,445	17.1
DIFFERENT INDUSTRY	74.3	9.9	4,221	5,414	28.3
NET MILITARY AND OTHERS	4.3	.6			
ENTERED COVERED WORK FORCE	180.3	24.1		2,829	
LEFT COVERED WORK FORCE	175.0		3,689		
FINAL COVERED WORK FORCE	749.7	100.3		5,573	

| | THOUSANDS OF WORKERS | % OF TOTAL | 1965-1970 | | |
			1965 MEAN WAGES	1970 MEAN WAGES	% CHANGE MEAN WAGES
INITIAL COVERED WORK FORCE	749.7	100.0	5,573		
INMIGRANTS	84.8	11.3	5,901	9,656	63.6
OUTMIGRANTS	85.6	11.4	5,582	9,131	63.6
NET MIGRATION	-.8	-.1			
NONMIGRANTS:					
SAME INDUSTRY	390.2	52.0	6,167	8,465	37.3
DIFFERENT INDUSTRY	81.1	10.8	4,326	7,065	63.3
NET MILITARY AND OTHERS	-15.0	-2.0			
ENTERED COVERED WORK FORCE	243.2	32.4		3,848	
LEFT COVERED WORK FORCE	162.8		4,523		
FINAL COVERED WORK FORCE	814.3	108.6		7,040	

Source: Regional Analysis Information System, Bureau of Economic Analysis.

Table 7-6
Migration Summary by Industry, Pittsburgh SMSA (Based on Social Securit: Continuous Work History Sample (1%) First Quarter of 1960-65-70)

THOUSANDS OF WORKERS

GOVERNMENT AND OTHER,
INCLUDING UNCLASSIFIED

FINANCE, INSURANCE AND REAL ESTATE

WHOLESALE AND RETAIL TRADE

TRANSPORTATION, COMMUNICATION
AND PUBLIC UTILITIES

MANUFACTURING

CONTRACT CONSTRUCTION

MINING

AGRICULTURE, FORESTRY AND FISHERIES

INITIAL COVERED WORK FORCE, 1960	2.5	15.4	35.2	312.3	47.6	169.4	33.4	131.3
1960-1965								
INMIGRANTS	.7	2.2	5.2	32.4	3.8	14.9	4.2	10.2
OUTMIGRANTS	.6	1.8	7.3	25.4	5.9	22.9	4.2	12.5
NET MIGRATION	.1	.4	-2.1	7.0	-2.1	-8.0	.0	-2.3
NONMIGRANTS:								
SAME INDUSTRY	*	8.2	13.7	207.8	25.0	72.9	17.0	65.6
LEFT THIS INDUSTRY	.8	2.0	6.9	19.0	7.4	23.7	3.4	11.1
ENTERED THIS INDUSTRY	3.2	.6	3.6	24.6	4.9	14.2	5.9	17.3
NET MILITARY AND OTHERS	-.1	.1	.1	4.8	.9	-2.3	1.1	-.3
ENTERED COVERED WORK FORCE	1.4	.8	7.3	35.8	6.5	61.1	8.2	59.2
LEFT COVERED WORK FORCE	.8	3.4	7.1	59.3	9.1	46.2	8.8	40.3
FINAL COVERED WORK FORCE, 1965	5.5	11.9	30.1	306.2	41.2	164.5	36.4	153.8
1965-1970								
INMIGRANTS	.6	2.5	10.8	26.7	5.5	20.8	4.4	13.5
OUTMIGRANTS	.8	3.7	6.8	23.6	6.1	25.2	5.2	14.2
NET MIGRATION	-.2	-1.2	4.0	3.1	-.6	-4.4	-.8	-.7
NONMIGRANTS:								
SAME INDUSTRY	*	5.0	12.4	182.8	23.8	69.2	16.8	79.8
LEFT THIS INDUSTRY	3.2	1.0	4.2	20.8	4.7	27.9	3.8	15.5
ENTERED THIS INDUSTRY	.5	1.8	7.9	21.2	6.9	14.9	5.8	22.1
NET MILITARY AND OTHERS	.1	.1	.6	-16.0	1.1	-1.3	.7	-.2
ENTERED COVERED WORK FORCE	1.0	1.9	9.9	46.2	9.2	80.9	12.4	81.7
LEFT COVERED WORK FORCE	1.1	2.2	6.2	57.0	6.2	37.5	10.5	42.1
FINAL COVERED WORK FORCE, 1970	2.5	11.3	42.1	282.9	47.0	189.2	40.2	199.1

Source: Regional Analysis Information System, Bureau of Economic Analysis.
*Statistically insignificant

non-migrants consistently, but non-migrants who changed industry in the 1965-1970 period did quite well, especially those leaving government and services or entering manufacturing.

Pittsburgh's 1970 population age profile (fig. 7-2) is intermediate in type, not so top heavy as Wilkes-Barre or St. Joseph, but not so tapered as Savannah or even Montgomery. The cohorts aged fifteen to thirty shrank markedly from 1960 (when they were five to twenty) and a similar notch up to age forty in the 1960 profile shows that those age groups have been undergoing erosion for at least three decades. The small cohorts under five years in 1970 will fit much more easily into the labor force than those now in their teens.

Under the administration of Pete Flaherty, the mayor since 1969, and perhaps before his election, the Renaissance lost momentum and the old coalition weakened. Flaherty was elected on a platform of reduced spending. Major new projects did not enter the pipeline for several years.

One very divisive issue has been the Port Authority Skybus system. It was conceived in the mid-sixties by Westinghouse Electric and Parsons-

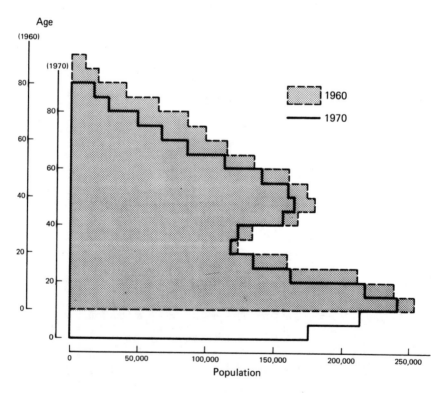

Figure 7-2. Population Age Profiles, 1960 and 1970 Pittsburgh, Pa. SMSA

Brinkerhoff-Quade-Douglas as a moderate-capacity, automatically-controlled, rubber-tired, high speed urban mass transit system, with steep grade capability, to replace the commuter rail lines, the last of which were then being retired, and to relieve automobile loads on some of the main approaches to the city center. The concept included a good deal of un-proven technology. Working with the Port Authority and the state, but not with the local city governments, plans and financial arrangements were prepared for a first line to serve the prosperous southwestern suburbs, and two busways. Construction had already begun when the mayors of fifteen cities affected by the system sued successfully for an injunction to stop work until a plan was published and accepted. Judicial hearings lasted from January through September of 1972. Construction resumed in 1973, but four different agencies, the mayor, the governor, the Port Authority, and the Southwest Pennsylvania Regional Planning Commission, have or are making conflicting plans for the rest of the system.

It may be too early to pass judgment on the Pittsburgh Renaissance and its sequelae. After all, the economic die had been cast decades earlier in the building of Big Steel, the "good trust," in the late nineteenth century, and the playing out of its advantages in the early twentieth century. Whereas the makers of the Renaissance made little direct effort at social or economic change, they did erect a symbolism of change, or at least of public well-being. Symbols can take on a life of their own and the place may now seem less forbidding. Perhaps, but just perhaps, the future holds something different for the Pittsburgh SMSA.

8

Case Study: Pueblo SMSA, Colorado

Figure 8-1 illustrates the long-term trends of population, relative income per capita, natural increase, and net migration for the Pueblo SMSA as defined in 1970 (Pueblo County). It shows that the area's population was nearly constant in the 1920s and 1930s, grew in the war and postwar decades, and stabilized again in the 1960s. Employment fell in the 1930s, grew moderately during the 1940s and slowly afterwards. Income per capita was consistently below average, with relative declines in the 1950s and late 1960s. The components of population change, natural increase, and net migration show an interesting pattern. Migration accounted for over half the growth in the initial decade of expansion. As will be seen later,

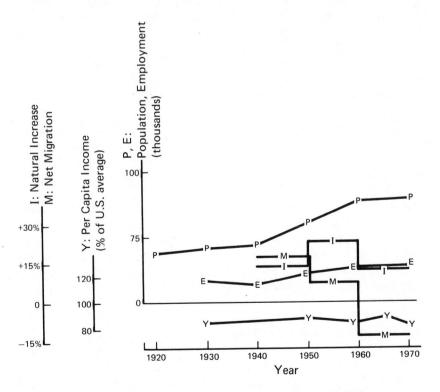

Figure 8-1. Composite of Trends, Pueblo SMSA

95

employment growth tailed off in the early 1950s, depressing the net migration rate, but natural increase rose enough to sustain the same total growth rate. Only in the 1960s did net migration finally overcome the demographic momentum of an expansion whose economic sources had peaked two decades earlier. This one-generation lag in downward adjustment of population will appear repeatedly in other case studies.

General Description

Pueblo is a fairly typical small American industrial city, but a slight anachronism on the high western edge of the prairies. Its dominant employer, the CF and I Steel Corporation, looms grimly on the south edge of the city, but the prairie opens on the east and the spectacular Sangre de Cristo Mountains rise on the west. In a region where the cities are composed mostly of suburban areas, Pueblo has hardly any suburbs. Its Democratic labor-oriented politics have separated it politically from the Republican state and congressional delegations over the years (Shomaker 1953; Bloom 1974). Its entry into the tourism, defense, and high technology industries has been slower than the more prosperous western cities like nearby Colorado Springs.

Pueblo is predominantly a working-class city of the progressive era and shows some of the amenities of early twentieth century corporate paternalism as well as its defects. It was built largely in a period when steel was the "good trust." Workmen's houses of that era are on high ground with decent sized lots, on streets lined with cottonwood trees. There are many small and medium-sized public parks. There has been an unusually high degree of homeownership since at least 1940 (Elazar 1970, p. 48). The poorest districts, however, are on low land with unpaved streets on the fringes of the original developments.

A profile of the Pueblo SMSA population as of 1970 (table 8-1) shows the solid working class character of the area; moderate income levels, blue-collar occupations, homeownership, and a high school education predominate. Home values and rents are low, but this appears to be due more to lower incomes and perhaps housing quality than to slow growth, as homeowner vacancy rates are very low and rental vacancies are moderate.

Chronological Development to 1940

Pueblo lies where the old Santa Fe Trail (U.S. Highway #50) reached the foot of the Rockies, nearly a thousand miles above the Mississippi. There were a fort and intermittent settlements in the area from 1842. A gold rush

Table 8-1
Selected Population and Housing Characteristics Pueblo SMSA, 1970

	Pueblo SMSA	Mountain Division	243 SMSAs
Black %	1.8	2.2	12.0
Under 5 years %	8.2	9.0	8.5
65 years and over %	9.4	8.4	9.3
Median years of education[1]	12.0	12.3	12.2
Unemployed %	5.9	4.8	4.3
White collar %[2]	44.5	50.5	52.4
Craftsmen and Foremen %[2]	16.0	13.3	13.6
Laborers and other %	39.5	36.2	34.0
Family incomes over $15,000 %	11.9	17.6	24.5
Family incomes below low income %	11.2	10.9	8.5
Housing owner occupied %	72.8	65.5	59.5
Median house Value[3]	$12,713	16,432	19,027
Median Gross Rent	$ 82	104	117
Homeowner vacancy rate %	1.0	1.4	1.1
Rental vacancy rate %	7.9	7.8	6.0

Source: *County and City Data Book*, U.S. Bureau of the Census, 1972.

Notes:

1. Persons 25 years and over.

2. Percentage of employed civilian labor force,

3. Single family owner-occupied.

brought a few permanent settlers in 1858. Rail access was brought in from Denver and water from the Rockies in 1872 by a land developer named Palmer. A grant of $350,000 from the county brought the main line of the Santa Fe Railroad through Pueblo rather than a shorter route to the East in 1876. A gravity railroad was extended west into the coal fields. The rail access to coal, ores, and markets made Pueblo an outstanding location for energy-intensive metallurgical industries. Four small but permanent towns were founded in the present central area of Pueblo by 1882, when the first zinc smelter and steel mill were both opened and the real boom started (table 8-2). Three more railroads extended service to Pueblo in 1887 and 1888, and daily service reached a level of seventy-eight passenger trains. More smelters were built in 1888 and 1902. All were soon controlled by the Guggenheims' American Smelting and Refining Company (ASARCO). New steel mills were built in 1889. Capacity expanded rapidly up to 1918 and was brought mainly under the control of Colorado Fuel and Iron Company (now CF and I Steel). Only fuel and transportation were available in adequate quantity for this rush of industrial growth, however. Water, most ores, and especially labor had to be imported. Labor was recruited from Italy and Eastern Europe, and later from Mexico. With each wave of expansion, a new company town would be developed, populated

Table 8-2

Historical Population and Employment, Pueblo SMSA (Pueblo County, Colorado)

Year	Population	% Change in Population	Employment	% Change in Employment	% of Total Employment Female
1870	2,265	—			
1880	7,617	236.2			
1890	31,491	313.2			
1900	34,448	9.4			
1910	52,233	51.6			
1920	57,638	10.4			
1930	66,038	14.6	25,093	—	20.3
1940	68,870	4.3	20,972	−16.4	22.4
1950	90,188	31.0	31,366	49.6	25.3
1960	118,707	31.6	38,452	22.6	30.2
1970	118,238	−0.4	40,420	5.1	34.8
1973	123,000	4.1			

with a single ethnic group, and provided with water, housing, and a company store (Taylor 1963; Taylor 1974; Taylor, n.d.).

Despite the growth of the steel and smelting industries, the Pueblo area remained economically diversified through the 1880s. The State Insane Asylum, a large employer, was opened there in 1879. Stock raising and farming grew, as did banking, outfitting, and other services to westward migrants and prospectors in the successive gold and silver rushes of the Rocky Mountain region. Water, gas, and telephone utilities were formed in the early 1880s. Despite the opposition of the steel interests, the four original towns were consolidated, although the major steel and smelting company towns remained independent. To celebrate the new prosperity a large number of grandiose· buildings went up in the 1890s, including an opera house designed by the great Chicago architect, Louis Sullivan (Taylor 1963; Schomaker 1953).

But the boom was already past as the new monuments were being topped off. Steel declined in the 1890s, but not so badly as several other industries. The price of silver fell, ending serious prospecting and closing many mines. Prolonged drought decimated commercial agriculture in the area. The general strike of 1903-1904 depressed production in the coal mines and coke ovens, crippling smelting and rail revenues in turn. Steel production alone rebounded, and by 1910 the area was well on its way to being a one-industry, one-firm city. The greatest degree of concentration was probably reached at the peak of CF and I Steel's growth in 1918, although a similar steel boom occurred in World War II which may have matched it (Taylor 1963; Taylor 1974; Schomaker 1953).

A second decline occupied most of the period between the wars. New gas-fired smelters, also ASARCO-owned, were built in the Texas-Oklahoma gas fields from 1916 to 1920, and the old coal-fired ones were phased out. By 1923, all the Pueblo area smelters were closed. Taking advantage of the imported water supply, many of the former laborers bought small farms in or near the former company towns and continued in production until the 1940s. CF and I Steel also declined. In 1933 the company entered receivership, was refinanced, and was severely cut back in employment. Compounding the problems of the period, the Arkansas changed its course in a flash flood in 1921, killing a hundred people and destroying a large part of the central Pueblo area. Much of the recovery and protection cost was borne by local government, leaving little revenue for developing schools and municipal services. There was no high school in the industrial half of the city until 1922; only twenty-six high school students graduated as late as 1926. By 1930 the area's population was largely depleted of potential outmigrants, for although total employment in Pueblo County fell from 25,093 to 20,972 by 1940, reflecting severe distress, the county population actually increased from 66,038 to 68,870 in the same depression decade (Taylor 1963, pp. 402-414; Pueblo Area Council of Governments 1972).

Development in the 1940s and 1950s

Most of the remaining physical and economic growth of the Pueblo area until very recently occurred in the 1940s and early 1950s. The main sources of growth were the wartime recovery of the CF and I Steel, and the establishment of the Pueblo Army Depot, an ordnance and supply depot, located 16 miles east of the city. It was a rough town in those years with a thriving prostitution and gambling industry (Schomaker 1953, p. 80). CF and I Steel reached its greatest employment in 1957, and the Army Depot in 1953.

The 1960s and Early 1970s

The Pueblo area entered the 1960s with the third major "bust" of its history well under way, due to employment cutbacks at CF and I and the Army Depot, which have continued through 1973. The Colorado State Hospital staff grew through 1963, but was severely cut back in the late 1960s with a change in emphasis from custodial to outpatient care and decentralization of the state mental health system (Pueblo Area Council of Governments 1972; Ward 1971).

The near-stability of total employment in the decade of the 1960s and slight decline of population masked profound compositional changes, some of which are visible in table 8-3. Male employment actually fell; all the net growth was accounted for by increased female employment, which nevertheless remained a smaller part of total employment in the Pueblo area than in the United States as a whole (table 8-2). The jobs eliminated were largely those of craftsmen and operatives near the middle of Pueblo's income range, plus some thousand low-paid service jobs at the hospital. The jobs created were largely professional or technical as the steel plant converted to more automated technology, a new state college campus was established, and the school system expanded considerably.

A development commission was formed in 1970. An EDA grant was provided to extend water to the airport area for industrial development, but despite the entry of small steel-using manufacturers, the decline of manufacturing employment has continued.

Social changes noted by Bloom (1974) reflecting the influx of professionals in the period included a declining frequency of membership in YMCA and golf clubs, and fewer public health nursing visits. The presence

Table 8-3
Pueblo SMSA Work Force Summary: Selected Annual Averages 1964-1971

	1964	1967	1970	1971
TOTAL CIVILIAN WORK FORCE	41,120	43,160	45,200	45,490
1. Unemployment	1,600	1,990	2,180	2,300
Percentage of Work Force	(3.9)	(4.6)	(4.8)	(5.1)
2. Employment—Total	39,520	41,170	43,020	43,190
a. Non-agricultural Wage and Salary	34,180	36,070	37,560	37,700
Mining	10	10	20	10
Contract Construction	1,310	1,220	1,570	1,480
Manufacturing	9,200	8,970	8,710	8,270
Transportation and Public Utilities	2,580	2,400	2,570	2,670
Wholesale & Retail Trade	5,950	6,370	6,930	7,080
Finance, Insurance and Real Estate	1,100	1,150	1,250	1,370
Services	4,500	4,840	5,570	5,930
Government	9,530	11,110	10,940	10,890
b. All Other Non-agricultural Employment[1]	4,220	3,970	4,150	4,310
c. Agricultural Employment	1,120	1,130	1,310	1,180
3. Labor Disputants	0	0	0	0

Source: Colorado Division of Employment

Note:

1. Includes the self-employed, unpaid family workers and domestics in private households.

of an aging resident, non-mobile group of earlier immigrants, however, was indicated by rising numbers of people living alone, more unemployment, and more families receiving public assistance. There was also rising juvenile delinquency (Bloom 1974, p. 47), but a fall in the total crime rate.

Population age profiles for 1960 and 1970 have been superimposed in figure 8-2. Each five-year age group, referred to as a cohort, is kept at the same level in the diagram so that actual population changes can be observed for a more or less constant group of people. The third group from the bottom, for example, is the cohort which was 0-4 years old in 1960 and 10-14

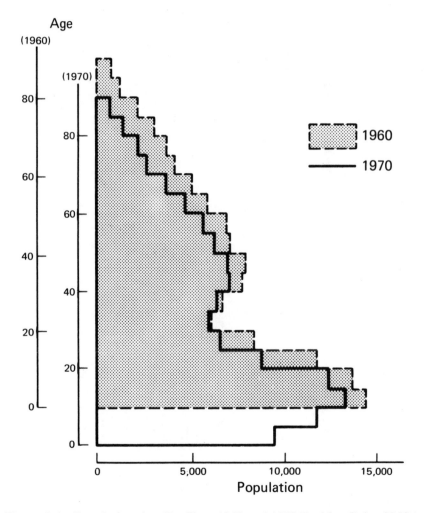

Figure 8-2. Population Age Profiles, 1960 and 1970 Pueblo, Colo. SMSA

Table 8-4
Migration Summary, All Industries, Pueblo SMSA (Based on Social Security Continuous Work History Sample (1%) First Quarter of 1960-65-70)

	THOUSANDS OF WORKERS	% OF TOTAL	1960-1965		
			1960 MEAN WAGES	1965 MEAN WAGES	% CHANGE MEAN WAGES
INITIAL COVERED WORK FORCE	25.7	100.0	4,418		
INMIGRANTS	2.6	10.1	4,033	5,328	32.1
OUTMIGRANTS	4.2	16.3	3,905	4,696	20.3
NET MIGRATION	-1.6	-6.2			
NONMIGRANTS:					
SAME INDUSTRY	13.0	50.6	5,373	6,361	18.4
DIFFERENT INDUSTRY	1.7	6.6	2,958	3,878	31.1
NET MILITARY AND OTHERS	.6	2.3			
ENTERED COVERED WORK FORCE	6.9	26.8		2,516	
LEFT COVERED WORK FORCE	6.7		3,259		
FINAL COVERED WORK FORCE	24.9	96.9		4,968	

1965-1970

	THOUSANDS OF WORKERS	% OF TOTAL	1965 MEAN WAGES	1970 MEAN WAGES	% CHANGE MEAN WAGES
INITIAL COVERED WORK FORCE	24.9	100.0	4,968		
INMIGRANTS	3.1	12.4	4,510	6,287	39.4
OUTMIGRANTS	3.1	12.4	4,314	7,351	70.4
NET MIGRATION	.0	.0			
NONMIGRANTS:					
SAME INDUSTRY	13.7	55.0	6,024	7,836	30.1
DIFFERENT INDUSTRY	1.2	4.8	3,741	6,375	70.4
NET MILITARY AND OTHERS	.5	2.0			
ENTERED COVERED WORK FORCE	10.2	41.0		2,632	
LEFT COVERED WORK FORCE	6.7		3,475		
FINAL COVERED WORK FORCE	28.9	116.1		5,746	

Source: Regional Analysis Information System, Bureau of Economic Analysis.

Table 8-5
Migration Summary by Industry, Pueblo SMSA (Based on Social Security Continuous Work History Sample (1%) First Quarter of 1960-65-70)

THOUSANDS OF WORKERS

GOVERNMENT AND OTHER,
INCLUDING UNCLASSIFIED

FINANCE, INSURANCE AND REAL ESTATE

WHOLESALE AND RETAIL TRADE

TRANSPORTATION, COMMUNICATION,
AND PUBLIC UTILITIES

MANUFACTURING

CONTRACT CONSTRUCTION

	1.4	11.9	1.8	5.2	1.4	3.7
INITIAL COVERED WORK FORCE, 1960						
INMIGRANTS	.7	.5	*	.6	*	.5
OUTMIGRANTS	*	1.6	*	1.4	*	*
NET MIGRATION	.4	-1.1	-.2	-.8	-.3	.4
NONMIGRANTS:						
SAME INDUSTRY	*	7.5	1.5	1.0	.5	2.2
LEFT THIS INDUSTRY	*	*	*	.5	*	*
ENTERED THIS INDUSTRY	*	*	*	.6	*	*
NET MILITARY AND OTHERS	.	.5	.	.1	-.1	.1
ENTERED COVERED WORK FORCE	.5	1.0	*	3.8	*	1.0
LEFT COVERED WORK FORCE	.7	2.4	*	1.8	*	1.1
FINAL COVERED WORK FORCE, 1965	1.7	9.8	1.8	6.6	1.0	4.0

1960-1965

	1.4	11.9	1.8	5.2	1.4	3.7
INMIGRANTS	*	1.0	*	1.2	*	.5
OUTMIGRANTS	.7	.6	*	1.0	*	*
NET MIGRATION	-.6	.4	-.1	.2	-.2	.3
NONMIGRANTS:						
SAME INDUSTRY	*	7.7	.8	2.6	.7	1.7
LEFT THIS INDUSTRY	*	.7	.	*	.	*
ENTERED THIS INDUSTRY	*	.7	.	*	.	*
NET MILITARY AND OTHERS	.1	.1	.1	.1	.	.1
ENTERED COVERED WORK FORCE	*	1.2	.7	4.1	.6	3.1
LEFT COVERED WORK FORCE	.6	1.4	.6	2.4	.	1.7
FINAL COVERED WORK FORCE, 1970	.9	10.7	1.8	8.3	1.4	5.7

1965-1970

Source: Regional Analysis Information System, Bureau of Economic Analysis
*Statistically insignificant

years old in 1970. It can be seen that this cohort shrank slightly in the 1960s, due mainly to outmigration. (There was a trivial reduction due to mortality.) There were strong losses due mostly to migration in the 20-29 year (1970) cohorts as would be expected. More surprising is the shrinkage of the 40-49 year (1970) cohorts. Formerly they had been an extreme bulge which probably expanded to that size or more in the 1940-1950 period. Many of the steelworkers laid off in the 1960s by CF and I would have been in that group. The small size of the 0-5 year cohort (1970) reflects two factors: the small population of potential parents in the area (note the hollow in the profile between ages 20 and 40), and the general decline of birthrates nationally.

Pueblo's covered work force within the Social Security 1 percent Work History Sample declined during 1960-1965, then grew moderately during 1965-1970 (table 8-4). An increase of new entries to the covered work force absorbed most of the job growth, although outmigration of covered workers declined slightly. Wage gains to outmigrants were surprisingly low in the first half-decade, possibly because laid-off steelworkers would have little chance of using their trade elsewhere and would have to take less-skilled work in another industry. Otherwise, wage gains followed the familiar pattern, favoring migrants and those who change industry in good times.

The industry breakdown of the sample (table 8-5) shows a growing proportion of trade, service (unclassified) and government employment. Again the major factor was the differential rates of flow in and out of the covered work force, although the flows of net migration and interindustry transfers were generally in the expected directions.

The impetus for the two major recent developments has been non-local, and both are now located well outside the city of Pueblo; Pueblo West, a large, handsomely promoted land development by McCulloch Corporation, overlooking a huge new reservoir; and the DOT High Speed Test Track. Their objective seems to have been to exploit Pueblo's accessibility and labor supply, while evading its image. This neocolonial attitude is well illustrated by the new director of the Test Track, who bought a house in Colorado Springs and tried to influence the Pueblo County Commissioners to build a highway from there to the Track. Asked in a press interview why he hadn't chosen to live in Pueblo, he blamed his wife: "Well, Pueblo just isn't a wife's kind of town" (*Cervi's Rocky Mountain Journal,* May 4, 1974).

9

Case Study: St. Joseph SMSA, Missouri

St. Joseph is distinguished by the longest history of population loss of any present SMSA. Now about 87,000 people, it peaked in 1900 at a plausible but disputed 122,000 (Mo.-Kan. Bi-State Planning Commission 1970). It was once a major cattle market, meat packing and commercial center, and a serious rival of Kansas City, only 40 miles South. Kansas City definitely won the competition. In recent years, St. Joseph's modest revival has been in a new role as a subsidiary part of the greater Kansas City area, benefiting from Kansas City's new airport (between the two cities) and its general prosperity.

Figure 9-1 shows almost everything in motion but the population, while

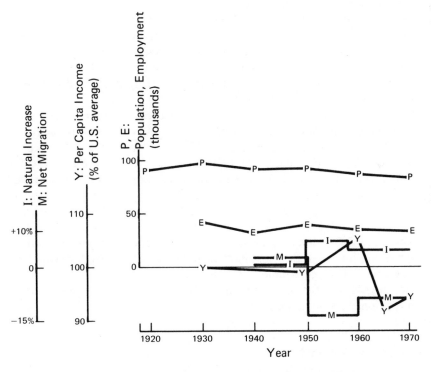

Figure 9-1. Composite of Trends, St. Joseph SMSA

107

the city was being buffeted by a series of economic shocks and partial recoveries. Employment plunged by 23 percent in the 1930s, net migration by 15 percent in the 1940s, and relative income per capita by 12 percent in the 1960s.

General Description

The historic central area of the city, actually located on its west side near the river, reflects both the boom of 1860-1900 and the erosion of succeeding decades. It is now an island of kinky Victorian ten-story terra-cotta pomposity, half vacant in a sea of parking lots. The lots are empty, too, but bristle with parking meters, the legacy of an urban renewal project with a serious marketability problem. The vast stockyard which is nearly empty dominates the south side of the city and is surrounded with the shells of abandoned packing houses and grain elevators. The metropolitan area has no suburbs, but a mid-city boulevard east of the center has taken the place of the ring-road of most Midwestern cities as the locus for an enclosed mall shopping center of the late 1960s style, and a strip of lesser clusters of shops. (This development, with free parking and a far more convenient location, must have compounded the problems of the renewal project.) The residential areas are hilly and often very pleasant, but a majority of the houses are either tiny or immense. The portion of the SMSA (Buchanan County) outside St. Joseph's city limits is sparsely populated farmland, lush and apparently quite productive.

St. Joseph is not unusually poor as measured by income per capita, which *is* unusual among non-growing SMSAs. Income per capita was 94 percent of the national average, down 12 points from 1959, but has been near the national average since 1929 (*Survey of Current Business* May 1972). Table 9-1 shows that a fairly large percentage of all families (9-1/2 percent) had incomes below poverty level, however, and only 11.6 percent had above $15,000, suggesting a large number of incomes only slightly above the mean. Several factors may help explain this, including the strong position of labor unions in the area, the near absence of ethnic minorities, and the dominance of the meat packing industry with its traditionally long hours and high wages (table 9-2). The last factor may well be the most important, as it is the only one which changed importantly in the 1960s, when income dropped abruptly.

Historical Background

The St. Joseph area had two eras of headlong growth, one from the Gold Rush of 1858 to the Civil War and a second more important one between the

Table 9-1

Selected Population and Housing Characteristics St. Joseph, Missouri SMSA 1970

	SMSA	West North Central Division	243 SMSAs
Black %	2.8	4.3	12.0
Under 5 years %	7.8	8.2	8.5
Sixty-five years and over %	14.8	11.8	9.3
Median years of education %[1]	12.0	12.2	12.2
Unemployed %	3.9	3.9	4.3
White collar %[2]	44.3	46.1	52.4
Crafts and Foremen %[2]	13.4	12.5	13.6
Operatives, laborers and other %	42.3	41.4	34.0
Family incomes over $15,000	11.6	16.8	24.5
Family incomes below low income[3] %	9.5	10.1	8.5
Housing owner occupied %	67.8	69.3	59.5
Median house value[4]	$11,307	14,571	19,027
Median gross rent	79	99	117
Home owner vacancy rate %	1.4	1.3	1.1
Rental vacancy rate %	11.0	8.3	6.0

Source: *County and City Data Book*, U.S. Bureau of the Census 1972

Notes:

1. Persons 25 years and over,

2. Percentage of employed civilian labor force,

3. As defined by 1970 Population Census Based on Family Size,

4. Single family owner-occupied.

Table 9-2

Hours and Earnings of Nonsupervisory Production Worker 1968, St. Joseph SMSA

	All employees (thousands)	Average weekly earnings-($)	Average weekly hours	Average hourly earnings-($)
Durable Goods	2.3	94.04	38.7	2.43
Non-durable[1] (except meat products)	4.6	107.25	39.2	2.81
4 Meat products	3.0	173.54	50.3	3.45

Source: BLS Bulletin 1370-9, p. 342

Note:

1. Calculated from totals for meat products and for nondurable goods.

Panic of 1873 and about 1900. Both were terminated abruptly. (The historical population figures, table 9-3, tend to smooth the trends somewhat because

Table 9-3

Historical Population and Employment, St. Joseph SMSA (Buchanan County, Missouri)

Year	Population	% Change in Population	Employment	% Change in Employment	% of Total Employment Female
1850	12,975	—			
1860	23,861	83.9			
1870	35,109	47.1			
1880	49,792	41.8			
1890	70,100	40.8			
1900	121,838	73.8			
1910	93,020	−23.7			
1920	93,684	0.7			
1930	98,633	5.3	41,487	—	24.7
1940	94,067	−4.6	31,994	−22.9	27.9
1950	96,826	2.9	37,101	16.0	30.9
1960	90,581	−6.5	34,789	−6.2	35.4
1970	86,915	−4.1	32,888	−5.5	38.2
1973	87,000	0.1			

Source:

Population: 1920, 1940, and 1970 *Censuses of Population*.

Employment: 1930, 1940, 1950, 1960, and 1970 *Censuses of Population*.

Note: 1930 employment is for ages 10 or more.
1940-1970 employment is for ages 14 or more.

of their inflexible ten-year rhythm.) In the first growth period as a supply and marketing point, St. Joseph acquired some 24,000 people, paved streets, and a rail line eastward, plus the beginning of a pork packing industry and a public school system (Rutt 1904, p. 67). It was also the eastern end of the Pony Express route. It failed, however, in efforts to lobby for selection as the eastern end of the first transcontinental rail line, which was awarded to Council Bluffs (Omaha), believed to be more secure and to be loyal Union Territory (Campbell 1945, p. 64). The second boom began in 1873-74 with the construction of the Missouri River Bridge, numerous civic buildings and the State Hospital for the Insane (Rutt 1904, p. 68). A livestock market was established in 1887 along with a major packing industry. Four more rail lines entered the area by 1893, but none continued west. The city stockyard, packing houses, and produce market thrived on the agricultural growth of the near hinterlands and access to the eastern markets. After the depression of 1893 weakened many of the independent packers, and helped by the passage of federal inspection laws only the larger firms could comply with (Kolko 1963), Swift and Company

Table 9-4
Employment in Buchanan County, 1950-1972

	April 1950	April 1955	April 1960	Average 1965[4]	Average 1970	Average 1972
Total Non-Agricultural wage & salary	31,420	34,350	31,060	30,950	32,170	32,830
Manufacturing Total	9,570	11,100	11,920	10,180	9,890	9,380
Food & Kindred	5,600	6,300	6,400	5,350	5,070	3,730
Textiles & Apparel	900	1,150	910	770	3,060	810
Chemicals & Allied	300	500	670	570	590	630
Other Manuf.	2,770[1]	3,100[1]	3,310[1]	3,490[1]	3,560[1]	4,210[1]
Contract Construction & Mining	1,550	1,950	1,140	1,600	1,740	1,790
Trans., Comm. & Pub. Util.	3,050	3,150	2,770	2,500	2,070	2,020
Wholes. & Retail Trade	8,700	10,000	8,220	7,840	7,830	8,230
Finance, Ins. & Real Est.	1,200	1,100	1,160	1,250	1,310	1,400
Service Exc. Domestic	4,400	4,100	3,170	3,890[2]	4,810[2]	5,060[2]
Government	2,900	2,900	3,260	3,690	4,570	4,920
Agricultural & Other Non-Agricultural	N.D.	N.D.	6,500	5,610[3]	4,900[3]	4,710[3]
Unemployed %			8.7	3.7	4.4	4.6

Source: Missouri Employment Security Dept., St. Joseph Area Office.

Notes:

1. Includes lumber and wood prod., paper prod., fabricated metal prod., electrical equipment and other,

2. Includes miscellaneous,

3. Includes nonagricultural self-employed workers and unpaid family workers and domestic workers in private households, and agricultural workers,

4. Estimation methods changed in 1965.

bought the stockyards. In 1897, Swift and the Nelson Morris firm built "two of the largest (meat packing) plants in the world" (Rutt 1904, p. 76). In a flurry of land speculation, most of the present city area was platted out in the 1880s and most of it was built upon by 1900.

The large packers, after gaining control of the industry, diverted their subsequent growth to the larger cities, and St. Joseph stopped growing. Events from 1900 to the present have apparently not attracted much interest from historians. Population dropped precipitously to 93,000 by 1910 and has remained near that size since. There was a small drop in rural population which rebounded in the 1930s to the 1900 size and fell again by some 44 percent in the 1940s and 1950s (Mo-Kan 1970). It can be inferred that the city's development consisted mainly in the taking over of smaller firms by larger ones and in the increasing age and falling mobility of the population.

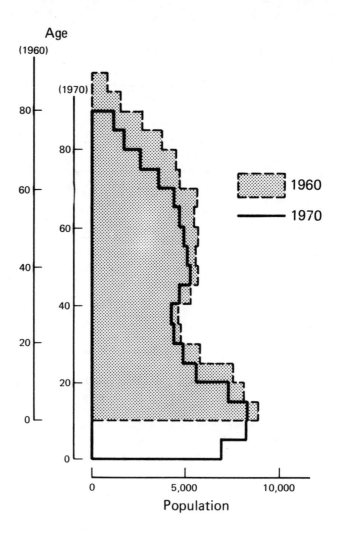

Figure 9-2. Population Age Profiles, 1960 and 1970 St. Joseph, Mo. SMSA

Development Since 1950

Employment trends since 1950 are illustrated in table 9-4. (Unfortunately, B.E.A. data could not be obtained for St. Joseph separately from Kansas City, so the State Employment Security estimates will have to do.)

There has been a steady decline in transportation, offsetting the growth

Table 9-5

Migration Summary, All Industries, St. Joseph SMSA (Based on Social Security Continuous Work History Sample (1%) First Quarter of 1960-65-70)

	THOUSANDS OF WORKERS	% OF TOTAL	1960-1965			
			1960 MEAN WAGES	1965 MEAN WAGES	% CHANGE MEAN WAGES	
INITIAL COVERED WORK FORCE	29.2	100.0	3,239			
INMIGRANTS	3.3	11.3	3,608	5,040	39.7	
OUTMIGRANTS	4.6	15.8	3,449	4,128	19.7	
NET MIGRATION	-1.3	-4.5				
NONMIGRANTS:						
SAME INDUSTRY	13.0	44.5	4,113	4,849	17.9	
DIFFERENT INDUSTRY	2.4	8.2	2,299	2,600	13.1	
NET MILITARY AND OTHERS	.1	.3				
ENTERED COVERED WORK FORCE	7.9	27.1		2,572		
LEFT COVERED WORK FORCE	8.9		2,081			
FINAL COVERED WORK FORCE	27.0	92.5		3,977		

Table 9-5 (continued)

	THOUSANDS OF WORKERS	% OF TOTAL	1965-1970		
			1965 MEAN WAGES	1970 MEAN WAGES	% CHANGE MEAN WAGES
INITIAL COVERED WORK FORCE	27.0	100.0	3,989		
INMIGRANTS	4.5	16.7	3,574	5,593	56.5
OUTMIGRANTS	5.1	18.9	4,073	6,578	61.5
NET MIGRATION	-.6	-2.2			
NONMIGRANTS:					
SAME INDUSTRY	12.6	46.7	4,714	6,758	43.4
DIFFERENT INDUSTRY	1.7	6.3	2,124	4,091	92.6
NET MILITARY AND OTHERS	-.2	-.7			
ENTERED COVERED WORK FORCE	11.0	40.7		2,570	
LEFT COVERED WORK FORCE	7.3		3,205		
FINAL COVERED WORK FORCE	29.9	110.7		4,874	

Source: Regional Analysis Information System, Bureau of Economic Analysis.

of government. There was extraordinary stability in virtually every other sector except for meat packing's decline after 1967. Twenty-three years of such stability and, perhaps, much longer represent a failure to participate in the strong national trends of the period, the growth of the trade, services, communication, and the high technology industries, and has resulted in an increasing specialization relative to the nation in slow-growth sectors. In light of this, it is interesting that promotional efforts (begun by the Chamber of Commerce only in the late 1960s) have brought in mainly more of the same: two pet food makers, paper products, food, and apparel manufacturers.

The St. Joseph population age profile (figure 9-2) seems to have been very near a sort of non-growth equilibrium by 1960. It changed by 1970 only in that smaller cohorts of children were born, reflecting a national trend.

Meat packing employment fell by several thousand after Swift closed its packing house in 1967, and Armour converted to a highly automated operation it calls a "pork arboretum." According to an Employment Security official, those laid off went principally to the Carnation factory, the State Hospital or service jobs, at much lower pay, or withdrew from the labor force. Women employees were hardest hit as female pay scales at the packing houses had been far above area norms.

St. Joseph's covered work force within the Social Security 1 percent Work History Sample declined in the first half of the 1960s and returned by 1970 to nearly the same level as before (table 9-5). Entries to the covered work force grew from 27 percent to 40 percent of the initial covered work force, while migration rates changed little. Wage gain patterns are not surprising in view of the high former wage scales in the declining packing industry. The industry breakdowns of the sample are omitted because they are inconsistent with the state data (table 9-4) and field observations. A classification error in the Social Security data is suspected.

10

Case Study: Savannah SMSA, Georgia

Figure 10-1 shows that Savannah's decade of non-growth in the 1960s followed two decades of moderate population growth and an earlier period of nearly stable population. Employment growth was negative in the 1930s, recovered in the 1940s, and fell to near zero in the 1960s. Income per capita, while low, remained steady relative to the nation through most of the period, but became oddly unstable in the 1960s. Net migration fell progressively from its moderate level of the 1940s, the accelerated growth in the 1950s being due entirely to a temporary rise in the rate of natural increase.

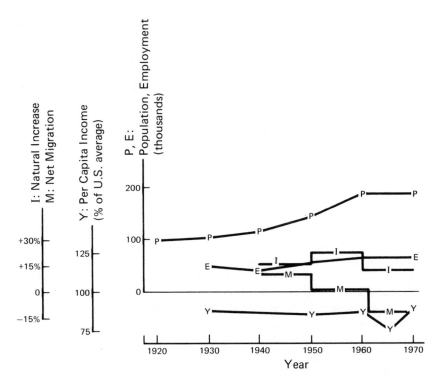

Figure 10-1. Composite of Trends, Savannah SMSA

General Description

Savannah's metropolitan area is composed of a lovely colonial center city, a heavily forested hinterland with scattered summer and year-round home development, and in between an astonishingly malodorous clump of industrial suburbs. Although separately incorporated to escape the city's taxes, the industrial suburbs penetrate almost to the center of the city, giving its boundaries somewhat the shape of an asterisk. There are only a few moderate-sized suburban commercial developments; most business and some shopping are still conducted downtown. The area has no university.

Population and housing characteristics of the Savannah SMSA at the end of the 1960s are outlined in table 10-1. A third of its people are black. Good educations are more common than good incomes in the area, and the poverty rate is high.

It had a fairly typical Southern small-city income distribution with 16.9 percent of its families below poverty level and 14.4 percent over $15,000 in 1969, compared with 14.0 percent and 17.0 percent for the South Atlantic Division.

Savannah's black population, while severely disadvantaged compared to the white population, is considerably better off than Montgomery's in terms of income and housing conditions (table 10-1). It is equally restricted from home and car ownership.

Considering its small size, slow growth, southern location, and impoverished hinterland, Savannah's income level is not exceptionally low. Its relative position fell between 1929 and 1949, but returned to near its former level by 1969, with 91 percent of the U.S. level per capita income and 152nd rank among SMSAs.

Chronological Development before 1940

Georgia was the last founded of the North American colonies. Savannah, its port, was a latecomer in the eighteenth century cotton trade and remained low in the hierarchy of information flows among pre-industrial cities analyzed by Pred (1966). Nevertheless, Savannah grew quite wealthy in the first half of the nineteenth century while the population was still concentrated near the Atlantic Coast, and its only important markets were reached by sea. It traded primarily cotton and the pine products—spars, pitch, and turpentine—needed to maintain wooden ships. Some ships were built there, including in 1819 the S.S. Savannah, the first steamship in transatlantic service. Railroads were extended from the city into the coastal plains before the Civil War. Sherman's march across Georgia spared

Table 10-1

Selected Population and Housing Characteristics Savannah SMSA, 1970

	SMSA	South Atlantic Division	243 SMSAs
Black %	34.1	20.8	12.0
Under 5 years %	8.8	8.4	8.5
65+ years %	8.2	9.6	9.3
Median years of education[1]	11.8	11.5	12.2
Unemployed %	4.3	3.5	4.3
White collar %[2]	47.2	46.4	52.4
Crafts & Foremen %[2]	15.3	14.2	13.6
Laborers & others %	37.5	39.4	34.0
Family incomes over $15,000 %	14.4	17.0	24.5
Family incomes below low income %	16.9	14.0	8.5
Housing owner-occupied %	57.3	63.5	59.5
Median house value[3]	$13,468	$15,236	$19,027
Median gross rent	$77	$103	$117
Homeowners vacancy rate %	1.5	1.5	1.1
Rental vacancy rate %	7.5	7.5	6.0

Savannah SMSA by Race

	Black	White & Other
Population change 1960-70	0.3%	−0.6%
Median family income	$4723	$9769
Housing units owner occupied	42.7%	67.0%
Housing units with 1.01 or more persons/rm	18.3%	5.9%
Housing units with no automobile available	49.9%	9.2%

Source: *County and City Data Book*, U.S. Bureau of the Census, 1972.

Notes:

1. Persons 25 years and over.

2. Percentage of employed civilian labor force.

3. Single family owner-occupied.

Savannah—the city was surrendered to him in 1864—but his destruction of the region's plantations, railroads, and factories probably did the city nearly as much economic damage as shelling it would have. Population, however, continued to increase (table 10-2).

After the war the major growth of the cotton industry was west of the mountains in the Gulf states, and as described earlier, Atlanta with the lesser piedmont cities increasingly captured the trade areas once tributary to the coastal cities like Savannah. The city grew slowly without diversifying, still trading mostly cotton and naval stores until the 1920s despite falling demand for the products and a weaker competitive position in those

Table 10-2
Historical Population and Employment, Savannah SMSA (Chatham County, Georgia)

Year	Population	% Change in Population	Employment	% Change in Employment	% of Total Employment Female
1850	23,901	—			
1860	31,043	29.7			
1870	41,279	33.0			
1880	45,023	9.1			
1890	57,740	28.1			
1900	71,239	23.3			
1910	79,690	11.9			
1920	100,032	25.5			
1930	105,431	5.4	49,221	—	32.8
1940	117,970	11.9	42,692	−13.3	31.5
1950	151,481	24.8	54,714	28.2	33.4
1960	188,299	24.3	68,004	15.2	36.2
1970	187,816	−0.3	66,347	5.3	39.2
1973	179,700	−3.1			

Sources:

Population: 1920, 1940, and 1970 *Censuses of Population*.
Employment: 1930, 1940, 1950, 1960, 1970 *Censuses of Population*.

Note: 1930 employment is for ages 10 or more.
    1940-1970 employment is for ages 14 or more.

industries. Nevertheless, population continued to grow, partly because of migration out of the destitute and overpopulated surrounding rural areas.

The industrialization of Savannah began during the First World War with the dredging of the Savannah River to permit deep-draft navigation for five miles above City Hall, the former end of the harbor. The work was done to accommodate the Savannah Sugar Refinery, opened in 1917. The refinery processed cane from Cuba.

In 1923 the city formed the Savannah Port Authority to develop a city-owned terminal and later, industrial land. In 1933 the Industrial Committee of Savannah was founded to seek new industry. This committee found the Union Bag and Paper Company (now Union/Camp Corporation) then on the verge of bankruptcy; the committee shored them up with local (C&S Bank) financing and brought them to town with a large package of concessions and subsidies (detailed in a Nader Study Group Report—Fallows, 1971). However, according to the report the firm had disastrous effects on water quality, fisheries, groundwater availability, air quality, and public finances while becoming the "world's largest integrated bag plant" in the succeeding four decades. This company is still the largest employer in the area. Because of the highly cyclical demand for packaging materials, its large corps of unskilled labor is kept semi-employed, hired on a short-term basis and frequently laid off. American Cyanamide and Continental Can also have large, vile-smelling plants pouring wastes into the river near Savannah. All these plants are located in Chatham County but outside the Savannah city limits, and are protected by an amendment to the State Constitution from being annexed.

Development in the 1940s and 1950s

Despite its industrial growth and commercial decline, Savannah retained unusually large employment in lodgings and personal services, and railroad transportation well into the mid-century (table 10-3). Employment growth continued in the 1940s and 1950s despite declines in railroads and household services, with the strongest growth in military employment, professional services (probably education), and construction.

The shift-share analysis shows mainly that the Savannah area failed to keep up with national trends in the high growth sectors, even the ones in which it once specialized. Transportation, communication and public utilities, trade, and armed services all contributed favorably to its mix effect in 1940, but none were significantly above national norms by 1960 except railroads, which were by then a negative influence.

Savannah and Chatham County acquired remarkably few new activities after the opening of the big plants, from the mid-1930s to the mid-1960s, except for the development of Hunter Air Force Base. The start-up of airline service in the 1940s and of a small motor vehicle (truck-body) industry in the 1940s and 1950s were the most noticeable and neither had an important structural effect; they were weak reflections of national trends. The more important changes were ones of accretion and attrition, the growth of the established heavy industries, the gradual destruction of the area's fisheries, groundwater resources, and air quality, and the deterioration of the central area's beautiful parks, garden squares, buildings, fine hotels, and restaurants. Employment growth picked up to 34 percent in the 1940s but slowed to 19 percent in the 1950s and had severe drops in 1958 and 1961 (Georgia Dept. of Employment Security). Military employment was the only important growth sector in the 1950s and net migration was near zero. Nevertheless, population continued to grow almost as fast in the 1950s due to the high fertility of the recent immigrants, amplified by the postwar baby boom.

Development in the 1960s

It was only in the 1960s, when employment growth was actually recovering temporarily but the baby crop was old enough to become mobile, that

Table 10-3

Employment by Selected Industrial Sectors, 1940-1970, Savannah SMSA

	1940	1950	1960	1970
TOTAL EMPLOYMENT (FULL AND PART TIME)	42,692	57,284	68,140	72,244
AGRICULTURE,FORESTRY,FISHERIES AND OTHER	1,196	976	496	447
AGRICULTURE	892	754	382	346
FORESTRY,FISHERIES AND OTHER	304	222	114	101
MINING	16	11	18	45
CONTRACT CONSTRUCTION	2,436	3,821	4,796	4,970
MANUFACTURING	7,785	12,370	14,879	12,848
FOOD AND KINDRED PRODUCTS	1,592	2,075	2,730	1,599
TEXTILE MILL PRODUCTS	42	15	13	14
APPAREL AND OTHER FABRICATED TEXTILE PRODUCTS	119	95	89	459
PRINTING,PUBLISHING AND ALLIED INDUSTRIES	337	461	677	441
CHEMICALS AND ALLIED PRODUCTS	1,642	1,121	1,420	1,417
LUMBER AND FURNITURE	917	1,735	1,687	1,210
MACHINERY	98	210	253	215
MACHINERY EXCEPT ELECTRICAL	--	177	148	150
ELECTRICAL MACHINERY	--	33	105	65
TRANSPORTATION EQUIPMENT	53	258	1,122	2,011
MOTOR VEHICLES AND MOTOR VEHICLES EQUIPMENT	13	83	309	486
TRANSPORTATION EXCLUDING MOTOR VEHICLES	40	175	813	1,525
OTHER MANUFACTURING	2,985	6,400	6,888	5,482
PAPER AND ALLIED PRODUCTS	--	4,968	5,300	3,969
PETROLEUM REFINING AND RELATED PRODUCTS	--	450	487	404
PRIMARY METALS INDUSTRIES	--	57	45	184
FABRICATED METALS + ORDNANCE	--	584	416	240
MISCELLANEOUS MANUFACTURING	--	341	640	685
TRANSPORTATION,COMM.,PUB. UTILITIES	6,854	7,084	6,866	6,739
TRANSPORTATION	6,016	5,784	5,115	4,689
RAILROAD TRANSPORTATION	3,260	3,579	2,357	1,438
MOTOR FREIGHT TRANSPORTATION AND WAREHOUSING	805	514	830	1,041
OTHER TRANSPORTATION SERVICES	1,951	1,691	1,928	2,210
COMMUNICATIONS	274	559	881	1,091
ELECTRIC,GAS,AND SANITARY SERVICES	564	741	870	959

WHOLESALE AND RETAIL TRADE	8,493	12,099	13,009	15,313
WHOLESALE TRADE	1,508	2,176	2,403	3,155
RETAIL TRADE	6,985	9,923	10,606	12,158
EATING AND DRINKING PLACES	1,021	1,705	1,823	2,194
FOOD + DAIRY STORES	2,026	2,224	1,955	1,888
OTHER RETAIL TRADE	3,938	5,994	6,828	8,076
FINANCE,INSURANCE AND REAL ESTATE	1,319	1,919	2,837	3,306
SERVICES	12,662	14,009	16,775	18,369
BUSINESS SERVICES	9,986	9,696	9,637	7,524
LODGING PLACES AND PERSONAL SERVICES	2,568	2,982	2,802	2,641
BUSINESS AND REPAIR SERVICES	667	1,019	1,433	1,645
AMUSEMENTS AND REC. SERVICES	346	447	474	449
PRIVATE HOUSEHOLDS	6,405	5,248	4,928	2,789
PROFESSIONAL SERVICES	2,676	4,313	7,138	10,845
TOTAL GOVERNMENT	1,931	4,995	8,464	10,207
CIVILIAN GOVERNMENT	736	2,397	3,153	4,310
FEDERAL MILITARY	1,195	2,598	5,311	5,897

Source: Regional Economics Information System, Bureau of Economic Analysis, from Census Data.

population growth dropped below zero in response to the lack of job opportunities. Unemployment was severe in the first half-decade (table 10-4). (It was suggested by both a Port Authority official and a former county planning official that the 1960 census population figure may have been inflated by overzealous enumerators.)

Heavy industry in Savannah declined sharply in several sectors in the 1960s (table 10-3). The boycott of Cuban cane shut down the sugar refinery about 1961, paper-making employment fell by 1,400 in the decade and railroad employment by about 1,000. Military employment increased slightly from 1960 to 1970 but declined in mid-decade with the closing of Hunter Air Force Base, later reopened as Hunter Army Airfield for the duration of the Vietnam involvement. Total employment growth was down by 6 percent for the decade, and population fell by 0.3 percent. Nevertheless, there was some diversification of the economy in the period, together with major investments in the public sector.

Employment growth was near national averages for most sectors except heavy industry and railroads in the 1960s, with strongest gains in trade, professional services, government, and apparel. Shipping declined. One reason given by a local official for the decline of the Savannah port was that the interstate highway system gives easier access from Atlanta to the port of Charleston. A new link being completed in the early 1970s may restore the balance.

The population age profile of the Savannah area (Fig. 10-2) showed very substantial decreases in all the cohorts below age 50 in 1970, except for ages 20-25 in which civilian outmigration was apparently balanced by military growth. The profile thus became higher-shouldered. The population lost was slightly more white than black.

Summary migration and workforce data from the Social Security Continuous Work History Sample (table 10-5) show a decline in the covered work force from 1960 to 1965 and a substantial gain from 1965 to 1970. The additional labor demand was met almost entirely by additional new entrants to the covered work force, the other components changing only slightly in the expected directions. Wage gains, which were very low for inmigrants in the early 1960s, increased substantially in all classes. Mobility of non-migrants between industries was high in the area and changed little in spite of doubling of their mean wages from 1965 to 1970.

The industry breakdown of the same source (table 10-6) shows that the big change was in covered "government and other" employment, which went from 7 percent decline to 70 percent increase in the second half-decade. There was net interindustry mobility out of government into trade in the bad times and the reverse in the good, but the major structural adjustments were accomplished by variations of the flow of new entrants.

In the past ten years or so, a new wave of civic energy seems to have

Table 10-4
Selected Annual Average Unemployment Rates, Savannah SMSA

1960	1961	1966	1969	1972
6.1	8.0	3.5	3.2	4.2

Source: Georgia Dept. of Labor.

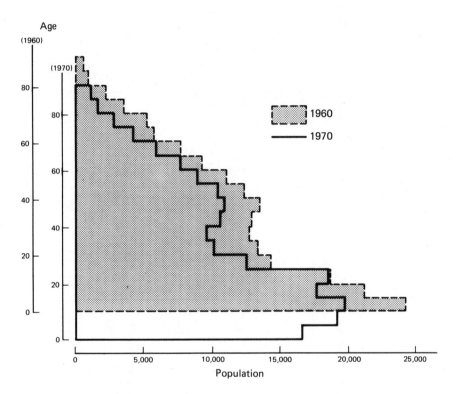

Figure 10-2. Population Age Profiles, 1960 and 1970 Savannah, Ga. SMSA

come into the Savannah area. Major public investments were made in a wide range of fields, many of them aimed at enhancing the quality of life, although the interests of Union/Camp and the C&S Bank were clearly not ignored. Some of these investments included:

1. the restoration of public spaces, rehabilitation of historic buildings, and imposition of architectural controls in the historic central city and waterfront district;

2. the construction of an immense city auditorium and concert hall;

Table 10-5
Migration Summary, All Industries, Savannah SMSA (Based on Social Security Continuous Work History Sample (1%) First Quarter of 1960-65-70)

	THOUSANDS OF WORKERS	% OF TOTAL	1960-1965		
			1960 MEAN WAGES	1965 MEAN WAGES	% CHANGE MEAN WAGES
INITIAL COVERED WORK FORCE	56.5	100.0	3,375		
INMIGRANTS	6.0	10.6	3,623	3,911	7.9
OUTMIGRANTS	10.6	18.8	3,672	5,024	36.8
NET MIGRATION	−4.6	−8.1			
NONMIGRANTS:					
SAME INDUSTRY	25.3	44.8	3,909	4,826	23.5
DIFFERENT INDUSTRY	6.2	11.0	2,677	3,638	35.9
NET MILITARY AND OTHERS	.7	1.2			
ENTERED COVERED WORK FORCE	14.3	25.3		2,090	
LEFT COVERED WORK FORCE	13.8	25.3	2,584		
FINAL COVERED WORK FORCE	53.1	94.0		3,834	

1965-1970

	THOUSANDS OF WORKERS	% OF TOTAL	1965 MEAN WAGES	1970 MEAN WAGES	% CHANGE MEAN WAGES
INITIAL COVERED WORK FORCE	53.1	100.0	3,834		
INMIGRANTS	7.5	14.1	4,930	6,970	41.4
OUTMIGRANTS	10.4	19.6	3,709	6,414	72.9
NET MIGRATION	−2.9	−5.5			
NONMIGRANTS:					
SAME INDUSTRY	24.5	46.1	4,673	6,924	48.2
DIFFERENT INDUSTRY	6.4	12.1	2,665	5,410	103.0
NET MILITARY AND OTHERS	.9	1.7			
ENTERED COVERED WORK FORCE	23.0	43.3		2,885	
LEFT COVERED WORK FORCE	11.1		2,974		
FINAL COVERED WORK FORCE	63.0	118.6		5,279	

Source: Regional Analysis Information System, Bureau of Economic Analysis.

Table 10-6
Migration Summary by Industry, Savannah SMSA (Based on Social Security Continuous Work History Sample (1%) First Quarter of 1960-65-70)

THOUSANDS OF WORKERS

GOVERNMENT AND OTHER,
INCLUDING UNCLASSIFIED

FINANCE, INSURANCE AND REAL ESTATE

WHOLESALE AND RETAIL TRADE

TRANSPORTATION, COMMUNICATION
AND PUBLIC UTILITIES

MANUFACTURING

CONTRACT CONSTRUCTION

AGRICULTURE, FORESTRY AND FISHERIES

	.6	5.5	17.8	4.6	13.8	3.7	10.5
INITIAL COVERED WORK FORCE, 1960	.6	5.5	17.8	4.6	13.8	3.7	10.5
INMIGRANTS	*	*	1.8	.8	1.7	*	.8
OUTMIGRANTS	*	1.2	3.4	.7	3.5	*	1.3
NET MIGRATION	-.1	-.8	-1.6	.1	-1.8	.1	-.5
NONMIGRANTS:							
SAME INDUSTRY	*	2.6	8.8	1.8	5.6	1.9	4.6
LEFT THIS INDUSTRY	*	*	1.6	1.5	1.5	*	1.0
ENTERED THIS INDUSTRY	*	*	1.6	.8	2.0	.7	.7
NET MILITARY AND OTHERS	-.1		.4	.2	-.1	.1	.2
ENTERED COVERED WORK FORCE	-.*	.7	3.9	.7	4.9	.6	3.5
LEFT COVERED WORK FORCE		1.3	3.9	.6	2.8	1.3	3.6
FINAL COVERED WORK FORCE, 1965	*	4.1	16.6	4.3	14.5	3.7	9.8
INMIGRANTS	*	1.0	2.3	.6	1.6	.5	1.5
OUTMIGRANTS	*	1.1	3.2	.5	3.5	.7	1.3
NET MIGRATION	-.1	-.1	-.9	.1	-1.9	-.2	.2
NONMIGRANTS:							
SAME INDUSTRY	*	1.5	9.4	1.5	5.4	1.5	5.2
LEFT THIS INDUSTRY	*	.7	1.2	1.0	2.3	.5	.7
ENTERED THIS INDUSTRY	.	.7	1.4	1.0	.7	*	2.3
NET MILITARY AND OTHERS	*	.6	.3	.2	-.3		.1
ENTERED COVERED WORK FORCE	-.*	1.3	2.7	1.4	9.1	.9	7.6
LEFT COVERED WORK FORCE	.	.8	2.7	1.1	2.9	1.0	2.6
FINAL COVERED WORK FORCE, 1970	*	5.1	16.2	4.9	16.9	3.2	16.7

1960-1965

1965-1970

Source: Regional Analysis Information System, Bureau of Economic Analysis.

*Statistically insignificant.

3. the funding of water pollution control facilities (including the sale of revenue bonds by the Port Authority to build a treatment plant for Union/Camp);

4. the upgrading of the port to handle container and LASH operations;

5. the construction of a bridge to Skidaway Island, opening a vast area for residential and recreational development (much of it owned by Union/Camp);

6. the creation of two vocational-technical schools and expansion of two local junior colleges to a four-year curriculum.

The Civil Rights Movement came to Savannah with a successful, non-violent series of sit-ins at lunch counters and hotels in June 1963 (Stahl 1966). Black politicians were later elected to both the County Commission and the City Board of Aldermen. There has apparently not been much consolidation of power on either a neighborhood or coalition basis by the black politicians, however, although there has been sufficient wariness on the part of the public agencies to avoid proposing new urban renewal or highway sites which would displace blacks. One respondent felt that race relations are again deteriorating in the area.

Savannah has experienced an era of diversification and civic enrichment. It has faced up to at least some of its long-ignored problems. Even its relative isolation may turn to advantage, for that has preserved the more distant surrounding swamps and pine forests, and in time perhaps fish and wildfowl will return even to the nearby estuaries. Still, the old factories remain; a block or two west of the historic district begins a wasteland of vacant or deteriorating industrial property; dense, pungent steam from the paper plant and occasional black or yellow smoke from some exotic chemical process drift through the city despite stricter air quality standards. Perhaps it will remain in many ways a company town, but the era of the 1960s in Savannah remains a lively example of development without growth.

11

Case Study: Scranton and
Wilkes-Barre-Hazleton
SMSAs, Pennsylvania

Wilkes-Barre-Hazelton and Scranton are in many ways separate and distinct areas, although they have been included along with Monroe County in the Northeast Pennsylvania SMSA since 1973. Before 1880 they occupied the same county. Since they share a common historic origin in the anthracite industry, and since some data do not distinguish them, they will be treated for convenience in the same chapter.

Their populations and incomes moved along parallel paths for most of this century, as figures 11-1 and 11-2 show. The major loss of employment occurred in the 1930s. Population was static until 1940, however, and then declined sharply for two decades. Relative income per capita for the

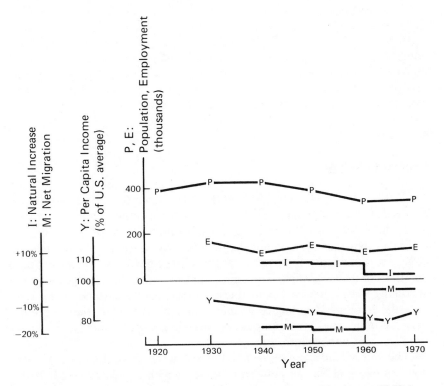

Figure 11-1. Composite of Trends, Wilkes-Barre-Hazleton SMSA

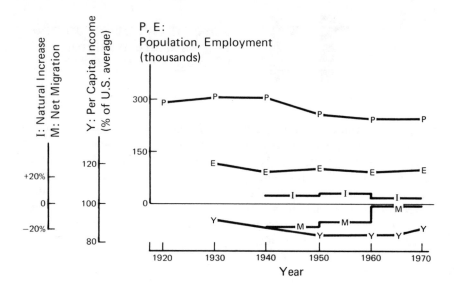

Figure 11-2. Composite of Trends, Scranton SMSA

combined areas was already low in 1929 and continued to fall until the mid-1960s. Natural increase rates in both areas were consistently among the lowest in the country so that both populations declined in the 1960s despite a slackening of net outmigration to near zero.

General Description

The Wilkes-Barre-Hazleton SMSA (Luzerne County, Pa.) contains two clusters of small to medium-sized cities and towns built to mine anthracite along the Northern Field and the Eastern Middle Field of the anthracite region of Northeastern Pennsylvania. Wilkes-Barre city, although the largest of the seventy-three municipalities in the SMSA, contains less than one-third of its population. The cities and towns lie edge to edge along the Wyoming Valley, where the Northern Field is near the surface. Many were once the domains of mining companies which controlled for their profit not only the mines and breakers but also housing, stores, electric and water supplies, and public transportation. The valley landscape of Wilkes-Barre is a record of dreadful exploitation. Smoke and flames pour from mines which have burned for half a century. There are black, bare heaps of mine wastes a hundred feet high and thousands long on the treeless hillsides and the narrow valley floor. Thousands of mobile homes are lined along the bulldozed tops of bare black waste heaps, housing the victims of the 1972 floods. Tattered frame houses and factory buildings fill the interstices. In the little business district of Wilkes-Barre, a domed marble courthouse overlooks a few rows of stodgy brick and granite commercial buildings and a very large hotel. Outside of the Wyoming Valley and the Hazleton area the county is rough but scenic, an uneven plateau, wrinkled by low, steep ridges and narrow valleys, with thick second growth forest cover.

Wilkes-Barre-Hazleton has a negligible black population of 0.6 percent. It is, nevertheless, an area of strong ethnic division between neighborhoods and municipalities. People of foreign stock are 30 percent of its population, only slightly more than average for the division. Perhaps the slow turnover of population and the fact that few new neighborhoods have been built in the past sixty years have helped the survival of churches and other ethnic institutions. Another factor might be the limited opportunities for upward social mobility in the area because of both the lack of growth and the predominantly blue collar job structure (table 11-1).

The population of Wilkes-Barre-Hazleton is exceptionally old, with a median age of 37.4 in 1970, relatively few children and 40 percent more people over 65 than would be typical for an SMSA its size. It is also a predominantly blue-collar area. High incomes are unusual, although poverty incomes are only a little more frequent than the average for SMSAs. There is a high rate of home ownership. The housing data in table 11-1 based on conditions before the floods, show low values and rents, but a tight market according to the vacancy rates. Post-flood conditions are much tighter and will doubtless become worse with the eventual removal of the mobile homes that now provide temporary shelter.

The Scranton SMSA (Lackawanna County, Pa.) is similar in general type, but more strongly dominated by a single city which, at 103,000 population, is by far the largest in the two SMSAs. Scranton, seen in context with the horribly disfigured former mining towns that occupy over half the SMSA, appears almost dignified. The city is not cheerful; there is too much wreckage of its former wealth in plain view; but it is stolid, reasonable, and surviving. The destruction of land and people—the mine wastes and dismal workmen's towns on which it grew—are largely out of sight from the central area. (The few wealthy Scranton suburbs, which were not visited, are the hermetic scene of several John O'Hara novels.) While the main shopping street is definitely worn, it is not a disaster area: decent hotels and offices have been put up near the grandiose County Courthouse and there is a new office building being built by a local bank.

Table 11-1

Selected Population and Housing Characteristics Wilkes-Barre-Hazleton and Scranton SMSAs, Pennsylvania 1970

	W-B-H SMSA	Scranton SMSA	Middle Atlantic Division	SMSAs 243
Black %	.6	.4	10.6	12.0
Under 5 years %	6.9	7.0	8.1	8.5
65+ years %	13.0	13.4	10.6	9.3
Median years of education[1]	11.5	11.7	12.1	12.2
Unemployed %	4.0	5.2	3.9	4.3
White collar[2] %	36.8	39.5	51.6	52.4
Crafts & Foremen[2] %	14.5	14.1	13.3	13.6
Operatives, laborers and other %	48.7	46.4	35.1	34.0
Family incomes over $15,000[3]	10.9	12.2	24.5	24.5
Family incomes below low income %	9.0	7.8	7.9	8.5
Housing owner occupied %	66.6	63.4	56.6	59.5
Median house value[4]	$11,086	$12,303	19,037	19,027
Median gross rent	$ 80	$ 78	112	117
Homeowner vacancy rate %	.7	0.8	0.8	1.1
Rental vacancy rate %	4.2	7.3	3.5	6.0

Source: *County and City Data Book*, U.S. Bureau of the Census, 1972.

Notes:

1. Persons 25 years and over.
2. Percentage of employed civilian labor force.
3. As defined by 1970 Population Census Based on Family Size.
4. Single family owner-occupied.

Several movie theatres are doing well and a nourishing if unpretentious meal can be bought. The noon crowds of office workers are passively observed by old men sitting shoulder to shoulder on the benches that surround the courthouse square. An old photograph in the city library shows an identical scene in the mid-1920s.

The Scranton SMSA population (table 11-1) is even older than that of the Wilkes-Barre-Hazleton area, but slightly better off. It has more white-collar workers, less poverty, and a slightly higher proportion of family incomes over $15,000, although the last figure is less than half the average proportions for the division and for all SMSAs.

Housing conditions in the Scranton SMSA for 1970 were also similar to but less extreme than those of the Wilkes-Barre-Hazleton area. Homeownership was high, home values and rents low. Vacancy rates in homes for sale were average, and in rentals slightly high. Since the Wilkes-Barre floods, however, there has been considerable pressure on the whole area housing market, so these rates probably do not describe the current situation.

Early Development of the Anthracite District

The early anthracite coal development, about 1828-1840, was concentrated around the canal terminals in Luzerne and Schuylkill counties.

Luzerne County's major growth, based almost totally on anthracite production, began with the extension of railway access from the coastal cities to Hazleton in 1836 and to Wilkes-Barre in 1843-1848. Wilkes-Barre's Dundee shaft was sunk in 1857 and its first coal breaker was built in 1859 (League of Women Voters 1963, pp. 23-24). The area grew very rapidly for three decades.

Scranton was a late entry to the anthracite industry of Northwest Pennsylvania and never became so exclusively dependent on it as did Wilkes-Barre-Hazleton (Luzerne County) and Schuykill County. The deposits of the Scranton area were first developed after a rail connection was made with the New York area through the Nay Aug Gap in 1851, but rail service south to the Pennsylvania Railroad lines was not completed until 1871. Iron was made in Scranton from 1840 and steel from 1870 until 1902, cigars from 1880 and books from about the same time. Rail shops of the Lackawanna Railroad were established there in 1905 (Hitchcock 1914; Prince 1950; *Scranton Times* 1966).

The decline of the Northern Pennsylvania anthracite industry (table 11-2) was clearly impending before World War I, although the war was to delay it somewhat. Many mines had exhausted their principal deposits by 1900 and had taken to mining "pillar" coal which supports the earth above, a practice which led to a serious continuing problem of surface subsidence and the release of poisonous fumes in the Scranton area. (The city of Scranton finally took title to "pillar" coal in the 1920s, which discouraged but probably failed to end the practice within its city limits.)

Statewide anthracite employment reached its peak between 1910 and 1919, by which time virtually everything visible on the surface in 1960 had been built. Wages and incomes were high for a blue-collar area: miners were the best organized trade and the "kings of labor." Employment changed little in the 1920s and 1930s, but relative incomes must have declined as production fell. In the Great Depression, more than half the anthracite area's miners lost their jobs and mining employment has declined steeply ever since (table 11-2).

Both metropolitan areas' greatest populations were reached in 1930, more than a decade after mining passed its peak employment, but did not begin to fall substantially until the 1940s and 1950s (tables 11-3 and 11-4). Luzerne County's unemployment rate rose to 28.4 percent of the labor force by 1940, and remained generally above 10 percent until 1963. Early estimates for Lackawanna County were not found, but employment there was similarly in the 10-12 percent range in the 1950s.

Table 11-2
Northeastern Pennsylvania Anthracite: Total Employees, 1924-1972

	Scranton SMSA	Wilkes-Barre Hazleton SMSA
1924	35,846	63,308
1930	36,317	61,114
1935	20,889	43,701
1940	16,860	42,238
1945	11,400	32,888
1950	11,005	33,176
1955	4,954	14,399
1960	2,937	6,002
1963	1,239	4,626
1972	284	1,401

Source: Economic Development Council N.E. Penn., *A Statistical Analysis of the Anthracite Industry*, Avoca, Pa., May 1974.

Mining essentially dominated the economy of the area until the Great Depression. It paid high wages to and demanded long hours from a strongly organized, virtually all-male work force. When laid off, they were supposedly reluctant to accept factory work because of its lower wages, hierarchical organization, and regimented work as contrasted with flexible team methods used in the mines. Women, however, were underemployed and more amenable to factory work. With a lack of clerical, trade, and office employment in the area, there were few opportunities for women to work, despite the trend of the times.

When non-mining industries attracted by cheap surplus labor began to locate in the Wilkes-Barre-Hazleton and Scranton areas in the 1930s, notably textile mills and sewing shops, they hired mostly women, paid very low wages, and in the early decades steadfastly resisted union organization. Thus the industrialization of the area reversed the previous sex patterns of employment (table 11-5) and degraded the relative wage structure of the area.

Labor availability and low wage demands were not the only aspects of the anthracite district that were attractive to the textile and apparel industries. Eastern Pennsylvania was much closer to the former centers of those industries—New England and New York City, respectively—than the southern towns that were the main alternative for new plant location, and closer to their markets. In the case of apparel, they fit in with a unique pattern at that stage of the dispersing of women's fashions out of New York. Truckers were given batches of precut cloth at Manhattan factories to be returned sewn up as garments. The catch was that the trucker was then free to deal with a non-union sewing shop, which the factory was not

Table 11-3

Historical Population and Employment Wilkes-Barre-Hazleton SMSA (Luzerne County, Pennsylvania)

Year	Population	% Change in Population	Employment	% Change in Employment
1880	133,065	—		
1890	201,203	51.2		
1900	257,121	27.8		
1910	343,186	33.5		
1920	390,991	13.9		
1930	445,109	13.8	158,364	—
1940	441,518	−.8	119,951	−24.3
1950	393,241	−11.2	138,873	15.8
1960	346,972	−11.5	121,920	−12.2
1970	343,329	−1.3	136,180	11.7
1973	346,800	1.3		

Sources:

Population: 1920, 1940, and 1970 *Censuses of Population*.

Employment: 1930, 1940, 1950, 1960, and 1970 *Censuses of Population*.

Note: 1930 Employment is for ages 10 or more.
    1940-1970 employment is for ages 14 or more.

Table 11-4

Historical Population and Employment, Scranton SMSA (Lackawanna County, Pennsylvania)

Year	Population	% Change in Population	Employment	% Change in Employment
1880	82,269	—		
1890	142,088	72.7		
1900	193,831	36.4		
1910	259,570	33.9		
1920	286,311	10.3		
1930	310,397	8.4	112,994	—
1940	301,243	−2.9	81,165	−28.2
1950	257,396	−14.6	92,332	13.8
1960	234,531	−8.9	83,707	−9.3
1970	234,131	−0.2	92,615	3.1
1973	237,000	1.2		

Sources:

Population: 1920, 1940, and 1970 *Censuses of Population*.

Employment: 1930, 1940, 1950, 1960, and 1970 *Censuses of Population*.

Note: 1930 employment is for ages 10 or more.
    1940-1970 employment is for ages 14 or more.

Table 11-5
SMSA and U.S. Employment By Sex, 1930-1970

	1930	1940	1950	1960	1970
Wilkes-Barre-Hazleton					
Total Employment	158,364	119,951	138,873	121,920	136,170
Male	126,280	91,108	96,736	74,502	80,038
Female	32,084	28,843	42,137	47,418	56,142
% Female	20.3	24.0	30.3	38.9	41.2
Scranton					
Total Employment	112,994	81,165	93,322	83,707	92,615
Male	87,830	58,610	62,799	53,055	55,059
Female	25,164	22,555	29,533	30,652	37,556
% Female	22.2	27.8	32.0	36.2	40.6
U.S.					
% Female	22.1	24.7	28.0	32.8	37.7

Note: 1930 data are for employed persons aged 10 or more.
1940-1970 data are for employed persons aged 14 or more.

(Vance 1955). Another attraction was the availability of cheap existing factory space, some of it developed by local authorities, and a generally welcoming public attitude as contrasted with that of the dominant interests in many southern towns at the time. The pattern had been established when coal first began to falter. In 1914, the Scranton Board of Trade raised $1.1 million to develop factory buildings and encourage manufacturers to establish in the area; this was the first of several "Scranton Plans" which have been undertaken along basically the same line during this century.

Development in the 1940s and 1950s

The area's total employment increased during the 1940s but fell nearly to its prewar level in the mid-1950s. The overwhelming structural trends of these two decades in both SMSAs were the continued fall of mining and the rise of manufacturing within an otherwise nearly static industrial profile (table 11-6). The area hardly participated at all in the national trends of growing trade, service, and government employment during this period.

World War II temporarily halted the decline of coal demand and stimulated manufacturing industry in the area. In the postwar period, however, anthracite mining quickly resumed its decline, to 44,000 employees in 1950, 9,500 in 1960, and 2,600—1 percent of the area's total employment—by 1970.

There was a series of cave-ins after the war in which underground mines were flooded by river water from above, culminating in the Knox Mine Disaster of 1959 in Wilkes-Barre. The flooded mines would be too costly to reclaim even at vastly higher coal prices.

The growth of manufacturing was at first strongly concentrated in apparel which contributed 54 percent of its increase in the 1940s. Apparel growth fell to 22 percent of a much smaller manufacturing increment in the 1950s, and total employment declined.

Meanwhile, the area's population size, which had been essentially constant despite the catastrophic layoffs of the 1930s, began to decline toward a level more commensurate with their reduced economic base. Unemployment fell from its peak levels near 30 percent, but remained in the 10-12 percent range through these decades. Labor force participation rose slowly but remained far below U.S. averages, especially for males. As late as 1960, only 69.7 percent of working age males in Luzerne County were working or seeking work, compared to 77.4 percent for the United States. Strong negative net migration rates existed in the 1940s and 1950s, but were evidently inadequate to relieve the pressure of excess population for two full decades after the employment loss bottomed out.

Development Since 1960

The Wilkes-Barre-Hazleton and Scranton SMSAs grew in total employment from 1954 to 1960, then fell back to little or no growth. Employment in these areas seemed to respond in an exaggerated way to the downward movements of the national business cycle in the early 1960s and after 1969, especially in the manufacturing sector. The overall trend for the decade was a modest recovery of total employment with further specialization in manufacturing and a virtual disappearance of mining (table 11-6). Service employment finally began to grow but at nowhere near the national rates. Unemployment rates improved greatly in mid-decade (tables 11-7 and 11-8).

A number of new industrial parks were completed in the 1960s. The type of firm attracted began to shift toward higher-wage operations like the metal fabrication, although there was continued growth as well in low wage work like apparel, paper, and electronics assembly: It is unclear to what extent the shift was a conscious policy—the first articulation of such a policy seems to have come late in the decade—and to what extent it was due to a gradual tightening of the labor market due to a falling population, improved labor organization, and rising wage expectations.

The population age profiles (figures 11-3 and 11-4) suggest that the demographic aspect of labor supply was indeed tightening. The profiles are

Table 11-6
Employment by Selected Industrial Sectors, 1940-1970, Wilkes-Barre-Hazleton and Scranton SMSAs

	1940	1950	1960	1970
TOTAL EMPLOYMENT (FULL AND PART TIME)	201,116	231,410	205,896	229,233
AGRICULTURE,FORESTRY,FISHERIES AND OTHER	4,508	3,905	2,580	1,783
AGRICULTURE	4,436	3,866	2,550	1,738
FORESTRY,FISHERIES AND OTHER	72	39	30	45
MINING	57,966	44,154	9,490	2,608
CONTRACT CONSTRUCTION	6,412	9,424	8,747	12,218
MANUFACTURING	35,504	65,645	78,841	89,942
FOOD AND KINDRED PRODUCTS	5,180	5,986	6,535	5,056
TEXTILE MILL PRODUCTS	11,806	12,523	6,361	5,478
APPAREL AND OTHER FABRICATED TEXTILE PRODUCTS	6,639	22,900	25,485	29,258
PRINTING,PUBLISHING AND ALLIED INDUSTRIES	2,055	2,980	4,860	5,745
CHEMICALS AND ALLIED PRODUCTS	575	803	950	1,125
LUMBER AND FURNITURE	773	1,522	1,767	2,628
MACHINERY	1,144	4,960	10,153	11,850
MACHINERY EXCEPT ELECTRICAL	--	2,464	5,528	5,245
ELECTRICAL MACHINERY	--	2,496	4,625	6,605
TRANSPORTATION EQUIPMENT	363	647	3,150	2,092
MOTOR VEHICLES AND MOTOR VEHICLES EQUIPMENT	97	218	1,432	618
TRANSPORTATION EXCLUDING MOTOR VEHICLES	266	429	1,718	1,474
OTHER MANUFACTURING	6,969	13,324	19,580	26,710
PAPER AND ALLIED PRODUCTS	--	412	551	1,976
PETROLEUM REFINING AND RELATED PRODUCTS	--	107	121	115
PRIMARY METALS INDUSTRIES	--	1,798	1,043	1,430
FABRICATED METALS + ORDNANCE	--	1,795	3,514	7,086
MISCELLANEOUS MANUFACTURING	--	9,212	14,351	16,103
TRANSPORTATION,COMM.,+PUB. UTILITIES	16,326	19,455	15,686	13,326
TRANSPORTATION	12,050	13,924	10,150	7,718
RAILROAD TRANSPORTATION	8,361	8,600	4,565	1,822
MOTOR FREIGHT TRANSPORTATION AND WAREHOUSING	2,417	3,182	4,095	4,334
OTHER TRANSPORTATION SERVICES	1,272	2,142	1,490	1,562
COMMUNICATIONS	1,170	2,166	2,553	2,406
ELECTRIC,GAS,AND SANITARY SERVICES	3,106	3,365	2,983	3,202

WHOLESALE AND RETAIL TRADE	34,819	41,751	38,730	43,592
WHOLESALE TRADE	3,800	6,381	6,543	8,206
RETAIL TRADE	31,019	35,370	32,187	35,386
EATING AND DRINKING PLACES	4,506	5,929	5,320	6,969
FOOD + DAIRY STORES	9,118	8,809	7,011	7,584
OTHER RETAIL TRADE	17,395	20,632	19,856	20,833
FINANCE,INSURANCE AND REAL ESTATE	4,633	5,248	6,376	7,445
SERVICES	35,103	34,071	35,944	46,544
BUSINESS SERVICES	17,608	14,408	13,075	12,693
LODGING PLACES AND PERSONAL SERVICES	6,204	6,224	5,411	5,440
BUSINESS AND REPAIR SERVICES	2,982	3,986	3,874	4,729
AMUSEMENTS AND REC. SERVICES	1,371	1,521	1,277	1,086
PRIVATE HOUSEHOLDS	7,051	2,677	2,513	1,638
PROFESSIONAL SERVICES	17,495	19,663	22,869	33,851
TOTAL GOVERNMENT	5,845	7,757	9,502	11,775
CIVILIAN GOVERNMENT	5,845	7,549	9,217	11,937
FEDERAL MILITARY	--	208	285	438

Source: Regional Economics Information System, Bureau of Economic Analysis, from Census Data.

Table 11-7

Selected Annual Average Unemployment Rates, Wilkes-Barre-Hazleton SMSA

1950	1960	1965	1970	1972
9.0	12.1	6.3	5.2	8.9

Source: Pennsylvania Bureau of Employment Security.

Table 11-8

Selected Annual Average Unemployment Rates, Scranton SMSA

1950	1960	1963	1969	1971
9.8	11.9	11.1	4.1	6.4

Source: Pennsylvania Bureau of Employment Security.

exceedingly high-topped and deeply undercut by migration, not only in the younger cohorts but up to age fifty. The high, wide tops of the profiles mean that large numbers of people were leaving the labor force due to retirement or death. The gap in the younger working ages was growing rapidly, as can be seen by comparing the solid (1970) and dotted (1960) lines. The same comparison, incidentally, makes it clear that whereas total net migration returned to near zero in this decade, the outmigration of people in the younger working ages continued unabated. One must infer, therefore, that there was an increase of inmigration in the older age groups, much of it probably retired former residents, now on fixed incomes, attracted by cheap housing and the presence of friends and relatives.

The Social Security Work History Sample analyses (for Wilkes-Barre-Hazleton only, tables 11-9 and 11-10) show small and nearly balanced rates of inmigration and outmigration, but large rates of entering and leaving the covered work force. There were increases in both entries to the covered work force and outmigration in the second half of the decade when business was better. Improved business also allowed more and poorer people to upgrade their wages by changing industry. The general trend was out of trade and mining into construction, government and services, but there were also strong cross-flows in and out of manufacturing. The only significant structural change, the growth of government and service employment, was accomplished mainly by new entries to the work force rather than transfers or net migration.

The haphazard development of the area by the coal companies left it susceptible not only to economic exploitation but to "natural" disasters.

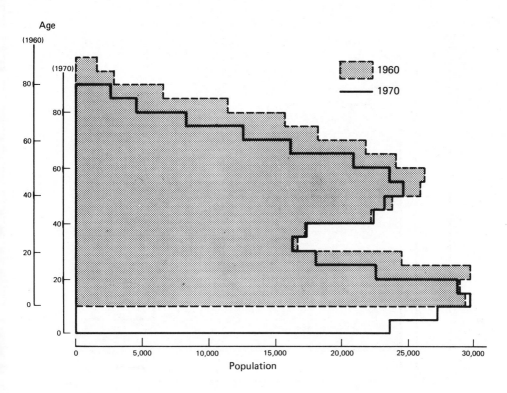

Figure 11-3. Population Age Profiles, 1960 and 1970 Wilkes-Barre-Hazleton, Pa. SMSA

The Wyoming Valley is a flood plain. The hurricane of 1936 had caused severe damage. In June 1972, Storm Agnes caused the Susquehanna to overflow the 1937 dike. Central Wilkes-Barre and the other Wyoming Valley towns were flooded; 60,000 persons were temporarily homeless and a large number of businesses and smaller factories were destroyed. The president had recently frozen disaster housing money. In part through the efforts of an informal group of homeowners which became the Wyoming Valley Flood Victims' Action Council (one of their tactics was a "children's crusade" to the White House), relief was eventually provided by the federal government. SBA provided forgiveness of up to $5,000 in outstanding indebtedness on damaged homes and financing of repairs or replacement at 1 percent interest. HUD moved in over 8,000 mobile homes for "temporary" housing, of which 3,400 were still occupied in November 1973, and provided for "Interim Assistance" home repairs of up to $3,000 per house through the local redevelopment agency. The relief was chan-

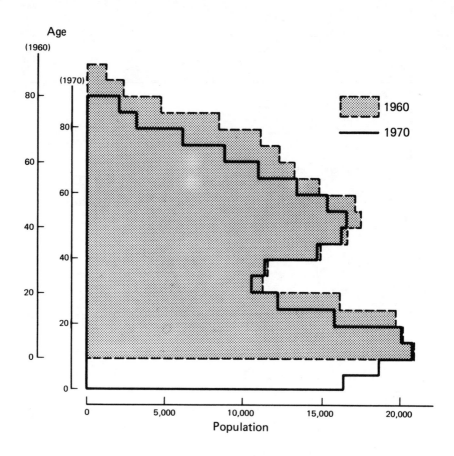

Figure 11-4. Population Age Profiles, 1960 and 1970 Scranton, Pa. SMSA

neled largely to homeowners and downtown businessmen, however, and was far short of even their needs, seemingly due in part to profiteering. Costs of building materials and contracting escalated in the area, and rents have tripled since the flood. The mud has been shoveled away, and unemployment has returned to pre-flood levels, but more persistent effects remain. Groundwater is polluted with mine wastes. All domestic water is supplied by private firms, a legacy of coal "company town" practices, and the last new treatment plant in the Wilkes-Barre area was built in 1911. There are severe shortages of housing and community facilities, and little impetus to provide more. Several dress factories and a large bakery never reopened, making the central areas more than ever dependent on outlying jobs in the industrial parks. A further blow to the area is that four of the five railroads serving the area were in bankruptcy and threatened to shut down freight service.

The major foci of growth in the two SMSAs—the newer industrial parks and Scranton's small central business district—were not damaged in the floods, and in a sense the modernization of the area's economy may even have been accelerated by the disaster. (Disaster recovery efforts, as Jones and Mar (1974) pointed out, may have been misguided in focusing on reconstruction of old homes and businesses rather than reinforcing the new growth sectors, but there would have been a serious problem of equity in doing otherwise.)

Market forces now seem to be aligned with local policy in seeking higher-wage and more stable sources of employment: the population age structure seems to insure continued low rates of natural increase, barring a major wave of inmigration. Thus the Wilkes-Barre-Hazleton and Scranton areas seem to be finally completing a fifty-year adjustment to the collapse of anthracite mining. The next question, however, is whether they can develop the resilience to weather the next shock that the national economy may send their way. If not, as the manufacturing industries in which they now specialize pass through their life cycles, the whole painful process may start again.

Table 11-9
Migration Summary, All Industries, Wilkes-Barre-Hazelton SMSA (Based on Social Security Continuous Work History Sample (1%) First Quarter of 1960-65-70)

	THOUSANDS OF WORKERS	% OF TOTAL	1960-1965		
			1960 MEAN WAGES	1965 MEAN WAGES	% CHANGE MEAN WAGES
INITIAL COVERED WORK FORCE	85.2	100.0	3,069		
INMIGRANTS	13.7	16.1	3,915	4,470	14.2
OUTMIGRANTS	11.4	13.4	3,128	4,362	39.5
NET MIGRATION	2.3	2.7			
NONMIGRANTS:					
SAME INDUSTRY	44.4	52.1	3,305	4,117	24.6
DIFFERENT INDUSTRY	6.4	7.5	3,066	4,111	34.1
NET MILITARY AND OTHERS	.8	.9			
ENTERED COVERED WORK FORCE	30.7	36.0			
LEFT COVERED WORK FORCE	22.5		2,601	2,451	
FINAL COVERED WORK FORCE	96.5	113.3	3,643		

			1965-1970		
	THOUSANDS OF WORKERS	% OF TOTAL	1965 MEAN WAGES	1970 MEAN WAGES	% CHANGE MEAN WAGES
INITIAL COVERED WORK FORCE	96.5	100.0	3,643		
INMIGRANTS	12.6	13.1	4,202	6,477	54.1
OUTMIGRANTS	16.0	16.6	3,954	6,971	76.3
NET MIGRATION	-3.4	-3.5			
NONMIGRANTS:					
SAME INDUSTRY	46.5	48.2	4,111	5,814	41.4
DIFFERENT INDUSTRY	10.5	10.9	2,753	5,231	90.0
NET MILITARY AND OTHERS	.7	.7			
ENTERED COVERED WORK FORCE	37.9	39.3		3,076	
LEFT COVERED WORK FORCE	23.1		2,945		
FINAL COVERED WORK FORCE	108.6	112.5		4,866	

Source: Regional Analysis Information System, Bureau of Economic Analysis.

Table 11-10
Migration Summary by Industry, Wilkes-Barre-Hazleton SMSA (Based on Social Security Continuous Work History Sample (1%) First Quarter of 1960-65-70)

THOUSANDS OF WORKERS

GOVERNMENT AND OTHER, INCLUDING UNCLASSIFIED

FINANCE, INSURANCE AND REAL ESTATE

WHOLESALE AND RETAIL TRADE

TRANSPORTATION, COMMUNICATION AND PUBLIC UTILITIES

MANUFACTURING

CONTRACT CONSTRUCTION

MINING

AGRICULTURE, FORESTRY AND FISHERIES

	.8	3.9	4.2	37.9	5.6	16.2	2.5	14.1
INITIAL COVERED WORK FORCE, 1960	.8	3.9	4.2	37.9	5.6	16.2	2.5	14.1
IMMIGRANTS	*	1.3	.8	6.2	.6	3.0	*	1.6
OUTMIGRANTS	.6	.7	*	3.5	.9	2.9	*	2.1
NET MIGRATION	-.6	.6	.5	2.7	-.3	.1	-.2	-.5
NONMIGRANTS:								
SAME INDUSTRY	.	2.2	1.2	24.3	3.3	6.1	1.2	6.1
LEFT THIS INDUSTRY	.	.5	.9	1.3	*	2.2	.5	1.2
ENTERED THIS INDUSTRY	*	*	*	2.5	*	1.3	.1	1.2
NET MILITARY AND OTHERS	.	.1	.	.5	.1	.0	.1	.0
ENTERED COVERED WORK FORCE	.	*	1.2	12.5	1.3	7.9	1.1	6.3
LEFT COVERED WORK FORCE	.	.5	1.8	8.6	1.2	4.8	.9	4.6
FINAL COVERED WORK FORCE, 1965	*	4.3	3.5	46.2	5.6	18.5	3.1	15.3
IMMIGRANTS	*	.5	1.7	3.5	.7	4.1	.7	1.4
OUTMIGRANTS	*	.8	.7	7.4	1.1	4.5	*	1.3
NET MIGRATION	.	-.3	1.0	-3.9	-.4	-.4	.5	.1
NONMIGRANTS:								
SAME INDUSTRY	*	1.4	1.2	25.5	3.0	6.5	1.6	7.3
LEFT THIS INDUSTRY	*	1.3	.5	3.2	*	3.6	*	1.5
ENTERED THIS INDUSTRY	.	*	.9	3.5	1.3	2.1	.6	1.7
NET MILITARY AND OTHERS	.	.	.1	.3	.1	.1	.	.1
ENTERED COVERED WORK FORCE	*	*	1.1	15.6	1.4	10.0	1.6	7.5
LEFT COVERED WORK FORCE	.	.8	1.1	10.0	1.2	3.7	1.2	5.1
FINAL COVERED WORK FORCE, 1970	.6	2.4	5.0	48.5	6.5	23.0	4.5	18.1

1960-1965

1965-1970

Source: Regional Analysis Information System, Bureau of Economic Analysis.
*Statistically insignificant.

12

**Case Study: Terre Haute
SMSA, Indiana**

It is hard to find a flatter half-century's population curve than that of the
Terre Haute SMSA from 1920 to 1970, shown in figure 12-1. Even the area's
sharp loss of employment in the 1930s is not matched by any disturbance of
the population trend. Income per capita was very low at 75 percent of the
U.S. average in 1929; it converged on the U.S. average more slowly than
that of other poor SMSAs so that its rank position actually fell. Figure 12-1
shows an interesting cooling-off of the components of population
change—attributable largely to the aging population—from a moderate
positive natural increase rate balancing moderate negative net migration in
the 1940s, to rates very near zero but still symmetric around zero in the
1960s.

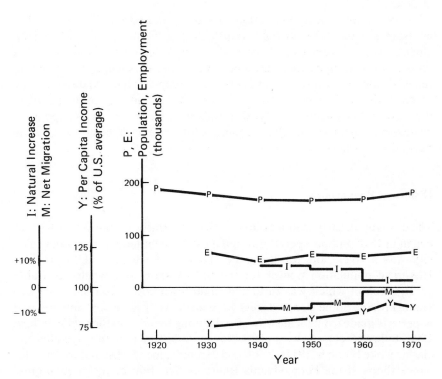

Figure 12-1. Composite of Trends, Terre Haute SMSA

General Description

Terre Haute city and region are by any standard depressed areas. The SMSA boundaries, however, include three large counties which are in considerably worse shape than the city and its surroundings: the convention of following county lines has made the statistical picture of the metropolitan area even worse than would one which eliminated the outlying rural areas and the abandoned mining towns.

A digest of 1970 population and housing conditions (table 12-1) shows an old, stable population, often poor but strongly inclined towards home ownership, and an exceptionally low-valued stock of owner-occupied housing.

Only one major industrial plant, the Commercial Solvents Corporation, is locally headquartered. A good many local businesses, however, including a shopping center, the two newspapers, the television station, and several gas stations, are owned not by big city investors, but by Tony Hulman, a local septuagenarian better known for his Motor Speedway in Indianapolis. (His surname also graces the local technical college and airfield.)

Terre Haute's accommodation to stagnation and relative decline has not been graceful. The city hall has a 1950-ish jet fighter on its lawn and the clock face on its tower has been replaced by a bare plywood disc with a crudely drawn happy-face, grinning over acres of vacant, razed, urban renewal land. The Indiana University main campus is located downtown, a recent addition. It is pleasantly built, very busy, and may in time enliven the surrounding business and residential districts, as well as local politics, professions, and the schools, but there is little effect on the city yet visible beyond its borders.

Historical Background

The city was an early frontier outpost. Steamer traffic on the Wabash River began in 1818 and prospered through most of the nineteenth century. The city was a river port for the grain, pork, and whiskey of the region. Historical population figures for the SMSA show steady growth (table 12-2), much of which was rural and small town population outside Terre Haute proper. Some iron and steel were made using local coal and ore, and paper was made from local straw. Coal mining boomed in the region before 1900, followed closely by a glass-blowing industry (which originated the classic Coke bottle in 1911), brick and ceramic pipe works, and the maintenance shops of the Pennsylvania Railroad. The four-county region grew rapidly on the coal boom to a 1920 population of 189,000.

Table 12-1

Selected Population and Housing Characteristics Terre Haute, Indiana SMSA 1970

	SMSA	East North Central Division	243 SMSAs
Black %	3.1	9.6	12.0
Under 5 years %	7.4	8.7	8.5
Sixty-five years and over %	13.5	9.5	9.3
Median years of education[1]	12.0	12.1	12.2
Unemployed %	4.2	4.3	4.3
White collar %[2]	43.5	45.7	52.4
Crafts and Foremen %[2]	14.1	14.7	13.6
Operatives, Laborers and others %	42.4	39.6	34.0
Family incomes over $15,000 %	14.1	23.5	24.5
Family incomes below low income[3] %	9.6	7.5	8.5
Housing owner occupied %	75.9	67.5	59.5
Median house value[4] %	$8,875	17,610	19,027
Median gross rent	$ 93	116	117
Home owner vacancy rate %	1.3	1.1	1.1
Rental vacancy rate %	8.3	6.8	6.0

Source: *County and City Data Book*, U.S. Bureau of the Census 1972

Notes:

1. Persons 25 years and over.

2. Percentage of employed civilian labor force.

3. As defined by 1970 Population Census Based on Family Size.

4. Single family owner-occupied.

In the few years after World War I, the rail maintenance shops were shut down; the breweries and distilleries were closed because of the Eighteenth Amendment; paper-making was abandoned; and local iron, steel, and ceramic industries entered a long decline. Coal mining collapsed in the late 1920s. As the surrounding rural population declined, people went primarily to the more prosperous cities like Indianapolis and Chicago rather than to Terre Haute (Drummond 1955). The region's population has remained near 175,000 ever since, while its relative income level and locational advantages have generally declined despite sporadic attempts to resuscitate the local economy. It has no scheduled airline passenger service (but does have a very large airfield) and has been generally last in line for state highway upgrading. According to Drummond (1955), plants which have located in the area since 1920 have come mainly for the surplus labor, not supplies or markets. There are food processing plants, he points out, but not enough to process even the locally-produced soybeans, vegetables, and pork. Even labor availability as an attraction is colored by a reputation for bad labor relations earned violently in the general strike of 1935,

Table 12-2
Historical Population and Employment: Terre Haute SMSA (Clay, Sullivan, Vermillion and Vigo Counties, Indiana)

Year	Population	% Change in Population	Employment	% Change in Employment	% of Total Employment Female
1850	42,035	—			
1860	59,164	40.7			
1870	81,926	38.4			
1880	103,873	26.8			
1890	115,852	15.3			
1900	137,577	11.9			
1910	171,769	24.9			
1920	188,914	10.0			
1930	176,711	−6.5	65,411	—	18.6
1940	173,875	−1.6	47,698	−27.1	23.1
1950	172,468	−0.8	61,985	30.0	26.0
1960	172,069	−0.2	59,830	−3.5	32.5
1970	175,143	1.8	66,247	10.4	38.3
1973	176,100	0.6			

Sources:

Population: 1920, 1940, and 1970 *Censuses of Population*.
Employment: 1930, 1940, 1950, 1960, and 1970 *Censuses of Population*.

Note: 1930 employment is for ages 10 or more.
   1940-1970 employment is for ages 14 or more.

although in fact many major plants are non-union. There was no significant economic growth during World War I in any sector except in the well-organized vice industry, which was shut down, officially, several times since 1945 (Farmer 1945; *Life* 1952; Wyden 1961; *Time* 1969).

The Great Depression was extremely hard on the Terre Haute area in that its employment was severely reduced but its population remained steady. The impact was greatest in heavy industry, with a preponderance of male employees. There may have been an influx of female-employing, low-wage employers such as canneries at this time. In any case, the percentage of women in the area's total employment rose from well below average in 1930 to near average in 1940, and has stayed there since (table 12-2).

Development in the 1940s and 1950s

Terre Haute's former distilling and heavy manufacturing base was largely gone by 1940. The area had declined in population since before 1920, but had remained a significant trade and service center, with considerable food-processing employment and a large coal mining sector in the outlying parts of the SMSA. Despite the closing of the Pennsylvania Railroad's western maintenance shops at Terre Haute, the percentage of railroad employment was still significantly more than the national figure.

The decade of the 1940s was relatively prosperous for the Terre Haute area (table 12-3). There was absolute growth in all sectors, but relatively slower growth in trade and services erased by 1950 the positive mix effect those sectors had contributed in the 1940s. The 1950s were disastrous: the agriculture, mining, railroad transportation, and food processing industries each shed several thousand jobs, while even wholesale trade, retail trade, communication, and government showed losses. Only the electrical machinery sector expanded significantly, far from enough to prevent a decline in total employment. Given a normal pattern of rising labor force participation in the period, this meant the area could support fewer people; there was indeed a substantial loss of population in that decade and the next. Unemployment was high throughout the 1950s (table 12-4).

The major components of employment change shown in the shift-share analysis were a negative mix effect, a normal (negative) allocation effect, and a steeply declining positive competitive effect.

The mix effect tells much of the story in Terre Haute. In 1940, surpluses of trade, most services, and transportation were the positive influences, offset by deficiencies of manufacturing, except food and government. By 1950 there were *no* strong positive influences, while the surplus of railroad and mining employment became a negative influence. Additional negative influences by 1960 were a surplus of food processing employment and a deficiency of finance, insurance and real estate.

Development Since 1960

The 1960s were not as bad as the previous decade but showed no real departure from the established pattern. Mining, agriculture, food products, and railroads continued to decline; trade and most services failed to keep pace (the exception being a major expansion of Indiana State University); and manufacturing grew, notably paper, chemicals, and electrical machinery. The loss of population triggered by the distress of the 1950s, combined with some growth of employment, made for improved income per capita, but unemployment and underemployment generated by the declining sectors contributed to a poverty level of 9.6 percent in 1969.

There was some employment growth during the late 1960s, the most significant gain being in government, reflecting the establishment of the main Indiana State University campus of 14,000 students in Terre Haute.

Table 12-3

Employment by Selected Industrial Sectors, 1940-1970, Terre Haute SMSA

	1940	1950	1960	1970
TOTAL EMPLOYMENT (FULL AND PART TIME)	47,698	62,047	59,905	66,400
AGRICULTURE,FORESTRY,FISHERIES AND OTHER	6,448	6,087	3,823	2,171
AGRICULTURE	6,438	6,049	3,803	2,166
FORESTRY,FISHERIES AND OTHER	10	38	20	5
MINING	4,461	4,960	1,826	854
CONTRACT CONSTRUCTION	2,179	2,884	3,370	4,509
MANUFACTURING	7,872	12,899	16,108	17,271
FOOD AND KINDRED PRODUCTS	2,979	3,820	3,593	1,934
TEXTILE MILL PRODUCTS	9	45	41	66
APPAREL AND OTHER FABRICATED TEXTILE PRODUCTS	234	414	554	641
PRINTING,PUBLISHING AND ALLIED INDUSTRIES	646	1,001	1,431	1,796
CHEMICALS AND ALLIED PRODUCTS	455	1,597	1,608	1,458
LUMBER AND FURNITURE	367	629	426	487
MACHINERY	252	514	3,138	3,890
MACHINERY EXCEPT ELECTRICAL	---	420	817	1,059
ELECTRICAL MACHINERY	---	94	2,321	2,831
TRANSPORTATION EQUIPMENT	65	140	428	530
MOTOR VEHICLES AND MOTOR VEHICLES EQUIPMENT	49	107	133	276
TRANSPORTATION EXCLUDING MOTOR VEHICLES	16	33	295	254
OTHER MANUFACTURING	2,865	4,739	4,889	6,469
PAPER AND ALLIED PRODUCTS	---	663	800	1,123
PETROLEUM REFINING AND RELATED PRODUCTS	---	164	165	42
PRIMARY METALS INDUSTRIES		1,148	1,118	1,597
FABRICATED METALS + ORDNANCE		798	972	1,652
MISCELLANEOUS MANUFACTURING		1,966	1,834	2,055
TRANSPORTATION,COMM.++PUB. UTILITIES	4,606	6,607	5,328	5,143
TRANSPORTATION	3,653	5,120	3,582	3,003
RAILROAD TRANSPORTATION	2,240	3,202	1,686	1,069
MOTOR FREIGHT TRANSPORTATION AND WAREHOUSING	1,021	1,374	1,650	1,523
OTHER TRANSPORTATION SERVICES	392	544	246	411
COMMUNICATIONS	353	630	590	953
ELECTRIC,GAS,AND SANITARY SERVICES	600	857	1,156	1,187

WHOLESALE AND RETAIL TRADE	9,827	13,108	12,856	14,156
WHOLESALE TRADE	1,650	2,568	2,216	2,435
RETAIL TRADE	8,177	10,540	10,640	11,721
EATING AND DRINKING PLACES	1,421	2,067	2,083	2,380
FOOD + DAIRY STORES	2,036	2,149	1,688	1,552
OTHER RETAIL TRADE	4,720	6,324	6,869	7,789
FINANCE+INSURANCE AND REAL ESTATE	1,126	1,379	1,685	2,103
SERVICES	9,712	11,330	12,202	17,190
BUSINESS SERVICES	5,509	5,929	5,128	4,459
LODGING PLACES AND PERSONAL SERVICES	1,912	2,070	2,012	1,783
BUSINESS AND REPAIR SERVICES	1,166	1,630	1,331	1,455
AMUSEMENTS AND REC. SERVICES	509	565	329	363
PRIVATE HOUSEHOLDS	1,922	1,664	1,456	858
PROFESSIONAL SERVICES	4,203	5,401	7,074	12,731
TOTAL GOVERNMENT	1,467	2,793	2,707	3,003
CIVILIAN GOVERNMENT	1,467	2,731	2,630	2,850
FEDERAL MILITARY	--	62	77	153

Source: Regional Economics Information System, Bureau of Economic Analysis, from Census Data.

Table 12-4
Selected Annual Average Unemployment Rates, Terre Haute SMSA

1950	1955	1960	1966	1970	1972
8.3	8.1	8.1	3.6	4.6	6.0

Source: Indiana Employment Security Division.

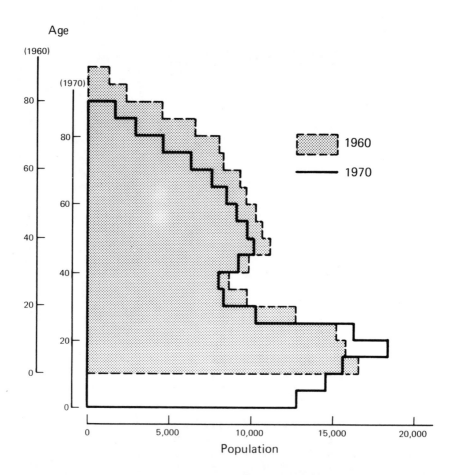

Figure 12-2. Population Age Profiles, 1960 and 1970 Terre Haute, Ind. SMSA

Gains in trade, non-electrical machinery (Allis Chalmers), other durables (Columbia Records distribution center), chemicals (Dupont and Commercial Solvents), and primary metals (Anaconda) were offset by long-term declines in transportation and public utilities, foods and agriculture. Most growth has been the expansion of existing plants rather than entries of new firms, according to a Chamber of Commerce representative. Total employment, however, has never since exceeded its 1951 annual average (Indiana Employment Security Division).

The irregularities of Terre Haute's population age profile (figure 12-2) became somewhat accentuated during the 1960s. There were relatively few births, reflecting the small size of the cohorts aged 15-25 in 1970. An increase in the cohorts aged 15-25 in 1970 was probably due to the growth of the university, and so the projecting "shelf" below age 25 does not represent as serious a threatened labor surplus as it might elsewhere.

The Social Security Work History Sample (tables 12-5 and 12-6) shows a decline in covered employment from 1960 to 1965, followed by a modest expansion up to 1970. The decline of the early 1960s was confined to the manufacturing sector. There were a great many exits from the covered work force out of manufacturing in this period, plus some outmigration and transfers to other industries. The gains of the second half-decade, on the other hand, were localized in the services and government sector. The growth difference was again mainly a function of entries to the covered work force, with the addition of a significant stream of interindustry transfers out of trade and into services and government, making strong wage gains in the process. Trade appears to have served as a kind of countercyclic or "flywheel" sector, absorbing workers at low wage levels during bad times, and giving them up to the higher-wage sectors in good times. Another surprising development in the relatively better years of the late 1960s was that gross outmigration rates rose rather than falling in the manner that conventional labor market theory predicts.

Table 12-5

Migration Summary, All Industries, Terre Haute SMSA (Based on Social Security Continuous Work History Sample (1%) First Quarter of 1960-65-70)

	THOUSANDS OF WORKERS	% OF TOTAL	1960-1965		
			1960 MEAN WAGES	1965 MEAN WAGES	% CHANGE MEAN WAGES
INITIAL COVERED WORK FORCE	42.1	100.0	3,419		
INMIGRANTS	5.8	13.8	4,996	5,486	9.8
OUTMIGRANTS	6.9	16.4	3,416	5,422	58.7
NET MIGRATION	-1.1	-2.6			
NONMIGRANTS:					
SAME INDUSTRY	17.0	40.4	4,103	5,125	24.9
DIFFERENT INDUSTRY	4.1	9.7	3,251	3,962	21.9
NET MILITARY AND OTHERS	-.1	-.2			
ENTERED COVERED WORK FORCE	12.9	30.6		2,527	
LEFT COVERED WORK FORCE	13.8		2,673		
FINAL COVERED WORK FORCE	40.0	95.0		4,225	

1965-1970

	THOUSANDS OF WORKERS	% OF TOTAL	1965 MEAN WAGES	1970 MEAN WAGES	% CHANGE MEAN WAGES
INITIAL COVERED WORK FORCE	40.0	100.0	4,225		
INMIGRANTS	11.0	27.5	5,900	8,697	47.4
OUTMIGRANTS	7.4	18.5	4,385	8,210	87.2
NET MIGRATION	3.6	9.0			
NONMIGRANTS:					
SAME INDUSTRY	18.0	45.0	4,914	7,400	50.6
DIFFERENT INDUSTRY	4.8	12.0	3,306	5,502	66.4
NET MILITARY AND OTHERS	.3	.8			
ENTERED COVERED WORK FORCE	16.5	41.3		3,590	
LEFT COVERED WORK FORCE	9.4		3,251		
FINAL COVERED WORK FORCE	51.0	127.5		6,269	

Source: Regional Analysis Information System, Bureau of Economic Analysis.

Table 12-6
Migration Summary by Industry, Terre Haute SMSA (Based on Social Security Continuous Work History Sample (1%) First Quarter of 1960-65-70)

THOUSANDS OF WORKERS

GOVERNMENT AND OTHER, INCLUDING UNCLASSIFIED

FINANCE, INSURANCE AND REAL ESTATE

WHOLESALE AND RETAIL TRADE

TRANSPORTATION, COMMUNICATION AND PUBLIC UTILITIES

MANUFACTURING

CONTRACT CONSTRUCTION

MINING

AGRICULTURE, FORESTRY AND FISHERIES

INITIAL COVERED WORK FORCE, 1960	*	1.6	1.1	14.2	2.2	11.4	.9	10.3
INMIGRANTS	*	.5	*	1.2	*	1.1	*	2.0
OUTMIGRANTS	*	*	*	2.5	*	1.7	.	2.0
NET MIGRATION	.1	.2	.1	-1.3	.2	-.6	.2	.0
NONMIGRANTS:								
SAME INDUSTRY	.	.9	*	5.9	1.5	3.7	.5	4.1
LEFT THIS INDUSTRY	.	.	.	1.4	*	1.6	*	.9
ENTERED THIS INDUSTRY	*	.	*	1.2	*	1.5	.	.5
NET MILITARY AND OTHERS	.1	.	.	-.1	.	.	.	-.1
ENTERED COVERED WORK FORCE	*	*	.8	1.9	.7	5.0	.5	3.5
LEFT COVERED WORK FORCE	*	*	.5	4.2	.5	4.4	*	3.2
FINAL COVERED WORK FORCE, 1965	.8	1.7	1.7	10.3	2.9	11.3	1.2	10.1
INMIGRANTS	.	3.5	1.1	2.4	.6	1.5	*	1.7
OUTMIGRANTS	*	1.2	*	2.0	*	1.8	*	1.6
NET MIGRATION	.0	2.3	.8	.4	.4	-.3	-.1	.1
NONMIGRANTS:								
SAME INDUSTRY	*	*	.8	4.6	2.0	4.4	.5	5.4
LEFT THIS INDUSTRY	*	*	*	1.2	.	2.4	*	*
ENTERED THIS INDUSTRY	.	*	*	1.9	*	.9	*	1.1
NET MILITARY AND OTHERS	.	.	.1	.3	.2	-.2	*	-.1
ENTERED COVERED WORK FORCE	.	.8	*	4.3	1.1	5.1	*	4.7
LEFT COVERED WORK FORCE	*	*	*	2.4	.7	2.5	*	2.7
FINAL COVERED WORK FORCE, 1970	*	4.7	2.7	13.6	4.1	11.9	1.0	12.9

1960-1965

1965-1970

Source: Regional Analysis Information System, Bureau of Economic Analysis
*Statistically insignificant.

Part II
Inferences

There are numerous similarities among non-growing metropolitan areas, not only in a static comparative sense but also in their historic origins and in the dynamic progressions through which they seem to pass after the cessation of growth. There is a strong presumption that these similarities are more than happenstance.

The final chapters constitute a search to explain them in ways which permit anticipation and ultimately perhaps control over the impacts of no growth on metropolitan areas.

13 The Dynamics of Not Growing

The case studies have shown that different SMSAs can have quite different responses to economic stagnation or decline. The very young and the very old—Amarillo and St. Joseph—seemed to absorb it most gracefully, losing population but maintaining or improving their levels of material welfare and, in Amarillo's case, aggressively promoting innovative sources of economic growth and diversity. The middle-aged cities, contrastingly, tended to maintain or increase their populations in bad times or to lose it at a much slower rate than employment with consequent underemployment, and to decline in income per capita while putting any public developmental resources into increasing their specialization in old, obsolete industries by protecting or expanding existing plants. Within the case histories, too, there are hints of a consistent progression from boom to "bust," actually a relatively benign if dramatic period of population loss, and from bust to stagnation, a long period of profound resistance to demographic or economic change which continues until the people, artifacts, and institutions which were assembled in the truncated growth era gradually erode away.

This chapter explores the reasons why such a progression might occur: the dynamics of not growing.

Demographic, economic, and institutional factors interact in the development of metropolitan areas, and national forces often overshadow local efforts to direct growth and change. These interdependencies are dramatized in the situation of non-growing areas, most of which seem bound up in a cycle of cumulative disadvantage. Population stability or decline, institutional stagnation, administrative dependency, and economic distress or exploitation in an area all "cause" each other in important ways, but are also part of larger processes at the regional and national scale.

Population Changes

The size and age structure of a local population are determined by its growth history, but also exert a powerful influence on the population's future growth. Each community's growth history is a unique path of changing yearly rates of birth, death, inmigration, and outmigration. Of these four components of growth, inmigration is the one component strongly

169

influenced by current economic conditions in the area: SMSAs with higher wages and more plentiful job opportunities have been shown to attract migrants disproportionately (Perloff 1960; Lansing and Mueller 1963; Lowry 1965; Alonso 1971a; Greenwood and Sweetland 1972).

It is understandable that traditional urban forecasting models ignore demographic processes and treat population size as a simple multiple of economic size. Population follows local economic growth fairly well so long as the economic growth is large enough to call for a positive net inmigration rate. It has often been noted, however, that metropolitan communities show a curious resistance to decline. Wilbur Thompson neatly called this phenomenon the "urban size ratchet." He ascribed it to economic factors like the advantages of economic agglomeration and the "response" of local entrepreneurs to the "challenge" of incipient decline (Thompson 1965).

Perloff noted another reason: an area's inmigrants are drawn from a whole world of potential movers, but its outmigrants are drawn only from the relatively small population of present residents in the area.

Peter Morrison has described the asymmetry of SMSA growth rates around the U.S. average (dispersed above it—concentrated below) and investigated in more detail the differential mobility mechanisms behind it (Morrison 1972). Morrison found that mobility is "longitudinally associated": people who enter or leave an SMSA in a given period are likely to move again, but people who don't, aren't. A large part of the moving therefore gets done by a small part of the population. What this means for a declining area is that net outmigration is rapidly self-limiting. The mobility-prone part of its population is distilled off at an early age and is not replaced. The potential mobility of the area's population falls and remains low as long as there is pressure for outmigration removing potential migrants before they accumulate and a lack of attraction to migrants from elsewhere. Frequently, the resulting net migration rate will not be strong enough to overcome the excess of births over deaths, and population will rise despite pressures to the contrary.

Since immobility is such a strong feature of non-growing populations, it is important to recognize its meaning in human terms as well as cold statistics. Choosing not to migrate when half or more of one's peers are doing so usually means putting higher value than others do on local attachments. These may include irretrievable equity in a house or business, ties with an extended family, and ethnic and religious associations. It may also reflect a realistic appraisal of one's skills and prospects in a modern job market. Arguments that migrating would be good for everyone based on the income gains of migrants (e.g., Hansen 1973, pp. 134-169) cannot overcome the subjective self-identified difference between migrants and non-migrants; for non-migrants expected income gains, if any, are not worth giving up a house and community. On the other hand almost every class of migrants tends "to attain higher occupational levels and to achieve more upward mobility" than comparable non-migrants (Blau and Duncan 1967, p. 272).

Closely associated with mobility is the population age structure, which in turn is a major determinant of population growth rates. Migration is done mostly by young people (see fig. 13-1); outmigration depletes the younger age cohorts while inmigration replenishes them. Places with young population (due to recent growth) will be subject to routinely high rates of gross outmigration, so these areas must have large gross inmigration rates or lose population. Young populations will also tend to have large crude birthrates and low crude death rates, regardless of minor variations in age-specific fertility and mortality. Places with low growth rates, conversely, will tend after a while to develop older age distributions which may in turn depress birthrates and outmigration rates and raise death rates. The maximum depression of birthrates in declining areas is likely to occur as the excessively depleted cohorts around age twenty-one move up through childbearing ages.

The transformations of a metropolitan area's age structure under nongrowth follow a predictable sequence determined by the considerable regularity in the ages at which people migrate, bear children, and die. The annual probability of migration (i.e., moving between counties) peaks sharply at age twenty-two (reflecting events like military discharges, college graduations, and marriages) but also has large values below age ten, reflecting the high mobility of parents in their twenties. The probability of childbearing has a more rounded peak in the mid-twenties while death rates begin to rise steeply in the mid-forties, by which time their fertility and mobility are nearly exhausted.

The expectancy of migration falls rapidly with each passing year after its peak at age twenty-two. Economic conditions appear to have a declining influence on the outmigration of older persons (see Chapter 15). Therefore, once a young person of twenty-two or more has migrated into an area, he or she soon becomes increasingly likely to remain there, and a population of recent migrants will tend to have declining gross outmigration rates soon after a slowing of inmigration. The population of recent migrants also has a very high natural increase rate, however, and this decays much more slowly. Natural increase is the difference between the birthrate and death rate. Referring again to figure 13-1, it should be clear that the most typical recent migrant, in his early twenties, has before him a decade of above-average fertility and about three decades of below average mortality. And so there is also likely to be a "shadow boom" of continuous rapid population growth for a decade or more after the cessation of rapid economic expansion in an area.

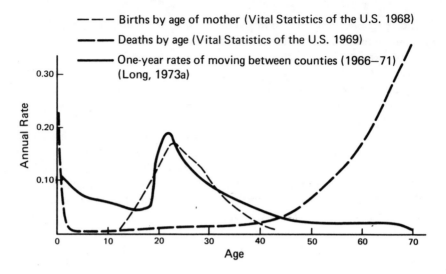

Figure 13-1. Age Profiles of U.S. Birth, Death, and Migration Rates

For purposes of illustration, a hypothetical small city will be followed through a boom-and-bust cycle touched off by a single 100 percent expansion of its labor force in a five-year period such as might follow the establishment of a large military base or the development of a new energy source in the area. This hypothetical situation is simplified, but not exaggerated: similar boom episodes occurred, for example, in Wilkes-Barre (1870s), Pueblo and Scranton (1880s), St. Joseph (1890s), Fort Smith (1900s), Midland and Odessa (1950s), and Amarillo (1960s). It will be assumed for simplicity that the new employment level is sustained (for example, short-term construction-related jobs would be replaced with new trade and service activities) although typically many of these sectors might experience an interim decline. National average age-specific rates given in figure 13-1 will be assumed, together with constant age-specific labor force participation rates.

The original age structure of the hypothetical city is shown in figure 13-2.[a] The age distribution of a typical group of 25,000 migrants is illustrated in figure 13-3. It is broader based and more sharply tapered than the age-specific rates because of the tapered distribution of the population to which they apply. For example, there are about 50 percent more people under ten than in their twenties, and so nearly as many migrants are under ten as are in their twenties despite the lower rate for the younger group.

The initial impact of the migrants upon the city is mainly additive as

---

[a]For simplicity a shape has been chosen which tapers smoothly with age, reflecting an uneventful history of steady growth at near its natural increase rate (i.e., its birthrate minus its death rate).

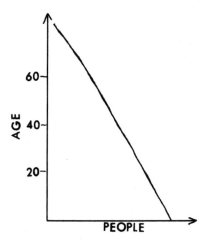

Figure 13-2. Age Distribution of Hypothetical Town: Median Age 24

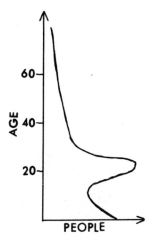

Figure 13-3. Age Distribution of Migrants: Median Age 24

shown in figure 13-4. Inmigration continues until the new jobs are filled and overshoots a little, depressing income levels and slowing the inflow. (The dotted area represents the original population structure five years older.) But by this time the annual number of births has already swelled by the disporportion of young adults to over twice its former level. Fertility continues high as the recent migrants pass through their most fertile years of age (fig. 13-5). There is little economic pressure for outmigration at this stage, however, as the number of persons of working age remains nearly constant once net migration approaches zero: deaths are balanced by the

174

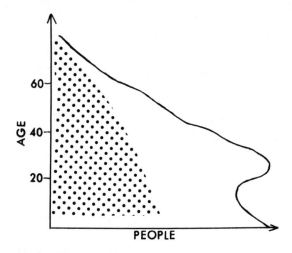

Figure 13-4. Result of 5-Year Boom: Median Age ~ 24

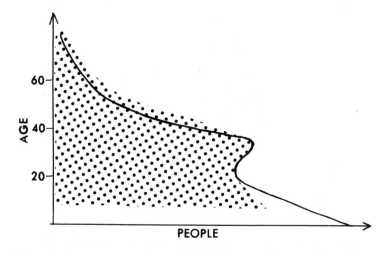

Figure 13-5. 10 Years After Boom: Median Age ~ 20

entry into the labor force of the relatively small age cohorts who were teenagers during the boom. Nevertheless, there is considerable population growth in the younger brackets.

The first real pressure on the job market comes fifteen years after the boom is over. The large age cohorts of children of the inmigrants start looking for work and cannot find it. But now, those entering the mobile age brackets, who are disposed by higher education, higher family income, and fewer children toward mobility will leave: more than half of their age groups in a typical former boom town do leave between ages fifteen and twenty. The original boomers, approaching age forty, are unlikely to move. By twenty years after the boom (fig. 13-6) there will have been considerable outmigration of the young and median age will rise dramatically.

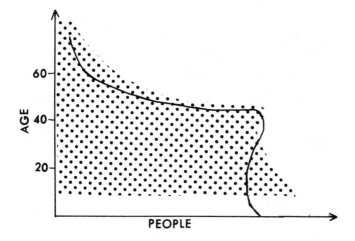

Figure 13-6. 20 Years After Boom: Median Age ~ 32

The outmigration of the baby surplus is only the first step in adjusting to the lack of employment growth, however; it will take another decade before the original inmigrants reach their fifties and begin to experience rising death rates (fig. 13-7). Once this stage is reached, births will only slightly exceed deaths. The newly born age cohorts will be somewhat larger than the yearly number of job openings available, however, so that there will be a chronic shortage of entry-level openings, causing constant pressure for outmigration. The population size and age structure will have achieved an approximate equilibrium relationship with the labor force size, however, except for minor fluctuations as the second generation offspring of the boom period pass through their life cycles. A rough no-growth equilibrium under the assumed mobility, fertility, and mortality profiles is illustrated in figure 13-8: a high-sided, blunt-topped distribution with a small "toe" of extra children below working age.

In sum, the community will experience a long period in which there is little turnover within its labor force. Due to the long erosion of its supply of younger and more mobile people, the community will be very resistant to downward adjustment of its labor force and population size. As will be

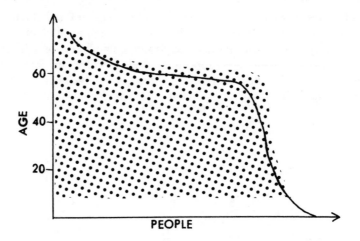

Figure 13-7. 30 Years After Boom: Median Age ~ 35

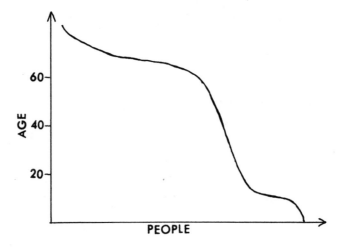

Figure 13-8. 50 Years After Boom: Median Age ~ 30

seen, this makes it particularly vulnerable to episodes of economic distress which a more mobile community would take in stride.

The process of demographic transformation under no growth just described may be summarized in six stages (table 13-1).

The non-growing SMSAs of the case studies fall historically reasonably well into the middle four stages of the classification scheme, as shown in table 13-2. Where the rate of employment growth changed abruptly from

Table 13-1
Stages of Transition from Growth to No Growth

Stage	Employment Growth Rate	Natural Increase Rate	Net Migration Rate	Population Growth Rate	Median Age
1. Stable growth	Moderate	Moderate	Near zero	Moderate	Average
2. Migration boom	High	Rising	High	High	Falling
3. Fertility boom	Near zero	High	Near zero	High	Low
4. Primary decline	Near zero	Falling	Large neg.	Large neg.	Rising
5. Secondary decline	Near zero	Very low	Small neg.	Small neg.	Very high
6. Non-growth equilibrium	Zero	Low	Small neg.	Small pos.	High

Table 13-2
Classification of Case Study Areas by Stage of Transition

	Stage 1 Stable Growth	Stage 2 Migration Boom	Stage 3 Fertility Boom	Stage 4 Primary Decline	Stage 5 Secondary Decline
Amarillo	Before 1950	1950-65		1965-70	
Fort Smith		Before 1910	1910-20	1930-40	1940-60
Montgomery		1940-50	1950-60	1960-70	
Pittsburgh[1]	Before 1880	1880-1920	1920-30	1930-40	
Pittsburgh[2]		1940-50	1945-60		1960-70
Pueblo[1]		1900-20	1920-30	1930-40	
Pueblo[2]		1940-50	1950-60		1960-70
St. Joseph		Before 1920	1920-30	1930-40	1940-70
Savannah		1940-50	1950-60	1960-70	
Scranton		1960-1920	1920-30	1930-40	1940-70
Terre Haute		Before 1910	1910-20	1920-30	1930-70
Wilkes-Barre-Hazleton		1850-1920	1920-30	1930-40	1940-70

Notes:

1. First cycle of boom and decline, followed by slight wartime growth.

2. Recurrence of decline, moving directly into secondary mode.

strongly positive to negative, as in Amarillo in the 1960s, stages 3 and 4
were superimposed: many of the adult population were very recent inmigrants still in a mobile stage of their life cycle and readily moved away when
laid off, so that the overall distortion of the age structure and resistance to

decline was less than in more gradually changing areas such as Montgomery or Terre Haute. Those which had brief wartime respites from otherwise long-term decline, like Pittsburgh and Pueblo, were not sufficiently rejuvenated to raise their mobility and fertility for very long and lapsed quickly back into secondary decline, rather than pass a second time through the primary decline stage.

The effects of demographic processes on a non-growing population are not limited to age. Other characteristics which are strongly correlated with high mobility are expected to be overrepresented in the "boom" phase and underrepresented in the "bust" phase of the cycle just described. These include low fertility (Long 1970), high education and white-collar occupation (Long 1973), and small families (Long 1972b), all of which were strikingly underrepresented in the profiles of the older declining areas examined earlier. The particular character of the location and its industries may of course modify the composition of the original inmigrant stream, as in the case of an oil town or a retirement community, but decline will still probably modify it in these directions.

Institutional Changes

The expected influences of non-growth upon the institutional style and structure of a metropolitan area include a contracting field of non-local communications and specialized business contacts, increasing non-local control over the local economy, smaller inflows of new personnel into organizations, and the selective survival of risk-avoiding styles of management.

A non-growing area within a growing national system gets in on a disproportionately decreasing proportion of the nation's communications. The actual performance of the non-growing area may tend to be even less than their random share, and perhaps grow not at all, because of the area's weak competitive position which underlies its decline. In business terms, stronger competitors can afford to enter distant markets, displacing the weaker ones from all but those in which they are most firmly established. Unable to afford development and promotional costs (and often being disposed to avoid risk, as discussed below), the weaker competitors will retrench to their largest, steadiest customers and try to hold them with price concessions, but thereby reduce their own likelihood of participating in growth-generating innovations. Airline service to the area may be cut back. Its newspapers are unlikely to be read elsewhere. It becomes increasingly unlikely to be selected as a center for important administrative activity by firms and public agencies operating at a multi-regional level. Pred

(1966, 1973, 1974a) and others have stressed the importance of such information flows in governing a metropolitan area's participation in the national development process by affecting its access to new ideas, new markets, new technologies, and venture capital.

Parallel with, and reinforcing, the area's descent in relative importance as a communication center is an impetus toward non-local administrative control. This is, of course, a trend affecting growing areas as well, a part of the increasing concentration of control in American industry and government, but it is one which may be accentuated by the risk-avoiding entrepreneurial style characteristic of non-growing areas, as discussed below, by economic weakness and by a shortage of trained professionals, managers, and technicians. These factors combine to encourage the takeover of local firms by stronger non-local competitors and to insure that any new organizations are likely to be pioneered by outsiders as branch operations.

An area whose economy is largely controlled by non-local multi-plant corporations faces a number of potential disadvantages. Rust (1973) showed that a small sample of administratively dominant areas experienced relatively steady, moderate growth and better resistance to the effects of a downturn in the business cycle when compared with near neighbors of similar size but greater dependency. He suggested that a major corporation's headquarters staff would tend to structure its holdings such that operations rewarding close attention would be kept close at hand in a carefully protected environment while only the most routine, inflexible activities would be entrusted to distant places. In such a pattern areas with few headquarters would become increasingly vulnerable to both product and process obsolescence. Areas with many headquarters, on the other hand, would give greater capabilities of economic innovation both within major firms and through breakaways and the formation of forward and backward linkages. Business cycles would be felt more sharply in the absentee-managed areas, both because a greater fraction of employment would be direct production labor, and because of a greater willingness to release trained labor in an area where most of them are likely to remain unemployed, on ice as it were, until they are needed again. Profits would be more likely to be reinvested or spent in headquarters than branch locations. Corporate support of education and the environment, both direct and through political pressure, would also be biased toward headquarters communities. The brunt of business cycles, market shifts, and technological obsolescence would therefore tend to fall on areas with absentee-owned plants.

The selective survival of risk-avoiding styles of management in a non-growing metropolitan environment[b] is hypothesized to be an important

[b] Suggested by Austin Burke, Research Director, Economic Development Council of Northeast Pennsylvania.

mechanism in the cycle of cumulative disadvantage accompanying long-term non-growth. Risk-taking is an essential characteristic of the successful entrepreneur or administrator in a growing area. Those who do not gamble on chances for expansion tend to be swallowed up by those who do. The reverse is true in a non-growing area: it is the gamblers who lose out. Within a generation or less of no growth, the risk-avoiding style not only prevails, but becomes deeply ingrained in all the area's institutions: its schools, churches, banks, and utilities as well as its business firms.

The demographic transformation described earlier results in a long period in which the labor force is aging, with few retirements and few new entries. Even at equilibrium there are considerably fewer new entries to the labor force in relation to its size than there would be in a growing area. Ansley Coale (1971) has pointed out that the top-heavy age profile of a non-growing population presents few opportunities for career advancement with increasing age. Organizations will have long periods without changes in management, and people at all levels will hold the same jobs for a long time, reducing the likelihood of innovation. Furthermore, the small inflow of new personnel will mean that a relatively small proportion of the labor force is available for training in new technologies at an age when they are willing to be trained at low wages or even pay for the privilege. Contracting fields of information exchange and growing administrative dependency may limit access to growth-generating innovations; this small inflow limits the rate at which an innovation can be implemented.

The foregoing suggests a somewhat broader hypothesis: it appears likely that the existing institutional characteristics which dispose the area toward decline, such as the dominance of a single group of decisionmakers, a low level of entrepreneurship, and a limited capacity for innovation, would seem to be reinforced during a period of stability or decline. This is not to deny Wilbur Thompson's more hopeful hypothesis of "challenge and response" (1965, pp. 18-21), but to suggest that the latter may best characterize only the early stages of distress.

Economic Changes

We have seen that the local economies of most non-growing metropolitan areas have been growing by such measures as employment and per capita income but have been doing so at less than normal rates for the nation. Although often specializing in low growth industries, they are also growing at less than national rates within those industries and have unusually slow-growing service sectors. Those areas which fail to grow for some time, then, are likely to get very poor. Behind the non-growing areas' slower employment and income growth are not so much lower wage rates for a given type of work—these appear to be remarkably similar to those of growing areas within a given region and industry—but higher and more unstable unemployment rates, lower rates of participation in the labor force, and a tendency to specialize in low-growth, low-wage industries and occupations.

The classical economic explanation—and justification—of these conditions is that the price system is signalling that greater national wealth per capita will result if labor and capital transfer to more productive locations. Several objections may be made to this view as a descriptive and normative guide. These objections, which will be developed below, are not intended to deny the need for unequal local growth rates, in the interest of national development, but rather to identify respects in which additional kinds of information may be needed to prevent a perverse outcome of economic development processes as they affect non-growth areas.

Not all production factors are equally mobile. As we have seen different rates of mobility for different classes of population (labor), so too are there mobility differences for different kinds of capital. Cash in savings is highly mobile outwards, credit somewhat less (a person must know the banker). Real estate improvements, public utilities, accessible land, and natural resources follow in approximately descending order of mobility. So long as a system is near equilibrium, needed adjustments can be made by small factor movements, involving only a highly mobile fraction of all labor and capital, and technological adjustments can be made to accommodate the slightly different factor mixes which result. A large or prolonged period of net factor outflow from a local area, however, may draw off the entire mobile fraction, leaving a relatively captive residual to suffer low returns because technologies are not forthcoming to utilize the surplus factors fully (Bolton 1971). The price system's "message" that the residual should also move is ineffectual because moving these factors is physically, socially or institutionally impractical. One might conceive of the point at which the mobile capital or labor fraction is depleted as an elastic limit of downward adjustment. Local economic decline short of the elastic limit would be an equilibrating influence supportive of both efficiency (national growth) and equity; it would raise the return earned both by the men and capital which leave and by those factors which stay behind. Economic decline beyond the elastic limit would have the reverse effect, and achieve little or no further factor relocation. (If this is so, then our present method of laissez-faire allocation of growth among areas is ineffectual, and places an impossible burden of adjustment on those which get too little.) Thus, non-growing areas face simultaneously a shortage of mobile factors and a surplus of immobile ones.

The outmigration of cash manifests itself in savings deposits. The savings institutions of non-growing areas, given little growth to invest in locally, must lend mostly outside the area. Savings deposits may tend to rise in such areas, after a period of no growth, in spite of falling income, because of the rising population age and the risk-avoiding tendencies of people in non-growing areas discussed earlier. Leisure spending is another way that cash leaks out. The Pittsburgh Regional Study (1963) points out that more local income is spent on non-local vacations than is received in tourist trade; it calls this an "unfavorable balance of vacations."

Another form of capital which selectively migrates away from non-growing areas is human "capital" in the sense that non-growing areas pay for the education of many people destined to migrate away.

Examples of surplus factors in non-growing areas may include labor over age thirty (especially the oldest, least educated or female), land, existing public facilities, and air, water, and mineral resources. Unregulated market processes will encourage the choice of technologies which allow the most substitution of these for more mobile factors and their use at low rates of productivity (unless there are market interventions by labor unions, public agencies or private interest groups to impose standards prevailing elsewhere). The result would be increased specialization in low-wage, low-growth industries, and a deteriorating physical environment.

Real estate provides an interesting illustration of differential capital mobility because such a large part of its real cost is discretionary. If services, maintenance, and, in the late stages, taxes and utilities are withheld, the yearly cost of owning a property is often less than half the cost of operating it in a way which would keep its value intact. In a falling market, a property can be written off and abandoned in a very few years by crediting the entire rental toward amortization and profit. Although legally a fixed facility, it can in fact be abandoned at little cost to the investor after relatively few years of disinvestment by withholding maintenance expenditures.

Indivisibilities in production based on the minimum workable size of investments such as dams, warehouses, airports, railway networks, and the like are sometimes referred to as a major source of scale economies in regional economic development. The absolute growth rate may have a similar effect, making larger threshold investments available to a growing city economy than to a stable one of the same size.

An alternative perspective from which to view the economic mechanisms of reduced metropolitan growth emphasizes demand rather than production factors. The Harrod-Domar type of growth models postulate that aggregate investment, while affecting the capacity to produce goods, has an even greater effect upon total income generated (the accelerator principle) and consequently upon demand (Ackley 1961, pp. 513-535; Richardson 1971, pp. 323-331). Underinvestment (slow growth), then, would result paradoxically in a surplus rather than a shortage of productive capacity relative to demand, forcing firms to operate at reduced productivity and to disinvest even more. The effect would be felt most strongly in sectors dependent largely on local demand such as construction, banking, real estate brokerage, electric power, retail trade and many services. Since trade and services tend to be labor-intensive industries, their negative accelerator effect should be particularly strong. The effects of this process may be only partially reflected in their employment figures, however, because of the large number of small proprietors in these industries who will absorb losses rather than go out of business, and the variability of work hours and productivity.

A somewhat more specific perspective on the demand multipliers of population changes in non-growing areas is provided by A.J. Brown (1972, pp. 16-25). He characterizes them as "short-term" effects, although the downward adjustment of population may require thirty to fifty years to reach equilibrium. He points out, however, that population movements may be relatively ineffective in restoring labor market equilibrium between areas because of the local demand that moves with the population. In an extreme case such as retired people moving to resort areas the multiplier effect on demand may easily exceed the supply effect of the withdrawal from the labor force of the non-growing area, contributing to an increased labor surplus in the non-growing area and a divergence of income levels between areas.

Opportunity and the Quality of Life

The quality of life that an area affords is reflected imperfectly in an aggregate, instantaneous concept like income per capita. When the average condition changes, it may be because individual circumstances changed, or because different kinds of people entered or left the population. The analysis is complicated by the fact that certain kinds of individual change are "normal," like a rise of income through most of the working life. The previous sections give a number of reasons to expect strong effects of no growth not only on income, but also on housing and other consumption options, on public service supply and quality, and on the kinds of physical and psychological stress these effects impose as a living environment. This section explores how and why the lack of growth may systematically change the quality of life and life opportunities afforded by a metropolitan area.

The first and pervasive impact of no growth is the depression of income. It begins from the lag of population growth in responding to a reduction of economic growth: more people means less income per capita. As the population moves into the primary decline phase, unemployment rises as the migrants' children seek work. It is conceivable that income per capita may also rise a little as population falls, but by this time the pressure of continued low income and labor surplus will be selectively encouraging the growth of lower-wage industries and occupations. In the secondary phase as older workers are laid off from declining industries there may be downward mobility into lower-paid work and, as was seen in the case studies, there may also be depressed labor force participation. Unemployment rates may fall merely because fewer people bother to seek work they know is not there, and so labor force participation rates may fall instead. The incidence of poverty, therefore, is expected to increase in the secondary phase, particularly among the older population but also including some less mobile members of all age groups. The lack of entry-level job opportunities for the generations born during and after the latest boom period is expected also to have a downward influence on intergenerational social mobility. Property income from local investments will be depressed by the soft real estate market and eroding service sector, encouraging small investors to buy securities or savings accounts instead, and perhaps favoring the large investors over small ones.

Despite an increasing federal role in the funding of local public services, the major costs of local government are still dependent upon local revenues. The resulting inequalities in education, welfare payments, and public health services between rich and poor metropolitan areas are exacerbated by further segregation of needs from resources by jurisdictional boundaries within metropolitan areas. We have seen that in some states (e.g., Georgia, Indiana, Colorado), constitutional prohibitions on annexation have been secured by lobbies for large employers located outside major cities. These reasons all contribute to a poverty of public services in non-growing areas. To the extent that these contribute to lower educational achievements, they will also tend to limit outward mobility, institutionally reinforcing the labor surplus and protecting low-wage employers.

Three factors are sometimes cited as compensations for the low incomes in non-growing areas: lower living costs due primarily to low housing costs, less crowding due to a large stock of low-cost housing, and a placid, relatively stress-free environment. The housing argument if true has two edges: housing may be cheap and plentiful, but it is low in quality. For less money, people consume a lower-quality service and have no option to upgrade. There is also a real question as to how long the housing stock can be allowed to deteriorate before abandonments begin to restore a housing shortage situation. The stress argument again has two sides: the residents who choose not to move away certainly protect themselves from the kind of "future shock" which Toffler (1970) describes in people subjected to a radically changing environment, but are opting for other kinds of stress:

dangerous work, periodic unemployment, and a limitation of upward social mobility which may put an increasing gap between reality and the expectations projected on them by national media and popular mythology.

This chapter has outlined an image of the character of a non-growing metropolitan area. The aggregate stability of a non-growth area masks a dynamic equilibrium of concurrent growth and decline. While structural change may be slow, this apparent lack of movement does not reflect simply a lack of impetus, but also reflects powerful change-resisting forces.

14 Influences of the Historical Growth Path

This chapter presents a cross-sectional analysis of a sample of growing and non-growing SMSAs. The analysis explores the influence of population growth upon a variety of social and economic conditions in metropolitan areas. It is essential, as the historical and case studies have shown, to take into account the differences between short-term and long-term decline, and between steady and fluctuating growth. Based upon the stage model of decline presented in Chapter 2, some influences of decline (such as a severe labor surplus) are expected to be felt most strongly a generation after the cessation of growth, and to persist for up to fifty years. Population growth is not treated as an instantaneous condition, therefore, but rather as a historical path extending from 1920 to 1970.

Interarea comparisons of aggregate data can provide only a clue about the real human impacts of non-growth. Used cautiously, however, these comparisons can help estimate the generality of some of the theoretical observations made in Chapter 13 and of the specific insights gained in the historical studies and case materials. While the possibility always remains that some unsuspected differences between the cities "caused" the differences ascribed to non-growth, the following precautions have been taken.

First, the reader now has some familiarity with the cases from historical and statistical perspectives, as well as from field observation. Second, plausible explanations have been offered for connecting the dependent variables with growth differences. Third, the sampling plan has been designed to minimize differences other than growth, which might otherwise account for the observed trends.

Defining the Sample

The sample of fifty-eight SMSAs contains all the non-growth SMSAs SMSAs as defined in Chapter 1 except Pittsburgh,[a] and a comparison group of similar SMSAs which had no decade of population stability or decline in

[a] Pittsburgh was omitted from the cross-section analysis because it is so radically different in size from the twenty-nine other non-growing areas, with a corresponding influence on income, migration ratio, and other factors of interest. The statistical measures such as correlation and regression generally used for this analysis are good for estimating trends among closely grouped values, but are sensitive to extreme values and might give a misleading overall picture if Pittsburgh were included, even if matched by a growing area of similar location, size and type.

1940-70, i.e., grew continuously at more than 1 percent per decade (table 14-1). No particular effort was made to provide cases of rapid growth and many of the comparison areas have in fact grown quite slowly.[b] Two actually declined earlier in the century: Lima, Ohio, and Macon, Georgia. The comparison group was matched as closely as possible with the non-growth group in its distribution of population (at about 1960) and industrial type, and comparison SMSAs are located geographically as close as possible to the non-growth sample. The resulting SMSAs are compared with the non-growth group in figure 14-1 and table 14-2. The entire sample is more eastern and somewhat smaller in population size than a random sample of fifty-eight SMSAs would be. It deliberately underrepresents the west and omits areas over one-half million because those areas offer so little experience with non-growth that aggregate comparisons could be misleading. The 50 percent incidence of non-growth within the sample is higher than in any region or size class. The statistics drawn from this sample then, will describe those groups of eastern, midwestern, and southern middle-sized and small SMSAs which are presumably the most susceptible to non-growth.

Defining the Growth Path

The consequences of population stability or decline are transmitted in a complex time pattern. Some effects strike immediately and diminish with time; some persist; others build up cumulatively; still others appear quite abruptly after a predictable lag period. A number of different dimensions of population growth were devised in order to estimate these effects.

The broad hypothesis which underlies this chapter is that not growing affects all SMSAs similarly in some respects. In particular, population loss is expected to follow a fairly regular pattern following a failure of some transient stimulus to inmigration, and that consequent effects will be transmitted to the structure, behavior, and welfare of the population in a similarly regular order. An idealized representation of the population growth rates resulting from the downward transition path described in chapter 13 would look something like figure 14-2. A particular non-growing SMSA may be placed somewhere on the path based upon its present and past growth rates.

Simply correlating community characteristics with current growth rates will reveal only those characteristics whose relationship is proportional to and simultaneous with the growth rate. A correlate of growth is unlikely to vary in such a way; more generally it may lead (change before) or lag (change after) the growth change, and its effect may accumulate or erode

---

[b]The choice of a quasi-random sample of growth rates permits a more sensitive analysis of their effects, at the expense of dramatic contrasts.

Table 14-1
Comparison SMSAs Which Grew Continuously, 1940-1970

Alburquerque, New Mexico
Asheville, North Carolina
Baton Rouge, Louisiana
Brockton, Massachusetts
Cedar Rapids, Iowa
Decatur, Illinois
Dubuque, Iowa
Evansville, Indiana - Kentucky
Fargo-Moorhead, North Dakota
Galveston - Texas City, Texas
Huntsville, Alabama
Jackson, Mississippi
Kalamazoo, Michigan
Lancaster, Pennsylvania
Lawton, Oklahoma
Lexington, Kentucky
Lima, Ohio
Macon, Georgia
Monroe, Louisiana
New London, Connecticut
Pine Bluff, Arkansas
Raleigh, North Carolina
San Angelo, Texas
Shreveport, Louisiana
Springfield, Illinois
Topeka, Kansas
Tyler, Texas
Wilmington, Delaware
York, Pennsylvania

with the passage of time. It is useful to separate out these possibilities, and then consider their combinations.

A correlate, C_s, which varies simply with the growth rate is illustrated in figure 14-3. It can be estimated for 1970 data using the model $C_{70} = f(G_{6070})$ where G_{6070} is the most recent population growth rate. If the relation is nearly proportional in the range under observation, it can be estimated by linear regression as $C_{70} = a + b\ G_{6070}$. In the illustration, a and b would be positive, with b less than one. A stepwise multiple regression of the available decade growth rates $C_L = f(G_t, G_{t-10}, G_{t-20}, G_{t-30}, G_{t-40})$ where G_t is the population growth rate for the decade prior to the observation[c] would yield the following table of coefficients.

$$G_t \quad G_{t-10} \quad G_{t-20} \quad G_{t-30} \quad G_{t-40} \quad \text{constant}$$
$$+ \quad\ \ 0 \quad\ \ \ \ 0 \quad\ \ \ \ 0 \quad\ \ \ \ 0 \quad\ \ \ \ +$$

(that is, only the coefficient of G_t and the constant would be significantly different from zero, and both would be positive.)

Growth correlates which change before the growth rate (C_b) or after the

_____
[c] For example, if C is observed in 1970, G_t would be the growth rate from 1960 to 1970.

Table 14-2
Comparative Distribution of Non-Growth and Comparison SMSAs

Geographic Division	Number of SMSAs	
	Non-Growth	Comparison Areas
New England	2	2
Middle Atlantic	4	3
South Atlantic	3	2
East No. Central	3	6
West No. Central	3	4
East So. Central	2	3
West So. Central	11	8
Mountain	1	1
Pacific	—	—
1950 Population*		
Less than 100,000	9	9
100,000 - 149,999	8	13
150,000 - 349,999	11	7
350,000 - 499,999	1	—
1960 Population*		
Less than 100,000	5	5
100,000 - 149,999	10	11
150,000 - 349,999	14	13
350,000 - 499,999	—	1
Industrial Type, 1960**		
Nodal	4	4
Manufacturing		
Government	2	2
Mixed	15	15
Other	—	—

Sources:

*1970 Area Designations.

**Stanback and Knight, *The Metropolitan Economy* (New York: Columbia University Press, 1970), pp. 132-137.

growth rate (C_a) are represented in figure 14-4. Here, no accurate correlation can be measured until the right period is selected at which to measure growth. In general, the model: $C = f(G_{t+k})$ will contain the best estimator, where k may be positive for leading correlates like C_b or negative for lagging ones like C_a. For linear relationships the estimating equation will be: $C_t = a + bG_{t+k}$. Multiple regression coefficients would be as follows:

	G_{t+10}	G_t	G_{t-10}	G_{t-20}	G_{t-30}	constant
$C_{a,t}$	0	0	+	0	0	+
$C_{b,t}$	+	0	0	0	0	+

Persistent, cumulative or diminishing correlates of growth (C_p, C_c, and

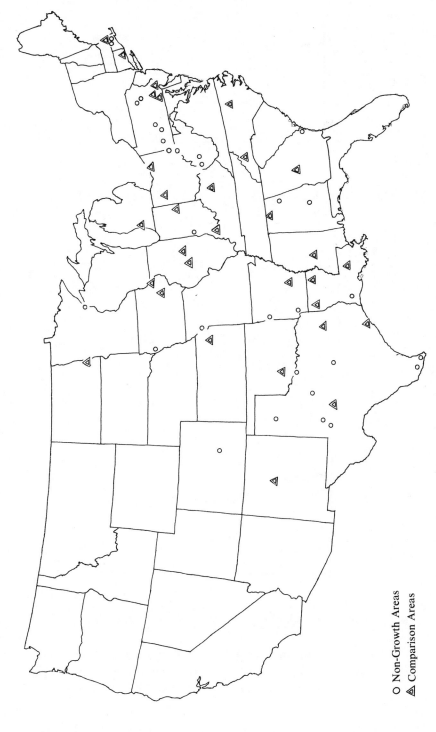

Figure 14-1. Geographic Distribution of the Sample

O Non-Growth Areas
△ Comparison Areas

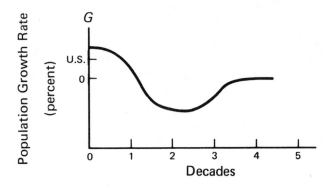

Figure 14-2. Idealized Downward Growth Transition

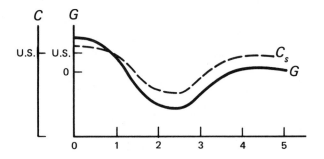

Figure 14-3. A Simple Correlate

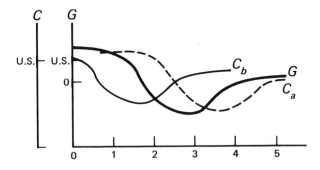

Figure 14-4. Leading and Lagging Correlates

C_d respectively) such as are illustrated in figure 14-5 may take a number of mathematical forms $C = f(t,M)$ in which the variables are the length of time since the occurrence of some event such as population loss, and some index of the magnitude of that event. These forms are poorly suited to the exploratory nature of the following analysis, however, in that they require narrow assumptions to be made in advance about what is the critical event and what form the function will take. In effect, a great many alternative formulations would have to be tried to exhaust the major possibilities. A relatively straightforward search procedure follows from an alternative, less rigorous concept of cumulative or diminishing effects, $C = f(G_t, G_{t-1}, \ldots, G_{t-n})$ where f is a simple linear equation using a non-overlapping series of available growth rates as predictors. A cumulative effect would respond in the same manner to growth rates in several prior periods. Coefficients from a linear stepwise multiple regression might look like this for a cumulative effect:

$$
\begin{array}{ccccc}
G_t & G_{t-10} & G_{t-20} & G_{t-30} & G_{t-40} \\
p \cong & q \cong & r & 0 & 0
\end{array}
$$

that is, coefficients for two or more adjacent periods would be of similar sign and magnitude. A place which had declines for a short time would be affected by p, for longer by $p + q$ and for longer still by $p + q + t$. A diminishing effect of decline would be visible only in those cases where a growth reduction had happened recently, i.e., between 1 and 2 on the horizontal scale of figure 14-5. A stepwise regression would yield coefficients in at least two periods with opposite signs, and the more recent one larger in absolute value, thus:

$$
\begin{array}{ccccc}
G_t & G_{t-10} & G_{t-20} & G_{t-30} & G_{t-40} \\
|p| > & |q| & 0 & 0 & 0
\end{array}
$$

Regressions for this kind of effect would tend to be rather weak because the expected underlying relation is non-linear.

A persistent effect like C_p in figure 14-5 is harder to recognize from the foregoing type of analysis. It will look essentially like a cumulative effect in that growth rate coefficients will keep the same sign for several successively earlier periods, but they will tend to diminish in absolute value:

$$
\begin{array}{ccccc}
G_t & G_{t-10} & G_{t-20} & G_{t-30} & G_{t-40} \\
|p| > & |q| > & |r| > & |s| & 0
\end{array}
$$

Defining the Dependent Variables

Data were compiled for the dependent variables listed in table 14-3 for each SMSA in the sample, except where noted in the text. Historical data were reconstructed for 1970 SMSA boundaries from county reports in most cases. In the New England cases, it was necessary to shift from SMSAs to

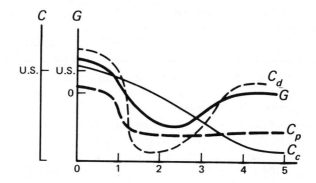

Figure 14-5. Cumulative, Diminishing, and Persistent Correlates

Table 14-3
Dependent Variables

Name (A/E = ratio of actual to expected) (see text)	Year(s) Observed	Source
Median age	1970	*1970 Census of Population*, vol. PC(1).
	1960	Table 24, State Reports
Administrative Dependency Index	1965	Calculated from *Fortune Directory* (Rust 1973)
A/E Total Labor Force	1970	1970 *Census of Population*, vol. PC(1)
A.E Total Female Labor Force	1970	1970 *Census of Population*, vol. PC(1)
Income of persons per capita	1969	1970 *Census of Population*, vol. PC(1) C table 89 State Reports
Income of persons per capita	1959	*1962 County & City Data Book*, U.S., Bureau of the Census, Table 4, item 22
% of family incomes over $15,000	1969	*1972 County & City Data Book*, U.S. Bureau of the Census, Table 3, items 56 & 57
% of family incomes below low income* level	1969	Ibid., table 3, item 62
Savings Deposits per capita	1970	Ibid., table 3, items 119 & 120

Table 14-3 (continued)

Median Value, owner-occupied Single Family Homes	1970	Ibid., table 3, item 88
Median Gross Rent	1970	Ibid., table 3, item 89
Percentage of occupied housing with 1.01+ persons/room	1970	Ibid., table 3, item 91
A/E Total Arrests	1970	*FBI Uniform Crime Reports for 1970*, U.S. Federal Bureau of Investigation
A/E Arrests for Aggravated Assault	1970	
A/E Arrests for Burglary	1970	
Physicians per 100,000 Population	1970	*Distribution of Physicians, Hospitals & Hospital Beds in the U.S.*, 1970 American Medical Association, 1971
A/E Total Births	1969	*Vital Statistics of the United States*, U.S. Public Health Service, 1968, Sec. I, *Natality*, Table 1-53.
Birthrates for Women by Age 15-19 to 40-45	1968	
Total Births as Fraction of 1970 Population	1968	
A/E Total Deaths	1969	*Vital Statistics of the United States*, U.S. Public Health Service, 1969, Sec. IIB, *Mortality*, Table 7-8
A/E Deaths Due to:		
Diseases of Heart	1969	
Malignant Neoplasms (cancer)	1969	
Cerebro-vascular diseases (stroke)	1969	
Accidents	1969	
Total Deaths Fraction of 1970 Population	1969	

*Census definition, based on family size.

State Economic Areas (SEAs) because only the latter followed county lines in that region.

Several of the original variables are not comparable in their raw form because of differences in the size and composition of the population to which they apply. In the cases of labor force participation, birth, death, and crime rates the following procedure was used to specify comparable index numbers:

$$R_L = A_L/E_L$$

where R_L is the index for the SMSA, A_L is the actual number of occurrences (e.g., deaths) and E_L in the SMSA is the expected number of occurrences if national average rates applied to the local population structure. The expected number E_L is calculated by

$$E_L = \sum_{i=1}^{n} \frac{A i_N P i_L}{P i_N}$$

where $A i_N$ is the national number of occurrences in age group i, $P i_N$ is the national population of age group i, and $P i_L$ is the SMSA population of age group i.

Growth rates are all based upon the value at the beginning of the period, rather than the middle. There is a resulting exaggeration of large positive rates (e.g., a doubling is made into a tripling) but there should be little bias within the range of most variables used. Rates per capita are based upon population at the nearest census period. In the case of 1965-1970 outmigration rates, this means the population at the end of the period, depressing slightly the calculated outmigration rates of rapidly growing areas.

General Observations

A stepwise multiple regression analysis was made in which the five decade growth rates 1920-1970 were used to estimate a number of suspected correlates of reduced growth. The results are summarized in table 14-4. The largest coefficients in each row are emphasized by underlining.

Most of the suspected correlates are significantly related to the growth path, but few of the relations are chronologically simple. Strong lag effects, as well as cumulative, persistent, and diminishing influences of growth are discernible. The locations of the largest coefficients form a striking pattern: all but one fall in the first or third columns, the latter corresponding to a period centered twenty-five years before the observation of the dependent variable. For example, this twenty-five year lag affects poverty, crowding, and deaths. It is consistent with the stage hypothesis (Chapter 13) which predicts that new responses to non-growth will appear when the children of the last inmigrant generation are unable to find jobs. There are also a number of strong coefficients in the fifth column, representing the delayed influence of growth which occurred forty to fifty years before and whose immigrants now are retiring and dying off.

Cumulative or persistent growth effects are seen among some of the wealth-related economic indicators like home values, rents, and incomes over $15,000. They last no more than two decades. They are followed by a coefficient reversed in sign, evidencing a boom-bust relationship: faster prior growth predisposes an area to a greater distress when it ends.

Age

The stage model suggests that under non-growth the median age of the population will rise in two distinct periods, first, as the more mobile of the recently arrived group depart, and twenty years later as the more mobile offspring of that group who remained in the area follow.[d]

$$\text{Age} = 30.1 - .094G_t - .082G_{t-20} + .034G_{t-30},$$

$R^2 = .46$

Consistent with the stage model, it was found that the downward influence of growth on median age is strongest for the most recent decade and is nearly as strong for the third.[e] Growth in the fourth decade previous to the observation tends to raise the 1970 median age due to the aging of large cohorts of adult inmigrants who arrived thirty to forty years earlier. Jointly these effects explain 46 percent of the variance in median age.

Administrative Dependency

A high degree of non-local administrative control in an SMSA's economy is expected to predispose it to uneven growth, with cyclic gains and losses of employment which are proportionally more severe than those of the national economy. The fraction of total SMSA employment which is in branches of major non-local corporations as identified by *The Fortune Directory* (1966) is referred to here as the "dependency index." It was calculated for thirty-five SMSAs of this sample in an earlier study by the author (Rust 1973).[f]

$$\text{Admin} = 26.9 - .79G_t - .11G_{t-40},$$

$R^2 = .14$

Administrative dependency appears to be negatively related with growth in the subsample analyzed.[g] Significant negative coefficients appear both in the 1960-1970 decade and in the 1920s. The long lag is probably

[d] See table 14-4 for standard deviations of coefficients and F statistics for the equation.

[e] The stage model suggests that age would yield negative coefficients of growth rates for the first and third decades. Non-negative coefficients for those decades, or larger coefficients of either sign in any decade, would tend to refute the stage model.

[f] See table 14-4 for standard deviations of coefficients and F statistics for the equation.

[g] A positive relation with short-term growth would not constitute refutation, however, as the growth could be a consequence of branch plant expansion. The relation with long-term growth should be conclusive.

Table 14-4
Stepwise Multiple Regressions on Decade Population Growth Rates, 1920-1970
Coefficients of Decade Population Growth Rates
(Standard Deviations in Parentheses)

Dependent Variable**	G_t	G_{t-10}	G_{t-20}	G_{t-30}	G_{t-40}	Constant	R^2	F
1970 Median Age	$-.94 \times 10^{-1}$ ($.34 \times 10^{-1}$)	*	$-.82 \times 10^{-1}$ ($.21 \times 10^{-1}$)	$.34 \times 10^{-1}$ ($.18 \times 10^{-1}$)	*	30.1 (.6)	.46	9.2
1965 Dependency Index	-.79 (.40)	*	*	*	-.11 (.07)	26.9 (6.5)	.14	2.7
1970 A/E Labor Force	$.13 \times 10^{-2}$ ($.08 \times 10^{-2}$)	$.12 \times 10^{-2}$ ($.06 \times 10^{-2}$)	$-.10 \times 10^{-2}$ ($.05 \times 10^{-2}$)	*	*	.956 (.014)	.22	2.9
1970 A/R Female Labor Force	$.22 \times 10^{-2}$ ($.16 \times 10^{-2}$)	*	$-.61 \times 10^{-3}$ ($.59 \times 10^{-3}$)	*	*	.966 (.028)	.09	1.5
1969 Income per capita	9.3 (4.6)	10.0 (3.4)	-7.2 (3.1)	*	*	2650 (79)	.34	5.5
1959 Income per capita	9.4 (2.3)	-5.6 (2.1)	*	*	*	1581 (50)	.35	8.9
1969 % of family incomes over $15,000	.20 (.05)	.07 (.02)	*	-.02 (.02)	*	12.4 (.8)	.49	10.1
1969 % of family income below low income	*	-.19 (.07)	.22 (.08)	-.12 (.06)	.04 (.03)	11.8 (1.4)	.28	3.0
1970 Savings deposits per capita	-7.8 (7.3)	7.9 (5.4)	-9.4 (4.9)	*	*	1642 (125)	.12	1.4
1970 Median Home Value	137 (34)	39 (19)	*	*	-18 (9)	12,229 (563)	.49	10.3
1970 Median Gross Rent	.66 (.18)	.31 (.13)	-.20 (.12)	*	*	80.7 (3.0)	.45	8.6

1970 % with 1 + persons/room	*	−.11 (.05)	$.16$ (.06)	−.07 (.04)	.02 (.02)	7.8 (1.0)	.29	3.1
1970 A/E Arrests	$.46 \times 10^{-2}$ ($.37 \times 10^{-2}$)	*	*	*	*	.309 (.055)	.04	1.5
1970 A/E Assaults	$.21 \times 10^{-1}$ ($.16 \times 10^{-1}$)	*	*	*	*	.986 (.232)	.05	1.8
1970 Burglaries	$.36 \times 10^{-1}$ ($.34 \times 10^{-1}$)	*	*	*	*	2.91 (.50)	.03	1.1
1970 Physicians per 100,000 Persons	1.20 (.89)	*	.88 (.59)	*	−.46 (.29)	113.7 (14.9)	.16	2.1
1968 A/E Total Births	$-.16 \times 10^{-2}$ ($.12 \times 10^{-2}$)	*	*	*	*	.242 (.018)	.05	1.8
1968 Total Births per Population	$.26 \times 10^{-3}$ ($.24 \times 10^{-3}$)	*	*	*	$-.45 \times 10^{-4}$ ($.44 \times 10^{-4}$)	$.307 \times 10^{-1}$ ($.040 \times 10^{-1}$)	.07	1.3
1969 A/E Total Deaths	$-.58 \times 10^{-2}$ ($.26 \times 10^{-2}$)	*	*	*	$-.48 \times 10^{-3}$ ($.48 \times 10^{-3}$)	.90 (.04)	.14	2.7
1969 A/E Deaths from: Heart Disease	$-.44 \times 10^{-2}$ ($.33 \times 10^{-2}$)	*	*	*	$-.77 \times 10^{-3}$ ($.59 \times 10^{-3}$)	1.02 (.05)	.08	1.5
Cancer	$-.36 \times 10^{-2}$ ($.32 \times 10^{-2}$)	*	*	*	*	.978 (.047)	.04	1.3
Stroke	*	$-.39 \times 10^{-2}$ ($.30 \times 10^{-2}$)	$.70 \times 10^{-2}$ ($.37 \times 10^{-2}$)	$-.42 \times 10^{-2}$ ($.22 \times 10^{-2}$)	*	.992 (.063)	.12	1.5
Accidents	$-.17 \times 10^{-1}$ ($.05 \times 10^{-1}$)	*	$.51 \times 10^{-2}$ ($.35 \times 10^{-2}$)	*	$-.17 \times 10^{-2}$ ($.17 \times 10^{-2}$)	1.11 (.09)	.27	3.9
1969 Total Deaths per Population	*	*	$-.94 \times 10^{-4}$ ($.88 \times 10^{-4}$)	$.79 \times 10^{-4}$ ($.78 \times 10^{-4}$)	$-.48 \times 10^{-4}$ ($.48 \times 10^{-4}$)	$.202 \times 10^{-1}$ ($.019 \times 10^{-1}$)	.16	2.1

1. A/E means actual/expected (see text),
2. As defined by 1970 Population Census based on family size,
*Not included due to F-Ratio below 1.0,
**See table 14-3 for definition.

a unique historical effect, reflecting the presence in the sample of several industrial cities in which large firms are based and which grew rapidly in the 1920s.

Labor Force Participation

Labor participation is one of three components which determine income per capita, the other two being unemployment and earnings per worker. It is a particularly interesting indicator when corrected for age. For this purpose a labor force ratio has been calculated which is the ratio of actual labor force to the expected labor force based on the age distribution of the population. A higher labor force ratio reflects the overall attractiveness of the local job market to potential workers. Conversely, a low labor force ratio can reflect the "discouraged worker effect," that is, the failure of people who would normally be working even to seek work in a climate of restricted opportunities.

$$\text{Labor Force Ratio} = .956 + .0013G_t + .0012G_{t-10} - .0010G_{t-20},$$

$R^2 = .22$[h]

The total labor force ratio tends to rise in association with recent growth, which is consistent with a "discouraged worker effect" under slow growth.[i] The sign of the relationship is significant but the coefficient is not very large. The female labor force ratio is also increased by growth in the first decade, but more strongly than the male labor force ratio. The female ratio is increased by *slow* growth, however, in the third decade. Growth apparently influences female labor force participation downward during the third decade later. This is opposite to the lagged effect of growth on the incidence of poverty (see below), and again is consistent with the "discouraged worker effect," because growth three decades earlier contributes to the low-mobility segment of the population and thus to a potential labor suplus.

$$\text{Female Labor Force Ratio} = .966 + .0022G_t - .00061G_{t-20},$$

$R^2 = .09$[j]

---

[h] See table 14-4 for standard deviations of coefficients and F statistics for the equation.

[i] A non-positive coefficient in the first decade would tend to refute the "discouraged worker effect." A positive coefficient in the third decade, in view of the stage model and the large proportion of declining areas in the sample, would also tend to refute the effect.

[j] See table 14-4 for standard deviations of coefficients and F statistics for the equation.

Steady growth would have the same size of upward effect on male or female labor force participation; only uneven growth would bring out this imbalance. The equations account respectively for 22 percent and 9 percent of the variance in the total and female labor force ratios.

Income

Income per capita proves as expected to be strongly enhanced by past growth and to be depressed by past non-growth.[k] Its time pattern is different for income observations taken in different years.

$$Y69 = 2650 + 9.3G_t + 10.0G_{t-10} - 7.2G_{t-20},$$

$R^2 = .34$[l]

$$Y59 = 1581 + 9.4G_t - 5.6G_{t-10},$$

$R^2 = .35$[m]

Income in 1969 is positively related to growth in the two previous decades in about equal degrees and has a strong negative relation with growth in the third previous decade (the 1940s). (It also has a weak positive relation with the fourth decade of previous growth.) Income in 1959, on the other hand, shows a similar positive coefficient for the most recent decade, but a negative one for the second (the 1940s again). In both instances, one-third of the variance of income is explained. Industrial growth in the 1940s, particularly the war years, emphasized heavy metallurgical and manufacturing industry in the area covered by the sample, and was also the last period of upturn for coal production. Thus, large growth in this period would be associated with those industries, in places like Pittsburgh, Peublo and the Appalachian coal cities which generally had stable or declining relative incomes per capita in the 1950s and 1960s.

---

[k] A negative coefficient of recent growth would be a strong refutation but is unlikely, because of the known influences of income on future growth and income, and of growth on future growth. A multiple regression of income on growth and prior income would overcome this difficulty. A regression was performed in which the dependent variable was the growth rate of income per capita, 1960 to 1970, which approximates such a test. The resulting equation strongly confirms that recent growth not only reflects income levels, but influences income levels as well.

$$\% \text{ Income Growth} = 70.2 + .40G_t - .27G_{t-10} + .05G_{t-40}$$
$$(2.4) \quad (.15) \quad\quad (.08) \quad\quad\quad (.04)$$

$R^2 = .23 \quad F = 5.46$

(Standard deviations in parentheses.)

[l] See table 14-4 for standard deviations of coefficients and F statistics for the equation.

[m] Ibid.

Income Distribution: High Incomes and Poverty, 1969

The percentage of families with incomes over \$15,000 in 1969 is strongly influenced upward by recent growth, slightly cumulative in two decades, and diminishing in the third.

$$\text{Percentage over } \$15K = 12.4 + .20G_t + .07G_{t-10} - .02G_{t-30},$$

$R^2 = .49$[n]

These are the families that benefit strongly from growth and that are willing to move to capitalize on non-local opportunities. The growth path equation accounts for 49 percent of the variance of this indicator.

The percentage of families with incomes below poverty level, on the other hand, is influenced upward just as strongly by growth in the third previous decade.

Percentage
below poverty $= 11.8 - .19G_{t-10} + .22G_{t-20} - .12G_{t-30} + .04G_{t-40},$

$R^2 = .28$[o]

Surprisingly, this effect largely accounts for the greater incidences of poverty in non-growing areas, which consequently is unaffected by recent growth or non-growth, in the regression analysis. The relative contributions of historical and demographic factors are hard to disentangle, since growth in the 1940s would contribute to a labor surplus a generation later, but also reflects concentration in subsequently slow-growing industries. Growth five decades earlier also appears to raise the poverty level and again historical and demographic factors coincide: a specialization in the boom industries of the 1920s and a large generation passing from working age into dependency are both indicated by large growth in that era. The second and fourth decades of non-growth in the stage model are periods of relatively inelastic population size. Non-growth two or four decades before the observation would contribute, then, to increased poverty, which is what the negative coefficients in these columns show. The negative coefficients are large enough so that constant positive growth would tend to reduce poverty levels, constant negative growth to increase them. Short spurts of high growth, however, would tend to produce abrupt increases in poverty twenty and forty years afterward. The growth equation accounts for 28 percent of the variance in poverty levels, considerably less than for high incomes.

---

[n] Ibid.

[o] Ibid.

Savings

Savings deposits per capita are surprisingly high in many low-income non-growing SMSAs, which seems to run against the familiar principle of the diminishing marginal utility of income (the more you earn the smaller fraction you spend of the earnings). The apparent anomaly is quickly dispelled by the following table of selected zero-order correlation coefficients.

	Income Per Capita			Population Growth			
	1969	1949	1929	1960-70	1950-60	1940-50	1920-30
1970 Savings Per Capita	.448	.471	.478	−.128	−.064	−2.11	−.119

Unlike the housing case, then, income and growth pull in opposite directions on savings. Furthermore, that income may have been earned a long time ago and still be in the bank.

$$\text{Savings Per Capita} = 1642 - 7.8G_t + 7.9G_{t-10} - 9.4G_{t-20},$$

$R^2 = .12$[p]

The regression of decade growth rates on savings shows a positive relation only with the second decade, and larger negative relations in the first and third decades. These are the periods when slow economic growth imposes the greatest pressures on the labor market, and there is apparently a tendency for those people who are still earning, but feeling more threatened, to save for a rainy day. The suggestion offered in Chapter 13 that a lack of alternative local investment opportunities in real estate and small businesses would encourage saving does not account for the positive coefficient of growth in the second decade, but may still be part of the picture. Since the equation accounts for only 12 percent of the variance in savings, it is clear that other factors, notably income, must be involved. If income were included in the equation, considerably stronger relationships of savings with growth might be uncovered.

Housing

Median values of owner-occupied homes, median gross rent, and percentage of housing units occupied by more than one person per room (crowding), were analyzed as indicators of housing market conditions at different

---
[p] Ibid.

levels of income. They are affected in quite different ways, as would be expected from the income trends just discussed:

$$\text{Home value} = 12229 + 137G_t + 39G_{t-10} - 18G_{t-40},$$

$R^2 = .49$[q]

$$\text{Rent} = 80.7 + 66G_t + .31G_{t-10} - .20G_{t-20},$$

$R^2 = .45$[r]

Percentage with 1+
persons per room $= 7.8 - .11G_{t-10} + .16G_{t-20} - .07G_{t-30} + .02G_{t-40},$

$R^2 = .29$[s]

Home values and rents follow much the same trends as does the percentage of family incomes over $15,000, rising cumulatively over two decades with growth. Growth becomes a negative influence on home values only after forty to fifty years, which may be a combined effect of both people and homes getting too old. Rents are depressed by growth in the third decade, as are high incomes. Crowding, like poverty, is positively affected by growth in the third and fifth decades, but negatively in the second and fourth. The positive coefficients are smaller, however, so that their sum, the influence of a steady high or low growth rate on crowding, is nearly zero.

Crime and Criminality

Low crime rates of non-growing areas have previously been observed (Alonso 1972), but were attributed to the older age structure of their populations. However, the non-growing areas' environment might also tend both to select and to foster less criminal behavior by persons of comparable age than would be found in growing areas. To test this hypothesis, ratios of actual to expected crime rates were calculated from national and SMSA arrest statistics for all offenses (total) and for two contrasting classes of major crime, aggravated assaults and burglary. Assaults are crimes between persons who frequently know each other, are often without economic motivation, and are only slightly more prevalent among young people than old. Burglaries, on the other hand, are usually impersonal, economically-motivated crimes, and most burglars arrested are in their teens or twenties. The ratio of actual to expected rates in all three classes were found to be lower for the non-growth areas than for the comparison

[q] Ibid.

[r] Ibid.

[s] Ibid.

areas with better than 95 percent confidence, supporting the hypothesis that criminality (not only crime) is lower in non-growing areas (table 14-5). The regressions show a similar pattern without important lag effects. They have very low R^2 values, however

$$\text{A/E Arrests} = .309 + .0046G_t, \quad R^2 = .04$$

$$\text{A/E Assaults} = .986 + .021G_t, \quad R^2 = .05$$

$$\text{A/E Burglaries} = 2.91 + .036G_t, \quad R^2 = .03$$

which may be due in part to random error in the data, for which crime statistics are notorious.

Table 14-5
Criminality in Growing and Non-Growing Areas

	All Offenses	Aggravated Assault	Burglary
Growing Areas			
Mean	.55	2.01	5.02
Stand. Deviation	.23	1.20	1.96
Non-Growing Areas			
Mean	.41	1.16	3.81
Stand. Deviation	.19	.71	1.70

Births

SMSA birthrates of women in five-year-age cohorts from fifteen to forty-four years old were regressed on prior growth rates. The only factors in this analysis with which birthrates show any large (.2 or more) zero order correlations are income, growth, and the death ratio (table 14-6).

The strong positive correlations between the birth and death ratios is probably due to the varying urbanization and racial compositions of areas in the sample. Areas with larger proportions of rural, black or Chicano families will tend to have both higher fertility and higher mortality. The regression studies did not control for these variables, so the findings must be regarded as weak and tentative.

There is, nevertheless, a theoretical possibility that growth may influence SMSA birth rates downward. Differential mobility selects out more mobile members of each age group, who also tend to be the less fertile ones (Long 1970b). A growing local economy provides more opportunities for women to work. A weaker role of the church and of traditional values generally in growing places may encourage contraception. On the other

Table 14-6
Zero-Order Correlations with Birthrates, By Age of Mother

Age of Mother	Income Capita 1970	Population Growth 1960-1970	Ratio of Actual to Expected Deaths
15-19	.02	−.12	.60
20-24	.04	−.27	.60
25-29	−.03	−.23	.60
30-34	−.11	−.23	.53
35-39	−.24	−.22	.32
40-44	−.18	−.22	.27

hand, it is remotely conceivable that people might perceive the limited job opportunities in non-growing areas and choose not to contribute further to the local labor surplus.

The empirical trend of the actual to expected birth ratio in the present sample is downward with increased growth, upward with less growth:

$$\text{A/E Total Births} = .242 - .0016G_t, \qquad R^2 = .05^t$$

The most recent growth rate appeared to have a downward influence on birthrates. This is particularly notable because those births are a part of the most recent growth figure and would tend to influence it positively, not negatively.

It should be emphasized that the generally downward influence of growth on fertility is for age-specific birthrates, not the total population rate. The overall influence of growth on total fertility in an SMSA is still upward, because it adds population in the younger age brackets:

$$\begin{aligned} &\text{Total Births} \\ &\text{Per Population} = .0307 + .00026G_t - .000045G_{t-40}, \end{aligned}$$

$R^2 = .07^u$

Doctors, Death Ratios, and Death Rates

Ratios of actual to expected crude death rates were calculated for total deaths and for deaths due to each of the four largest causes for 1969. High ratios might show generalized or specific health problems related to growth. Possible sources of health problems in rapid growth could include automotive air pollution and the stress of environmental change. On the other hand, a relative shortage of physicians, hazardous work, poor hous-

^{t} Ibid.

^{u} Ibid.

ing, and poverty are often associated with slow growth, which might have an opposite effect on the death ratio.

There appears to be a strong tendency for physicians to concentrate in wealthy, growing areas. The factors which correlate most strongly with the ratio of physicians to population are home value (.399), and incomes above $15,000 (.32). The regression coefficients suggest that their response to a downturn in growth is both rapid and persistent:

Physicians
per 100,000
population $= 113.7 + 1.20G_t + .88G_{t-20} - .46G_{t-40}$,

$R^2 = .16^v$

Total death ratios showed a negative relation with growth, accounting for 14 percent of the variance.

$$\text{A/E Total Deaths} = .90 - .0058G_t - .00048G_{t-40},$$

$R^2 = .14^w$

Reporting bias would probably go the other way: a tendency toward under-registration where there are more deaths and fewer doctors, so these trends may be notable. (It begins to look as if growth could be good for people.) Death ratios from heart disease and cancer were also influenced downward by recent growth or upward by decline in the sample, but the statistics are fairly weak.

A stronger effect of growth is the accidental death ratio:

$$\text{A/E Accidental Deaths} = 1.11 - .017G_t + .0051G_{t-20} - .0017G_{t-40},$$

$R^2 = .28^x$

The overall pattern is that abnormally high accident rates are associated with slow growth, especially in areas which boomed twenty to thirty years ago but declined forty to fifty years ago (Savannah, Georgia, is an example). Most of the effect comes from the recent growth rate, which has a substantial negative coefficient: decline raises the accident rate. The third decade partly offsets this with a positive coefficient (as in the case of poverty) and the fifth decade's coefficient turns negative.

The death ratio due to stroke is curious:

$$\text{A/E Stroke Deaths} = .992 - .0039G_{t-10} + .0070G_{t-20} - .0042G_{t-30},$$

$R^2 = .12^y$

---

[v] Ibid.

[w] Ibid.

[x] Ibid.

[y] Ibid.

The growth rate of the third decade previous raises the incidence of stroke. Were inmigrants of that time predisposed (because of the stress of moving and separation from home) to have strokes when they reached their forties and fifties? The growth rates of the second and fourth decades, however, lower it strongly enough to make the overall response to constant growth negative. The time pattern of the influences of growth on stroke is much like that of poverty, but stroke and poverty are nearly independent with a zero order correlation of .038. The trend seems ambiguous.

There is also some ambiguity about the effect of growth on the population death rate uncorrected for age differences.

$$\text{Total Deaths Per 100,000 Population} = 2020 - 9.4G_{t-20} + 7.9G_{t-30} - 4,8G_{t-40},$$

$R^2 = .16$[z]

The coefficient of the most recent growth rate is expected to be negative because it mainly adds young people—migrants or infants—to the population, but proves not to be significant. Growth apparently lowers the crude death rate thirty and fifty years hence, but raises it in the intervening decade.

---

[z] Ibid.

15

Age, Sex, and Rationality in Migration from Metropolitan Areas

Migration studies attempting to relate gross intermetropolitan migration flows with local economic conditions have often produced a surprising finding: the absence of a significant "push" effect of low per capita income on high unemployment (Lowry 1966, pp. 22-23; Lansing and Mueller 1967, p. 294; Fabricant 1970, Alonso 1971, 1973). "Push" has appeared only infrequently.[a] Apparently, a person's likelihood of becoming a migrant is about the same whether his home is in a poor or a prosperous area. This finding has not been readily accepted for several reasons. It conflicts with the predictions of classical factor mobility theory and with numerous studies of individual migration behavior in which economic distress at home apparently stimulated moves which would not otherwise have been made. The economic "push" idea, furthermore, has common sense appeal, a congruence with personal experiences and popular mythology, and people are reluctant to abandon it.

Perhaps the idea of economic "push" describes a real behavior pattern, but applies to a more limited part of a local population than is generally believed and is offset by a reverse tendency in other population groups. Economic distress could conceivably be a "push" when it affects people who are childless, own no real estate, are about to enter the labor force for the first time, or are forming a new family, all of which are more frequent among the young. At the same time, distress could be a barrier to mobility for other persons whom it deprives of resources needed for the move, or on whom it imposes a greater dependence on friends and relatives, property and community institutions. A homeowner or small businessman in a distressed community, for example, would be hard put to recover enough equity in the sale of his property to afford to buy elsewhere. Confirming the notion of a selective barrier effect, recent studies of migration of the rural poor in India (Greenwood 1971) and the United States (Collignon 1972;

---

[a] Alonso (1973) found the migration-elasticity of income and other variables to be highly sensitive to the design of the sampling plan. Greenwood and Sweetland (1972), using the same data base in which Alonso and others found no significant "push," got per capita income at origin to enter as a strong "push" factor. Their sampling plan, however, may have drawn excessively from small, long-distance moves in which younger, better educated and presumably more "rational" than average migrants would tend to be overrepresented. They took a random sampling of half the available SMSAs—thus increasing the average distance to begin with—and included as observations all possible flows between them, most of which contain only a few people. A more balanced representation of flow size can be achieved by a Neyman-allocated stratified random sample of flows by size, or, as in the present study, by using total gross migration rates at an origin or destination.

Abt Associates 1970) show that for some communities and individuals, better economic conditions can contribute to higher rates of outmigration, not the reverse.

The existence of large and relatively immobile subclasses of the American population, together with great inequality in local economic growth, has led researchers like Roger Bolton (1971) and Peter Morrison (1972) to conclude that spontaneous migration has a very limited capacity to adjust interregional labor imbalances, particularly as they affect slowly growing or declining areas.

An Age-Sex Outmigration Model

As a first test of the idea that economic distress may have counteracting "push" and barrier effects, age groups were selected in which the effects are expected to reach fairly extreme levels, the 20-25 age group for the "push" effect and the 55-65 age group for the barrier effect. An analysis was made of the effects of local economic conditions on outmigration in the period 1965-70 for the three groups and for total population using a sample of thirty-four Standard Metropolitan Statistical Areas (SMSAs).

The model tested was:

$$\frac{OM_{i,c}}{P_{i,c}} = e^{\alpha 0} y_i^{\alpha 1} u_i^{\alpha 2} P_i^{\alpha 3} (1 + m_{i,t-1})^{\alpha 4}$$

where $OM_{i,c}$ = outmigration of age class c from SMSA i in a given period

$P_{i,c}$ = average population of age class c at SMSA i during that period

y_i = average per capita personal income at SMSA i during that period

u_i = average unemployment rate at SMSA i during that period

P_i = average total population at SMSA i during that period

$m_{i,t-1}$ = lagged net migration rate at SMSA i for a previous period.

The model predicts the proportion of a population age class in an SMSA which will migrate away in a time interval. The population at risk is factored out so that the dependent variable may be interpreted as a class-specific propensity to migrate, and so that the residual differences between predicted and observed migration rates can be compared between cities. (A variation was also tested in which the dependent variable was a number, OM_i, not a ratio, in order to provide a form in which the coefficient of determination could be compared with previous studies.) A log-linear form was chosen because it had been used in previous studies which made no-push findings (Lowry 1966; Alonso 1971), and because its coefficients are easily interpreted as elasticities of the migration rate to the variable in question.

Two dimensions of local economic conditions are reflected in the model, personal income per capita (y_i) and the unemployment rate (u_i). Per capita income reflects the overall level of material welfare in the region. Per capita income is used instead of pay scales because it better reflects local differences in multiple job-holding, part-time work, labor force participation rates (particularly by women) and occupational opportunities, all of which are as much a part of a city's economic environment as its pay scales. The coefficient $\alpha 1$ will show the elasticity of outmigration to income. A negative value, showing greater outmigration from lower income places, would be consistent with the "push" thesis, a positive value with counter-push.

Unemployment (u_i) is treated as a distinct variable for several reasons. It changes much more rapidly in time than does income, providing a more sensitive indicator of recent labor market changes. It also indicates the relative size of a population subgroup, the unemployed, who have an obvious incentive to move away. The coefficient $\alpha 2$ will show the elasticity of outmigration to unemployment rates, and a positive value would be consistent with the "push" thesis.

The population size of the SMSA in question (P_i) is not to be confused with the population at risk to outmigrate, i.e., the population of age class $P_{i,c}$. Its purpose in the model is to reflect the "mass effect," the probability of achieving the same purposes as migration by moving within an SMSA rather than beyond it. Bigger areas contain more potential destinations, so the mass effect will increase with the size of the SMSA, and total outmigration will tend to be slighty less than proportional to total population (Alonso 1971). The elasticity of population size $(\alpha 3)$ with respect to per capita outmigration, then, is expected to be a small negative number. (In the case of model (2) for all age classes combined, $P_{i,c}$ becomes redundant with P_i and is deleted. In this case $\alpha 3$ is expected to become positive but less than unity.)

Substantial mobility differentials exist between persons of varying education, occupation, and family size, independently of age (Long 1972; 1973b). These characteristics of an individual change slowly, if at all. It is not surprising, therefore, that recent migrants are much more likely to move in a given period than are non-migrants (Morrison 1972). The recent net migration rate $(m_{i,t-1})$ indicates the rate at which such "habitual movers" have been accumulating in the population (Beale) and entered strongly in Alonso's equation for aggregate gross outmigration (Alonso 1973, p. 16).

Table 15-1

Comparison of Subsample with all SMSAs in U.S.

Division	Subsample	Number of SMSAs Total U.S.	Sample as % of Total U.S.
New England	0	26	0
Middle Atlantic	7	25	28
South Atlantic	6	37	16
East North Central	5	48	10
West North Central	4	20	20
East South Central	3	13	23
West South Central	7	37	19
Mountain	1	14	7
Pacific	0	22	0
1969 Per Capita Income of Persons			
Less than $2600	9	28	32
$2600-2999	12	65	18
$3000-3299	9	74	12
$3300-3699	4	42	10
More than $3700	0	33	0
1970 Population			
Less than 100,000	0	26	0
100,000 - 149,999	11	41	27
150,000 - 349,999	20	92	22
350,000 - 999,999	1	50	2
1,000,000 - 1,999,999	0	21	0
2,000,000 or more	2	12	17

The proper length of the period of previous net migration to be considered is debatable: presumably it should be long enough to recognize a long, gradual build-up of "habitual movers," but short enough to cancel out the attrition of past mobility as individuals have children, change jobs, age, die or outmigrate; Alonso used five years (Alonso 1973, p. 16), which might be a trifle short. Longitudinal studies, rather than the cross-sectional approach used in most migration work, would help clarify this issue. The elasticity of lagged net migration ($\alpha4$) is expected to be positive for total outmigration. Older people should be more sensitive to lagged net migration than young people for two reasons. First, the data used here were lagged five to twenty years, and include a time when the parents of the younger group would themselves have still been highly mobile, so its effects on the younger would die out sooner. Second, the older group has a relatively low normal mobility, and because of the longitudinal association of mobility discussed earlier, will have only a small fraction of even potentially mobile population. Sustained net outmigration could quickly exhaust this mobile subgroup, while sustained net inmigration could double or triple it, leading to much greater relative changes in overall mobility for this age group than would be caused in the younger ones.

Sample and Data Used

The sample is drawn from the group of sixty study and comparison areas used in the previous chapter. As 1965-70 migration data by age are available only for State Economic Areas (SEAs), (U.S. Bureau of the Census 1972), the subsample used here is the subset of thirty-four SMSAs within the group of sixty, which correspond approximately with one or more whole SEAs.[b] The subsample, like the larger one, contains somewhat more eastern cities, and considerably more small and poor cities than would appear in a random sample of American SMSAs (table 15-1).

Some compromises were accepted in compiling specific data to represent the independent variables. Averages of annual unemployment rates for 1965-69 were used only in the twenty-one cities for which such rates are published (U.S. Manpower Administration 1970, 1966). One-time rates from the 1970 Census had to be substituted in the others (U.S. Bureau of the Census 1970a). Per capita income was also taken from the Census (U.S. Bureau of the Census 1970a). Similarly, 1970 total and class population figures were used. They should ideally have been adjusted to an average for the period, 1965-70, but the differences would have been minor. The approximation used exaggerates the population of faster growing areas, deflating slightly their per capita outmigration rates. Lagged net migration was represented by Census Bureau estimates for the 1950-60 period (U.S. Bureau of the Census 1967), leaving a gap of five years before the beginning of the observed migration period.[c]

Findings

The model was calibrated on these data, using stepwise multiple regression. Results, given in table 15-2, confirm that while economic conditions are negligible in explaining total outmigration, they show a strong "push" effect in the 20-24 age group, especially for women. Lagged net migration

---

[b] Containing between 2/3 and 1-1/3 of the SMSA population in 1970.

[c] The 1960-65 gap could in principle be filled by subtracting the 1965-70 net migration estimates from the source used here out of the 1960-70 net migration estimates prepared by the 1970 Census of Population and Housing in *General Demographic Trends*, sec. PHC-2. The two sources proved incompatible, however. They apply to different universes: persons age five or more in 1970 in the first, and all persons alive in 1970 in the second. The allocation of migrants whose 1965 residence was "unreported" in the first source would be a further problem: if omitted, outmigration would be biased downward.

Table 15-2
Regression Statistics for Gross Outmigration Rates

Run #	Dependent Variable	α0 (Constant)	α1 (Income)	α2 (Unemployment)	α3 (Total Population)	α4 (Lagged Net Migration Rate)	R²	Standard Error of Estimate
1.	OM5+	-1.96	-.37 (.62)	-.06 (.20)	.76*** (.09)	1.30*** (.41)	.78	.30
2.	OM5+ / P5+	-1.96	-.37 (.61)	-.06 (.20)	-.24*** (.08)	1.30*** (.41)	.45	.30
3.	OM20-24 / P20-24	7.08	-.78* (.51)	.06 (.17)	-.09 (.07)	-.19 (.33)	.29	.25
4.	OM20-24 male / P20-24 male	6.43	-.65 (.54)	.04 (.18)	-.03 (.08)	-.39 (.35)	.19	.26
5.	OM20-24 female / P20-24 female	7.56	-.89** (.51)	.08 (.17)	-.14** (.07)	†	.37	.25
6.	OM55-64 / P55-64	-9.47	.18 (.73)	.10 (.24)	-.19** (.10)	1.61*** (.48)	.39	.36
7.	OM55-64 / P55-64	-5.39	.73 (.69)	†	-.27 (.11)	X	.15	.40

*   90% confidence that the estimated sign is correct
**   95% confidence that the estimated sign is correct
*** 99% confidence that the estimated sign is correct
†   Did not enter with .01 minimum F-level for inclusion.

X   Deleted

overshadows a weak barrier effect of low income in the 55-64 age group.

Compared with Alonso's similar outmigration equation, which he calibrated on all 242 SMSAs for the same period (Alonso 1973, p. 16), Run 1 shows that the small sample closely represents national trends.[d] Run 2 is a transformation of Run 1 to permit comparison with subsequent runs. Population (persons aged 5+) is divided into both sides of the equation. As a result the population coefficient, $\alpha 3$, becomes $(.76 - 1.0)$ or .24; the coefficient of determination drops, and the other parameters remain virtually unchanged.

Run 3 predicts outmigration for the 20-24 age class. The large positive constant and small coefficients reflect high and variable mobility, much of it unexplained by the model. Income does enter negatively with better than 90 percent confidence, however, and is the only significant coefficient for this group.

When the 20-24 group is separated by sex, the source of the problem is apparent. Run 4 shows that none of the variables is significant at the 90 percent level or better in explaining male outmigration of the 20-24 age group. Income comes the closest, and has the expected negative sign or "push" effect. Things outside the model clearly dominated the migration of young males, notably military service and military base employment. Two of the model's three worst underestimates of their outmigration rates were made for SMSAs with large air force bases, while two of its three worst overestimates were associated with SMSAs having army bases.

Economic rationality surfaced at last in the outmigration of women aged 20-24 (Run 5): the negative elasticity or "push" sign of income for them has a 95 percent confidence level. The influence of population size is also significantly negative for young women, but not so extreme as for all groups combined. Apparently most "habitual movers" effects have been captured by the age-sex control, for lagged net migration never reaches the .01 minimum F-level for inclusion.

The very large elasticity of lagged net migration in Run 6 essentially runs the model; the barrier effect of economic distress at the older working ages is neither confirmed nor denied. Run 7 shows that when lagged net migration is deleted, income enters much more strongly, with the expected

---

[d] In the present terminology, he found

$$OM_i = e^{-3.3}P_i^{.88} \quad y_i^{.29} \quad (1 + n_{i,t-1})^{3.3} \quad (1 + m_{1,t-1})^{.47}$$
$$\phantom{OM_i = e^{-3.3}P_i^{.88}} (.02) \quad (.15) \quad (.6)$$

$R^2 = .903$ Std. Error = .283

where $n_{i,t-1}$ is the lagged rate of natural increase, a proxy for age distribution.

Run 1 shows a smaller elasticity of population size, indicating a greater aversion to small cities. Apparently the sample slightly underrepresents attractive small cities, or overrepresents unattractive large ones. The other differences are probably unrelated to the sampling. The positive sign of income is weakly significant in Alonso's equation and indeterminate in Run 6. The elasticity of a lagged migration is probably larger in Run 6 because of the lack of a lagged natural increase term with which it would be positively correlated.

positive (barrier effect) sign to slightly less than a 90 percent level of confidence, but there is a substantial drop in the model's explanatory power. Lagged net migration, then, apparently has a greater influence than per capita income on this group's mobility.[e]

In sum, the "no-push" anomaly has been explained by the finding that the young have an economically "rational" outmigration trend, while the older age groups may respond to economic distress as a barrier rather than a stimulus to migration and are particularly unlikely to leave places which have had substantial net outmigration in the past.

Conclusions

This brief study confirms the view advanced in Chapter 13 that apparently the migration system is distilling the more mobile, economically "rational" people into the faster growing places while the less mobile or "rational" people are being concentrated in the slower growing ones. This implies a particularly vicious mode of labor market segmentation, in which only the faster growing communities can conform to the self-adjusting world of the classical factor mobility model, while the slowly growing or declining ones become increasingly imbalanced, disadvantaged, and isolated from the national economy.

While the segmentation of outmigration behavior between classically "rational" and non-rational or counter-rational age-sex groups has been shown, at least for a small sample, its boundaries have not been mapped. Further empirical research is needed along the lines of the present study, using a full array of available age, sex and race-specified gross outmigration data. Inmigration and the effects of destination characteristics on migration behavior of different age, sex, and race groups can be studied from the same sources used here. The distance variable, however, cannot be analyzed directly from Census data except for aggregate moves; new data are needed in order to study the differential effects of distance on the migration behavior of these groups.

---

[e] In reviewing the several runs of the model, it was clear that one variable had not reached a significant positive or negative elasticity for any age or age-sex group: the unemployment rate. Suspecting that the mixed unemployment data may have been a problem, the same runs were repeated using a "clean" subsample of twenty-one SMSAs for which five-year average unemployment data were available; again it failed to enter significantly. It could probably be "forced" to enter by deleting income, with which it has a zero-order correlation of -0.6, but contrary to expectations, unemployment adds no important information regarding mobility to what is already contained in the per capita income statistic. It would be very interesting to explore the relation of migration to age-specific SMSA unemployment rates. At present, these are available only from the Decennial Census, which reports an instantaneous rate rather than an annual average.

16 Conclusions

At this point some preliminary conclusions can be drawn about what generally happens to metropolitan areas that don't grow, and some objectives and guidelines can be proposed for public policy in dealing with such areas. This step is an audacious one in view of the exploratory nature of the preceding analysis, but a necessary one to explicate its meaning. The purpose of this chapter is partly to convey advice, but more importantly, to identify the parts of the analysis which because of their serious implications deserve the most rigorous testing and criticism.

Summary Interpretation of Findings

The historic origins of non-growing areas, while spanning three centuries and many different sources of growth, reflect several common factors. Most are former boom towns and several have been through two or more boom-and-bust cycles. Boom growth is as much a part of these areas' problems as is decline. Hastily building to exploit a transitory economic advantage before it evaporated, the developers of boom areas often picked sites prone to "natural" catastrophes and were lax in protecting them from hazards. Floods of national-disaster proportions have struck Johnstown, Pueblo, Fort Smith, St. Joseph, Wilkes-Barre, and other former boom areas over the years, often terminating their development for decades. Scars of fire, flood, and earth subsidence were visible in a majority of the cities visited.

The cross-sectional studies seem to confirm that booms of economic growth and inmigration tend to be followed by "shadow booms" of continued population growth due to the high fertility of the young recent migrants, setting the stage for unemployment and economic stress when their children mature and seek jobs that are not to be found.

The immediate, short-term consequences of population loss for those who remain appear to be those associated with employment loss and the selective outmigration of young, higher-income people. These include a lower participation in the labor force, greater unemployment, poorer health services and restricted wage gains, as well as a depressed real estate market. There is not a significant influence on the incidence of poverty in the short term but poverty appears in the later stages of no growth.

Under continued economic non-growth, metropolitan areas become extremely resistant to decline in population size. Only a fraction of any population is highly mobile. Once this fraction has been depleted by out-migration it is not readily replaced from within the community, and there will be powerful resistance to the downward adjustment of population. Rather than leave their home community, a great many people who lose jobs thereafter accept much lower paying jobs, commute to outside the area or withdraw from the labor force. This is accompanied by higher rates of poverty, crowding, accidents, and stress diseases, together with a further decline in income per capita.

Non-growth of population not only reflects economic distress, but within our present institutions, reinforces and prolongs it, partly because those institutions are not adapted to manage change in a no-growth setting. Lacking growth in local service demand, no-growth areas become increasingly specialized in the very sectors least likely to promote recovery, while their service sectors become relatively undersized and obsolescent. Public services mainly funded from the local tax base, such as education, are particularly severely eroded. In an atmosphere of uncertainty and decline, cautious investment attitudes and resistance to innovation become the dominant survival traits in business, finance and government. Perhaps most damaging of all, the pervasive atmosphere of low wage demands, low returns on land and capital and public desires for any kind of economic growth foster and protect low-productivity, high-risk activities which destructively exploit people and the environment.

The stability of the no-growth communities seemed to have positive as well as negative aspects in some of the case study areas. Church, family, and ethnic ties were strong. The incidence of stress diseases was low. They were relatively safe from crime. Housing was cheap, plentiful and to a large extent owner-occupied. The reluctance of so many people to leave was not perhaps irrational, but a reflection of a particular set of values in which these qualities outweigh the possible material gain associated for some of them with moving to a more prosperous area. It may also reflect a realistic self-appraisal by some of how well, with their limited education and experience, they might compete in other job markets. Doubtless there are others near the margin who would be happier and better off if helped to move, but it would be presumptuous and inhumane to assume this is the case for more than a small part of the population.

Public attempts to reverse or to cope with metropolitan non-growth have sometimes been harmful or irrelevant to the people most in need of help. The most successful of the captured new resources for an increased share of industrial growth, but none addressed the real issue of development without growth, the conversion of old resources to new uses in a changing economy, while retaining enough self-determination in the process not to be reduced to a neocolonial status.

There are good economic and historical reasons for the recent incidence of metropolitan non-growth. It reflects the abandonment of technologies and resources which are no longer competitive in an overall process of upgrading productivity. But there are also limits to how much and how long a metropolitan area can decline without hurting people. If the responsibility for reversing that harm were recognized as part of the process, the supposed productivity gains might be offset, and a more cautious and humane style of development might be encouraged. There is a need for greater public awareness of the acute and persistent distress imposed on the older and less mobile members of our society by excessively uneven metropolitan growth, especially when it leads to long-term decline. Despite the prevailing mythology that a self-equilibrating private market and an even-handed federal establishment are promoting social equality, uneven locational decisions in government and industry are a major source of poverty and limited life opportunities.

Proposed Public Objectives and Guidelines

The foregoing view of metropolitan non-growth in its context in the boom-bust problem has emphasized failure of equilibrating forces in the national growth allocation system. It is very different from the one which underlies virtually all overt regional development programs in the United States (cf. Gilmore 1958; Levitan 1961; Committee for Economic Development 1964; Hansen 1970; Cameron 1970; Wingo 1972). Programs such as the loan and grant programs of the Economic Development Administration, the Regional Commission activities, the M.D.T.A. manpower training programs, and the hundreds of quasi-public local regional and statewide industrial development organizations reflect an opposite philosophy: local economic distress and abnormally low growth are seen as a localized disease which needs localized treatment, mainly the upgrading of industrial capital and skills. They generally emphasize lessening the outmigration of the young and mobile who actually would not suffer from the problem. They take on promotional functions which would be privately done in more prosperous areas. At best, they attract outside investments away from other areas (but probably not from ones with any strong advantage) which mollify the local impact of long-established decline, decades after the precipitating changes occurred. At worst, they help marginal firms create short-term booms based on exploiting surplus labor at low productivity, depressing incomes by reducing net outmigration and setting the area up for an inevitable second round of distress, as in the promotion of the apparel industry in Northeast Pennsylvania.

The main public role in the metropolitan non-growth problem is the influence of localized government expenditures on national patterns of growth allocation between local areas. Alonso (1971) has demonstrated that there is now a strong concentration of federal expenditures in richer and faster-growing counties and identified the very small fraction of programs in which regional impacts are expressly considered. He reviews some of the powerful interregional influences implicit in the allocation of overtly non-regional spending programs as in areas such as tax laws, pollution control policies, access changes arising from government-supported research and development in transportation, and the activities of regulatory commissions. He emphasizes, however, that geographic distribution of consequences is not inherently the main consideration in these implicitly regional public activities. He concludes that "it is neither realistic nor desirable to force them into formal regional coordination" (Alonso 1971, p. 31), and opts for a purely informational accounting of "national geographic consequences of current or contemplated national policies or programs for these issues."

Such an accounting appears a necessary first step in dealing with the problem of which metropolitan non-growth is a part. Integral with it should be a similar accounting of the consequences of major development plans in the private sector, at least in the largest corporations and in sectors likely to trip off unstable local growth such as the fossil fuel industries. At a minimum, the large corporations could be required, as in Sweden, to submit periodic region-by-region employment projections to a national manpower planning agency. Made available to congressional delegations and local media, the resulting awareness of impending problems would certainly stimulate some corrective political actions.

The troublesome consequences of booms as well as busts are important to recognize and to moderate even in absence of such a comprehensive informational program. Public pressures should be exerted toward moderating upward as well as downward growth fluctuations. One basic strategy having this effect would be to require the firms profiting from a boom to share the costs of dismantling it afterwards, restoring land and relocating people. The responsibility to transfer workers brought in from outside would be a highly desirable policy to require of all multiplant firms: internalizing at least one element of the social costs imposed by their actions would reduce the disparity between optimum courses for the firm and for society.

Once a boom has ended, the subsequent shadow-boom and labor surplus are sufficiently predictable to allow time to counteract those effects. The most positive way to counteract them, unlikely as it sounds, would be by encouraging the relocation of young recent immigrants to other areas as soon as area labor needs have been met in the migration boom phase and before the fertility boom sets in. It is also the best time for intensive industrial promotion so as to smooth the downturn of employment growth.

The Amarillo experience suggests that excess population can be shed in this phase at far less cost than later, particularly where at least one major employer accepts responsibility to transfer its people to new jobs elsewhere.

Areas in a fertility-boom phase with slower employment growth than population growth can be reasonably sure of problems in two decades or less and should beware any complacent interpretation of population growth and low unemployment as signs of health. An impending supply pressure on an area's labor market can be readily predicted by demographic analysis. Preparations should be made during the fertility-boom phase for the over-large cohorts of juveniles to emigrate successfully when they become ready to enter the labor force. Competent education is a major influence on mobility and will need disproportionate subsidy because of limited local resources. Preparations might include school field trips or visiting programs aimed at growing areas, and inviting recruiters from non-local firms.

When the oversized juvenile cohorts reach working age, actual moving assistance will be needed. Hansen (1971) has reviewed some pilot programs for mobility assistance. Help might include job search, housing search, transportation, and personal counseling as needed, through the primary decline phase. Industrial promotion in this primary stage will merely attract more inmigrants and prolong the problem, unless there is already a labor surplus and unless there is a reasonable prospect of steady growth.

The secondary decline phase is one in which there are low mobility, low fertility, slowly rising death rates and a population size which has become exceedingly resistant to decline. In this phase main objectives should shift to helping the people who stay to cope with the changing context and capabilities of their community. Helping people move out will still be valuable, but will appeal to a smaller potential clientele. Promotion of employment growth by traditional means may be appropriate at this stage, but should be done with far more attention than is normally paid to the needs of the non-mobile community members. Emphasis should be on finding productive, well-paid work for the older and less mobile unemployed and underemployed, rather than just skimming the meager yearly accretions of young men and women. There is a growing recognition by bodies like the Commission on the Future of the South (1974) that local development efforts should be more selective, emphasizing income and environmental impact as well as sheer numbers of employment. Other priorities should include encouraging locally owned or administered enterprises, cultivating political influence and resisting destructive exploitation of non-mobile people and the natural environment.

An overriding public objective in the secondary decline and non-growth equilibrium stages should be to protect, enhance, and capitalize on the benefits of slow growth such as stability, strong community ties, and the opportunity for communicating the customs and values of an older era to a younger one. In a sense the place has become a refuge. In the minds of those who have chosen to remain into the secondary phase, these values may outweigh some degree of increased material consumption. They ought to be respected.

Bibliography

General Bibliography

Abt Associates. (1970) *The Causes of Rural to Urban Migration Among the Poor*. Report to the Office of Economic Opportunity, Contract No. 849-4841, Cambridge, Mass.

Ackley, Gardner. (1961) *Macroeconomic Theory*. New York: MacMillan.

Alonso, William. (1968) "Urban and Regional Imbalances in Economic Development." In *Economic Development and Cultural Change*, V. 17, pp. 1-14.

_____. (1971a) *The System of Intermetropolitan Population Flows*. Working Paper No. 155. Berkeley: Institute of Urban and Regional Development, University of California.

_____. (1971b) "Problems, Purposes and Implicit Policies for a National Strategy of Urbanization," Working Paper No. 158. Berkeley: Institute of Urban and Regional Development, University of California.

_____. (1971c) "The Economics of Urban Size." In *Papers of the Regional Science Association*, V. 26, pp. 67-83.

_____. (1973a) National Interregional Accounts: A Prototype. Monograph No. 17. Berkeley: Institute of Urban and Regional Development, University of California.

_____. (1973b) "Urban Zero Population Growth." *Daedelus* 102 (Fall): 191-206.

Alonso, William and Medrich, Eliot. (1970) "Spontaneous Growth Centers in Twentieth Century American Urbanization." Working Paper No. 113. Berkeley: Institute of Urban and Regional Development, University of California.

Barone, Michael et al. (1972) *The Almanac of American Politics*. Boston: Gambit, Inc.

_____. (1974) *The Almanac of American Politics*. Boston: Gambit, Inc.

Beale, Calvin L. "The Relation of Gross Outmigration Rates to Net Migration." Washington, D.C.: Economic Research Service, U.S. Department of Agriculture (unpublished paper, 8 pages, no date).

Berry, Brian J.L. (1964) "Cities as Systems Within Systems of Cities." *Papers of the Regional Science Association*, V. 13, pp. 147-163.

Berry, Brian J.L. and Pred, Allan R. (1965) *Central Place Studies: A Bibliography of Theory and Applications*. Philadelphia: Regional Science Research Institute.

223

Blau, Peter Michael, and Duncan, Otis Dudley. (1967) *The American Occupational Structure*. New York: Wiley.

Bolino, August C. (1961) *The Development of the American Economy*. Columbus: Charles E. Merrill.

Bolton, Roger E. (1971) "Defense Spending and Policies for Labor Surplus Areas." In Kain, John F. et al., *Essays in Regional Economics*, Cambridge: Harvard University Press, pp. 137-160.

Borchert, John K. (1972) "America's Changing Metropolitan Regions," *Annals of the Association of American Geographers* 62:2 pp. 360-369 (June 1972).

Borts, George H. and Stein, Jerome L. (1969) *Economic Growth in a Free Market*. New York: Columbia University Press.

Brown, A.J. (1972) *The Framework of Regional Economics in the United Kingdom*. Cambridge: University Press.

Cameron, Gordon. (1970) *Regional Economic Development: The Federal Role*. Baltimore: Johns Hopkins Press.

Caudill, Harry M. (1962) *Night Comes to the Cumberlands*. Boston: Atlantic-Little, Brown.

Center for Future Research. (1973) *The Economic Impact of Declining Population Growth in Los Angeles County*. Los Angeles: University of Southern California.

Coale, Ansley. (1970) "Man and His Environment." *Science* (Oct. 9).

Collignon, Frederick C. (1973) *The Causes of Rural to Urban Migration Among the Poor*. Ph.D. dissertation, Harvard University Department of Political Economy and Government.

Committee for Economic Development. (1964) *Community Economic Development Efforts: Five Case Studies*. New York: Committee for Economic Development.

Davis, Lance E. et al. (1973) *American Economic Growth*. New York: Harper & Row.

Doeringer, Peter and Piore, Michael. (1970) *Internal Labor Markets and Manpower Analysis*. (Mimeo).

Dunn, Edgar S. (1971) *Economic and Social Development*, Resources for the Future. Baltimore: Johns Hopkins Press.

Esteban-Marquillas, J.M. (1972) "A Reinterpretation of Shift-Share Analysis." *Regional and Urban Economics*, V. 2, pp. 249-255.

Fabricant, Ruth A. (1970) "An Expectational Model of Migration." *Journal of Regional Science*, V. 10, No. 1 (April), pp. 13-24.

Fallows, James M. (1970) *The Water Lords*. New York: Grossman Pub.

Friedmann, John R.P. (1966) *Regional Development Policy*. Cambridge: MIT Press.

_____. (1972) "The Spatial Organization of Power in the Development of Urban Systems." Prepared for the Social Research Council (July).

Gilmore, Donald R. (1958) *Developing the "Little" Economies*. New York: Committee for Economic Development.

Glaab, Charles M. (1963) *The American City: A Documentary History*. Homewood, Ill.: The Dorsey Press.

Glaab, Charles M. and Brown, A. Theodore. (1967) *A History of Urban America*. New York: MacMillan.

Greenwood, Michael J. (1970) "Lagged Response in the Decision to Migrate. *Journal of Regional Science*, V. 10, No. 3 (Dec.), pp. 375-384.

_____. (1971) "A Regression Analysis of Migration to Urban Areas of a Less Developed Country: The Case of India." *Journal of Regional Science*, V. 11, No. 2 (August), pp. 253-262.

Gruen, Gruen & Associates. (1972) *The Impact of Growth: An Analytical Framework and Fiscal Example*. Berkeley: Calif. Better Housing Foundation.

Hansen, Niles M. (1966) "Some Neglected Factors in American Regional Development: The Case of Appalachia." *Land Economics*, V. 42, No 1 (February).

_____. (1969) *Urban and Regional Dimensions of Manpower Policy*. Prepared for the U.S. Dept. of Labor, Manpower Administration. Lexington, Ky.: University of Kentucky.

_____. (1970) *Rural Poverty and the Urban Crisis*. Bloomington, Ind.: Indiana University Press.

Hirschman, Albert. (1965) "Interregional and International Transmission of Economic Growth." In J.R.P. Friedmann and William Alonso, *Regional Development and Planning*.

Hoover, Edgar M. (1971) "Economic and Demographic Models." *Population Index* (Fall).

Hoover, Edgar M. and Vernon, Raymond. (1960) *Anatomy of a Metropolis*. New York: Regional Planning Association.

Isard, Walter. (1960) *Methods of Regional Analysis*. Cambridge: MIT Press.

Jones, Kenneth and Jones, Wyatt. (1968) "Toward a Typology of American Cities." *Journal of Regional Science*, V. 10, No. 2.

Kelley, Allen C. (1969) "Demographic Cycles and Economic Growth." *Science* (November 14).

Kolko, Gabriel, (1963) *The Triumph of Conservation*. Glencoe: Free Press.

Lansing, John B. and Mueller, Eva. (1967) *The Geographic Mobility of Labor*. Ann Arbor: Survey Research Center, Institute for Social Research.

Lasuen, J.R. (1972) "On Growth Poles." *Urban Studies*, V. 6, No. 2, pp. 137-161.

Long, Larry H. (1970a) "On Measuring Geographic Mobility," *Journal of the American Statistical Association*, V. 65, No. 33 (Sept.), pp. 1195-1203.

_____. (1970b) "The Fertility of Migrants to and within North America." *Milbank Memorial Fund Quarterly*, V. 48, No. 3 (July).

_____. (1972) "The Influence of Number and Ages of Children on Residential Mobility." *Demography*, V. 9, No. 3 (August), pp. 371-382.

_____. (1973a) "New Estimates of Migration Expectancy in the United States." *Journal of the American Statistical Association*, V. 68, No. 341, Application Section (March), pp. 37-43.

_____. (1973b) "Migration Differentials by Education and Occupation: Trends and Variations." *Demography*, V. 10, No. 2 (May), pp. 243-258.

Lowry, Ira S. (1966) *Migration and Metropolitan Growth: Two Analytical Models*. San Francisco: Chandler Publishing Co.

Lubove, Roy. (1969) *Twentieth-Century Pittsburgh: Government, Business and Environmental Change*. New York: Wiley & Sons.

Mace, Ruth A. and Wielson, Warren J. (1968) *Do Single Family Houses Pay Their Way?* Urban Land Institute, Research Monograph 15.

McCarty, Harold Hull. (1971) *The Geographic Basis of American Economic Life*. Westport Conn.: Greenwood Press.

Mera, Koichi. (1973) "On the Urban Agglomeration and Economic Efficiency." *Economic Development and Cultural Change*, V. 21, No. 2 (January).

Morrison, Peter A. (1972) "Population Movements and the Shape of Urban Growth: Implications for Public Policy in Commission on Population Growth and American Future." Research Reports, V. 5, *Population Distribution and Policy* (ed.) Sara Mills Mazie, pp. 281-322. Washington: U.S. Government Printing Office.

North, Douglass C. (1966) *Growth and Welfare in the American Past*, Englewood Cliffs: Prentice-Hall.

Northam, Ray M. (1963) "Declining Urban Centers of the U.S.: 1940-1960." *Annals of the Association of American Geographers*, V. 53, No. 1 (March).

_____. (1969) "Population Size, Relative Location and Declining." *Urban Land Economics*, V. 45, No. 3 (August).

Olvey, Lee Donne. (1970) "Regional Growth and Inter-Regional Migration: Their Patterns of Interaction." Ph.D. dissertation, Harvard University (April).

Parr, John B. (1966) "Outmigration and the Depressed Area Problem." *Land Economics*, V. 42, No. 2 (May).

Perloff, Harvey S. et al. (1960) *Regions, Resources and Economic Growth: Resources for the Future*. Baltimore: Johns Hopkins Press.

Pittsburgh Regional Planning Association. (1963) *Region in Transition*, Edgar M. Hoover, Project Director, Pittsburgh: University of Pittsburgh Press.

Pred, Allan R. (1966) *The Spatial Dynamics of U.S. Urban-Industrial Growth*. Cambridge: MIT Press.

_____. (1974) "The Growth and Development of Systems of Cities in Advanced Economics." *Lund Studies in Geography*, pp. 8-81.

_____. (1973) *Urban Growth and the Circulation of Information: The U.S. System of Cities, 1740-1840*. Cambridge: Harvard University Press.

Rodwin, Lloyd. (1970) *Nations and Cities: A Comparison of Strategies for Urban Growth*. Boston: Houghton Mifflin Co.

Rust, Edgar. (1972) "Metropolitan Non-Growth." Unpublished. Berkeley. Calif. (March 1972).

_____. (1973) "Administrative Polarization and Metropolitan Employment Changes: An Exploration." In Stephen Cohen, *The New Strategic Alternatives for Development Programs*, a report to the U.S. Economic Development Administration under grant OER-432-G-72-10.

Schlesinger, Arthur M. (1933) *The Rise of the City*. New York: MacMillan.

Shepherd, William Robert. (1956) *Historical Atlas*. New York: C.S. Hammond & Co. Eighth Edition.

Spengler, Joseph. "Price Level Tendencies Under Reduced Growth." *Southern Economic Journal*, V. 38, No. 4.

Stanback, Thomas M. and Knight, Richard V. (1970) *The Metropolitan Economy*. New York: Columbia University Press.

Thompson, Wilbur R. (1965) *A Preface to Urban Economics*, Resources for the Future, Inc. Baltimore: Johns Hopkins Press.

_____. (1968) "Internal and External Factors in the Development of Urban Economics." In Harvey S. Perloff and Lowden Wingo (eds.), *Issues in Urban Economics*, Resources for the Future. Baltimore: John Hopkins Press.

_____. (1973) "Problems That Sprout in the Shadow of No-Growth." *AIA Journal*, V. 60: 30-35 (December).

Toffler, Alvin. (1970) *Future Shock*. New York: Bantam Books.

Tolley, George. (1971) "National Growth Policy and the Environmental Effects of Cities." University of Chicago.

U.S. Government, Bureau of the Census. (1970a) *1970 Population Census: General Social and Economic Characteristics*, Sec. PC(1) B-1.

U.S. Government, Bureau of the Census (1970b) *Mobility for Metropolitan Areas*, Ser. PC(2) 2D.

U.S. Government, Bureau of the Census. (1972) *1970 Population Census; Migration Between State Economic Areas*, Ser. PC(2)-2E.

U.S. Government, Bureau of the Census. (1967) *Current Population Reports*. Ser. P-23, No. 7.

U.S. Government, Manpower Administration. (1965-1970) *Area Trends in Employment and Unemployment*, July issues.

Vance, Stanley. (1955) *American Industries*. Englewood Cliffs, N.J.: Prentice-Hall.

Williamson, Jeffrey. (1968) "Regional Inequalities and the Process of National Development." In L. Needleman, *Regional Analysis*, Penguin Books.

Wingo, Lowdon. (1972) "Issues in a National Urban Development Strategy for the United States." *Urban Studies*, V. 9, No. 1, pp. 3-27 (Feb.).

Wolf, Stewart and Goodell, Helen. (1968) *Harold G. Wolff's Stress and Disease*. Second Edition. Springfield, Ill.: Charles C. Thomas.

Bibliographies of SMSAs

Pueblo, Colorado

Bloom, Bernard. (1974) *Changing Patterns of Psychiatric Care*. University of Colorado.

"The Development of Commercial Banking in Pueblo County, Colorado." (1940) School of Business, University of Colorado.

Elazar, Daniel J. (1970) *Cities of the Prairies: The Metropolitan Frontier and American Politics*. New York: Basic Books, Inc.

Pueblo Area Council of Governments. (1972) *Economic Survey and Market Analysis*, Report No. 6 (November).

Pueblo Area Council of Governments. (1974) *An Economic Development Strategy for Pueblo: Phase I*, Report No. 14 (May).

Pueblo Design Quarterly. (published by Pueblo Regional Planning Commission) (June 1973).

Shomaker, Gordon Alexander. (1953) "The Government of Pueblo, Col-

229

orado, 1908-1957." M.A. Thesis, Department of Political Science, University of Colorado.

Taylor, Ralph C. (1963) *Colorado South of the Border*, Denver: Sage Books.

_____. (1974) "Colorful Colorado." In Pueblo, Colo. *Star Journal & Sunday Chieftain*, pp. 3-17 (through April 14).

Ward, Bert D. (1971) "A Summary Appraisal of Pueblo's Recent Economic Performance. Pueblo Regional Planning Commission, Nevada.

Amarillo, Texas

Amarillo: A Young City Going Places. (1973) Amarillo: Board of City Development (March).

Archambeau, Ernest. (1970) *History of Amarillo*, American Globe Times (May 18).

Billion Dollar Business. Amarillo, Texas Cattle Feeders Association, N.D. (1972).

Hammond, Clara T. (1971) *Amarillo*, Amarillo: George Autry.

"A Historical Sketch of Amarillo." (1972) Amarillo: Amarillo Chamber of Commerce (November).

Key, Della Tyler. (1968) *In the Cattle Country: History of Potter County 1877-1966*, 2nd Edition (Quanali: Nortex).

Manpower Trends, Amarillo Area. (1973) Vol. 28, No. 1-IV (January-October) Texas Employment Commission.

Fort Smith, Arkansas

Bartholemew, Harland and Associates. (1966) *Fort Smith Urban Area Study*, prepared for the Fort Smith Sebastian County Joint Planning Commission, Memphis, Tenn. (April).

Butler, William J. (1972) *Fort Smith: Past and Present*, First National Bank of Fort Smith.

Fort Smith Chamber of Commerce. (1972) *Fort Smith Industrial Directory*.

Fort Smith Public Library, Clippings Files on Fort Smith and related topics.

Patton, J. Fred. (1967) *History of Fort Smith, Southwest Times-Record*, Sesquicentennial Edition (May 2).

Montgomery, Alabama

Alabama Development Office: Origins—Divisions—Responsibilities. Montgomery, Alabama Development Office (1972).

Alabama Development Office. (1973) *New and Expanded Industries in Alabama*, Montgomery.

Alabama State Chamber of Commerce. (1965, 1967, 1968, 1970, 1972) *Industrial Alabama* (Directory of manufacturers).

Alabama State Planning and Industrial Development Board. (Annual 1960-1971) *New and Expanded Industries in Alabama* (title varies).

Alabama State Employment Service. (1960-1972) "Estimated Civilian Work Force: Montgomery, Alabama SMSA." (Monthly estimates with industry detail) Montgomery.

Alabama State Employment Service. (1963-1971) "Annual Average Work Force Estimates, Autauga County, Alabama," Montgomery.

Gay, W.T. (1957) *Montgomery, Alabama*. New York: Exposition Press.

Junior League of Montgomery. (1969) *A Guide to the City of Montgomery*.

King, Martin Luther, Jr. (1958) *Stride Towards Freedom*. New York: Harper's.

Montgomery-Central Alabama Regional Planning and Development Commission. (1973) *An Assessment of Economic Growth in the Central Alabama Region 1960-1970*. (June).

Perkins, Almond E. (1938) *The South: Its Economic and Geographic Development*. New York: John Wiley.

Richardson, Jesse M. (ed.). (1965) *Alabama Encyclopedia*. Northport: American Southern Publishing Company.

Rivers of Alabama. (1968) Huntsville: The Strode Publishers.

Vance, Rupert B. and Nicholas J. Demerath. (eds.) (1954) *The Urban South*. Chapel Hill: University of North Carolina Press.

Savannah, Georgia

Chatham County-Savannah Metropolitan Planning Commission. (1973) *Historic District Zoning Ordinance*. Savannah (April).

Fallows, James M. (1971) *The Water Lords*. The Center for the Study of Responsive Law. New York: Bantam.

George Peabody College for Teachers. (1971) *Savannah-Chatham County Public Schools: A Survey Report*. Division of Field Services and Surveys. Nashville.

Georgia Annual Average Work Force Estimates by Area, (1958-65) (1966-69; 1969-72) Georgia Department of Labor.

Historic Savannah Foundation. (1973) "A Brief Chronology of Significant Achievements of Historic Savannah Foundation, Inc." and other fact sheets, staff.

Nix, H.L. and Charles Dudley. (1965) Community Analysis, Savannah-Chatham County, Georgia. Georgia Department of Public Health (May).

Reps, John W. (1969) *Town Planning in Frontier America*. Princeton: Princeton University Press.

Riggs, P.S. (1937) *Turpentine Made This City*. New York: McBride.

Savannah Port Authority. (1973) *Savannah Area Manufacturers Directory*, 1973-74. Savannah.

Savannah Port Authority. (1972) *Savannah Industrial Survey, Historic Savannah Foundation, Inc.* (1968) (brochure).

Savannah Port Authority Annual Report(s) 1949-51; 1953-54; 1956-60; 1962-72.

Sims, Ruth P. (1968) "The Savannah Story Education Design," In Raymond W. Mack (ed.). *Our Children's Burden: Studies of Desegregation in Nine American Communities*. New York: Random House, pp. 109-140.

Spencer, F.W. (1966) *The Waterfront*. Savannah: F.W. Spencer Co.

Sussman, Frederick B. and Neil J. Bloomfield. "Savannah" in *The Community and Racial Crises*, David Stahl (ed.). Practicing Law Institute.

Southern Living. (1972) "The Vamping of Savannah." (May) pp. 70-77.

Wilkes-Barre-Hazleton and Scranton, Pennsylvania

Candeub, Cabot & Associates (1961) "Economic Analysis." In *Master Plan for the City of Wilkes-Barre, 1960-1980*.

Economic Development Council of Northeastern Pennsylvania. (1974) State of the Region: 1974 and Beyond. Avoca, Pa. (January).

_____. (1973) *Annual Report, 1972-73*.

_____. (1973) *Northeastern Pennsylvania Population Shifts: Growth Areas and Urban-Rural Balance*. Avoca, Pa. (April).

_____. (1974) *Household Characteristics and Income*, Northeastern Pennsylvania. Avoca, Pa.

_____. (1972) *The People: A Profile of Age, Sex and Race*, Avoca, Pa. (June).

_____. (1974) Data Notes, IV:I "An Inquiry into the Long Term Economic Impact of Disasters in the United States," (March).

————. (1974) "A Statistical Analysis of the Anthracite Industry in Pennsylvania from 1970-1972." (May) Avoca, Pa.

Greater Wilkes-Barre Chamber of Commerce. (1973) Data Sheets and lists of new firms.

Hammond, Thomas J. (1965) "A Geographical Analysis of Population Trends in Luzerne County, Pa." Master's thesis, Geography Dept., Pennsylvania State University.

Hitchcock, Frederick L. (1914) *History of Scranton and the Boroughs of Lackawanna County*. New York: Lewis Historical Publishing Co. (2 vols.).

Lackawanna County Regional Planning Commission. (1973) *Comprehensive Plan Update: Economic and Population Study*. Economic Development Council of North East Pennsylvania, Avoca (June).

League of Women Voters of Wilkes-Barre and Hazleton Pennsylvania. (1963) *This is Luzerne County: History—Government—Services*. Wilkes-Barre.

Luzerne County Planning Commission. (1966) "Background Material for the Overall Economic Development Program for Luzerne County."

Pennsylvania Bureau of Employment Security. (1960-72) (1950-59) "Total Civilian Work Force, Unemployment and Employment by Industry." (Monthly) (Annual Averages).

Pennsylvania Department of Transportation. (1973) *Transit Development Program for Lackawanna and Luzerne Counties*. Harrisburgh (January).

Pennsylvania State Planning Board. (1967) *Pennsylvania's Regions*. Harrisburgh, Pa.

Prince, Paul Anthony. (1950) "Geographical Aspects of Lackawanna County, Pa." Masters' thesis, Clark University, Worcester.

Scranton Times Souvenir Centennial Edition. (1966) July 2 and 3.

Smith, Wilbur and Associates. (1973) *The Wyoming Valley, Pennsylvania Planning and Development Considerations*, Philadelphia (December).

U.S. Bureau of Labor Statistics, Mideast Regional Office. (1970) *The Anthracite Belt in the Sixties*. Philadelphia, Pa.

Walker, David M. Associates, Inc. (1968) *Comprehensive Plan Wilkes-Barre, Pennsylvania*. Philadelphia, Pa.

Pittsburgh, Pennsylvania

A.C.T.I.O.N.—Housing. (1973) *Executive Director's Report to the Board of Directors*. (Sept. 1964-65; 69-71; 72-73.)

Adams, Walter F. (ed.) *The Structure of the American Steel Industry: Some Case Studies*. 9th Edition. New York: MacMillan.

Board of County Commission. Allegheny County. (1973) *Commuter Rail Potential Pittsburgh Area*. Pittsburgh: Ford Bacon and Davis.

Brown, Robert Kevin. (1959) *Public in Action, The Record of Pittsburgh*. Pittsburgh: University of Pittsburgh.

Chamber of Commerce of Greater Pittsburgh. (1969) *Pittsburgh Area Organizations and Programs Oriented to the Urban Crisis*. Pittsburgh (looseleaf).

Klein, Philip, et al. (1939) *A Social Study of Pittsburgh: Community Problems and Social Service Allegheny County*. New York: Columbia University Press.

Longini, Arthur (ed.) (1960) *Economic Atlas of the Pittsburgh Economic Area*. Pittsburgh: The Pittsburgh and Lake Erie RR Co.

Lorant, Stefen (ed.) (1964) *Pittsburgh: The Story of An American City*. Garden City: Doubleday.

Lubove, Roy. (1969) *Twentieth-Century Pittsburgh: Government, Business and Environmental Change*. New York: Wiley & Sons.

Penn's Southwest Association. (1973) *Penn's Southwest*.

Pennsylvania State Employment Service. (1973) *Labor Market Letter, Pittsburgh Area*, V. 27. #1-10.

Pittsburgh Regional Planning Association. (1963) *Economic Study of the Pittsburgh Region*. Pittsburgh: University of Pittsburgh Press.

_____. (1953-54; 56-63; 1965; 1970) *A Report of Its Work and Activities*.

Port Authority of Allegheny County. (1967) *Allegheny County Rapid Transit Study*. Pittsburgh: Parsons, Brinkerhoff, Quade and Douglas (December).

Regional Industrial Development Corporation of S.W. Penn. (1973) *Report*. (1962/63).

Southwest Pennsylvania Regional Planning Commission. (1973) *Dimensions of the Year 2000: A Basis for Plan Preparation in Southwestern Pennsylvania* (April).

Stave, Bruce M. (1970) *The New Deal and the Last Hurrah: Pittsburgh Machine Politics*. Pittsburgh: University of Pittsburgh.

Warren, Kenneth. (1973) *The American Steel Industry 1850-1970: A Geographical Interpretation*. Oxford University Press.

Terre Haute, Indiana

"Ascertainment of Community Needs." (1970) Part of C.I.P. (located in Clipping File of Vigo County Library).

Buckner, Harold Kay. (ed.) *Terre Haute and Her People of Progress*.

Drummond, Robert Rowland. (1954) *Terre Haute: A City of Non-Growth* (Mimeo).

Drummond, Robert Rowland. (1955) *The Phenomenon of Non-Growth in Terre Haute* (Mimeo).

Drummond, Robert Rowland. (1969) *Terre Haute, Indiana, An Unplanned City* (Mimeo).

Farmer, Rufus. (1945) "Cleanup on the Wabash." *Saturday Evening Post*, pp. 14ff.

"Gambling Arrests in Terre Haute." *Life*, September 1, 1952, pp. 16ff.

Indiana Employment Security Division. (1950-1972) *Work Force Summary, Terre Haute Area, 1950-1972*.

Indiana Employment Security Division. (1973) *Indiana Labor Market Information: Terre Haute Area* (February-November).

League of Women Voters of Terre Haute, Indiana. (ND) *Who's in Charge Here? A Look at Local Government in Terre Haute and Vigo County*.

McGregor, John R. (1973) "Terre Haute, the 'No-Grow' Industrial Center." *Indiana Business Review*. V. 28, pp. 14-18 (March-April).

Public Service Indiana. (1972) "Terre Haute: A Community Resume" (March).

Reid, J.A. (Publisher) (1915) *Terre Haute Today*.

"The Sad Case of Terre Haute." *Time*, February 21, 1969.

Tennies, Arthur C. (1968) "Decision in Terre Haute." Master's thesis, Butler University.

Industrial Survey of Terre Haute, Indiana. Terre Haute Chamber of Commerce. (1970).

Industrial Directory. (1973) Terre Haute Chamber of Commerce (August).

The Terre Haute Heritage, Inc. (1966) *Terre Haute, 1816-1966*. Commerce Books of Terre Haute.

Terre Haute, Indiana. (1971) Encino, Ca: Windsor Publications.

Wyden, Peter. (1961) "Indiana's Delinquent City." *Saturday Evening Post* (February).

St. Joseph, Missouri

Campbell, Ruth. (1954) "St. Joseph, Missouri: Gateway to the West." Master's thesis, Department of History, University of Southern California, Los Angeles.

Directory of Principal Manufacturers and Major Employers. (1974) St. Joseph, Missouri.

"Industrial Growth in St. Joseph Metropolitan Area Since 1968." (1974) (Mimeo) (June).

Mo-Kan Bistate Planning Commission. (1970) *A.B.C.D. Regional Plan Phase 2*, Vol. 2. St. Joseph, Missouri (December).

Rutt, Chris L. (1904) *History of Buchanan County and The City of St. Joseph.* Chicago: Biographical Publishing Co.

St. Joseph Area Chamber of Commerce. (1974) *Business and Economic Data, St. Joseph Metropolitan Area.* St. Joseph, Missouri (June).

St. Joseph—Buchanan County Planning Commission. (1968) *St. Joseph Buchanan County, Missouri Comprehensive Plan, Phase 1, Report 2, Summary of Findings.* St. Joseph.

St. Joseph News-Press clippings on St. Joseph in St. Joseph Public Library.

Index

Index

About the Author

Edgar Rust is a senior analyst with Berkeley Planning Associates in Berkeley California. He attended Williams College and received the masters degree in city planning from the Massachusetts Institute of Technology. He holds the Ph.D. degree in city and regional planning from the University of California where he was a lecturer from 1968-1970. Dr. Rust is a full member of the American Institute of Planners, and has worked as a city planner in Anchorage, Alaska, San Francisco, and Berkeley since 1963.

Date Due